INNOVATION IN PLAY ENVIRONMENTS

Innovation in Play Environments

Edited by
PAUL F. WILKINSON

ST. MARTIN'S PRESS   NEW YORK

All rights reserved. For information write:
St. Martin's Press, Inc., 175 Fifth Avenue, New York, N.Y. 10010
Printed in Great Britain
First published in the United States in 1980

Library of Congress Cataloging in Publication Data
Main entry under title:

Innovation in play environments.

   Bibliography: p.
   Includes index.
   1. Playgrounds — Addresses, essays, lectures.
2. Recreation areas — Addresses, essays, lectures.
3. Play — Social aspects — Addresses, essays, lectures
4. City planning — Addresses, essays, lectures.
I. Wilkinson, Paul F., 1948-
GV424.155   1980   790'.06'8   79-3840
ISBN 0-312-41815-9

CONTENTS

Contents

ACKNOWLEDGEMENTS

Credit for the production of any book is never due solely to one person, even if the book is the product of a single author. When the book is an edited collection of papers, however, the list of persons involved grows to immense proportions. The following are some of the people involved in the production of these two volumes: Polly Hill (President), Arvid Bengtsson (Past-President), Muriel Otter (Treasurer), Jane Knight (Secretary), International Playground Association; Cor Westland, Chairman, Conference Planning Committee of the Seventh World Congress of the International Playground Association, and the chairman and members of all of the conference committees; in particular, the members of the Program Committee of the Seventh World Congress of the International Playground Association, of which I was a member — Alexandra Semeniuk (Chairman), Sue Alexander, Pat Artkin, Lynton Friedberg, Herb Gray, Halina Kantor, Paul Kemp, Nancy Mallett, Marilyn Muleski, Les Miller, Karen Oster, Yolanda Pluta, Debra Pepler, Swain Van Camp and Sheila Ward; the Ontario Ministry of Culture and Recreation, and the Honourable Reuben Baetz, Minister; Dean Rodger Schwass, Alice Reppert, Betty Peckhover, Al Turner, Donna Lytle, Claire Côté, and other members of the Faculty of Environmental Studies, York University; the authors who contributed their time and effort to these volumes; David Croom for his help and support; Barbara Allan, who acted as research assistant and editorial assistant, and who spent countless hours editing, cutting, pasting, deciphering hand-writing, typing and generally being supportive; Alexandra Semeniuk, who was a constant source of help and inspiration, and who assisted in editing the final manuscripts; Beverley Brady, who typed the manuscripts — including the constant changes and revisions; and Doh and Chris, who put up with me when I could not play because of my reading and writing about play.

ACKNOWLEDGMENTS

To Chris — the future is his

PREFACE

This book, *Innovation in Play Environments*, and its companion volume, *In Celebration of Play*, were inspired by the Seventh World Congress of the International Playground Association,[1] held in August 1978 at Carleton University in Ottawa, Ontario, Canada.

The International Playground Association (IPA) was formed in 1961 as an interdisciplinary organization designed to exchange ideas and experiences in the realm of children's leisure and to work for the improvement of play opportunities and play leadership. It is important to emphasize that, despite the name of the association, it is not solely concerned with 'playgrounds' in the formal sense; rather, it is concerned with the wide range of play environments that are — or should be — available to children. It is recognized that play opportunities can exist for the child in and around the home (playrooms, backyards), the school and public park (traditional, adventure and creative playgrounds), the institution (day-care centres, hospitals), and the city *qua* city (the streets, museums, shopping centres). IPA is concerned with all of these environments and, in addition, with the roles that adults play in planning, designing, managing, and providing leadership for those environments.

The theme of the IPA Congress, 'Play in Human Settlements: An Integrated Approach', was directly inspired by the United Nations' Habitat Human Settlements Conference held in Vancouver, Canada in June 1976. One component of the conference was a workshop on 'Children in Human Settlements' sponsored by the Non-Governmental Forum and attended by representatives of a number of co-operating international organizations, including IPA who acted as the workshop organizers.[2] Consistent with the spirit of the United Nations' Declaration of the Rights of the Child, Article 7, that 'The Child shall have full opportunity to play and recreation which should be directed to the same purpose as education . . .', this multi-disciplinary group of experts, practitioners and citizens concerned with the needs of children in human settlements formulated the following statement:

The child and youth population in human settlements is of prime importance. They are every nation's most valued resource. They comprise over a third of the inhabitants of this planet. Mankind owes

1

the child the best it has to give! Fully endorsing the *UN Declaration of the Rights of the Child* with its all-encompassing principles, we emphasize the following points that focus on Habitat issues:

1. Every national government should have a *policy on children* which addresses itself to their total needs and includes the mechanisms and financial resources for its implementation.
2. By 1990 every child should have access to *clean water*.
3. By 1980 every child should enjoy *clean air* through the mandatory elimination of lead in motor fuel and other air pollutants that are known to cause serious brain damage and mutilation in the young.
4. Immediate steps should be taken to ensure *adequate nutrition* for children and mothers in order to eradicate the devastating physical and mental disorders caused by malnutrition.
5. Immediate steps should be taken to reduce the effects of the *killer car*. The child's right to play and move about the community free from danger must be ensured by public transportation solutions, appropriate design and planning, and innovative redevelopment of settlements. The subordination of man to machine must be treated as a disease. This lethal epidemic must be given top priority by all levels of government.
6. The development and redevelopment of settlements must be on a more *human scale*. Children suffer most from the effects of big cities, ghettos of poverty and shanty towns. Children must grow into the Habitat at their own pace — it must be a function of planning to ensure that this happens.
7. The creation of *better balanced communities* with a mix of social groups, occupations, housing and amenities is vital. We must ensure that the total settlement is designed with the child in mind
8. Changes in *land use policy* should include, along with the essential municipal services, the laying out of spaces for play and family recreation, as well as pedestrian routes or play paths. These should be given the same priority as other elements of infrastructure. At the time of assembling land, moneys for development of play spaces should be set aside until people have moved in and can participate in the designing — children's contributions are particularly vital.
9. *Participation* by the community, including children, in environmental planning, building and maintenance is the key to meeting the needs of neighbourhood users of different ages, interests and handicaps.

10. *Planning consent* and *financial subsidies* should only be given to family housing composed of suitable housing types which have adequate provision for play and child safety. There is growing substantial evidence that high-rise living and inadequate play provision produce damaging physical and mental effects on children and their parents.

11. All levels of government should recognize that provision for the *out of school* life of children is as serious as formal education. Play is the child's way of learning about, adapting to, and integrating with his or her environment.

12. In addition to adequate sports and recreation facilities, children and youth need a wide variety of opportunities, choices and raw materials that they can use as they see fit for *free, constructive, creative play*.

13. The need for *leaders*, the training of leaders and the stressing of the importance of their role as facilitators for children's play, must be the concern of public authorities. People rather than hardware are what is needed.

14. Child development and environmental planning for children's play must be included in *educational programs preparing people* for all professions concerned with or affecting children in the design and planning of human settlements.

15. *Environmental education* should be an integral part of the school curriculum, to ensure that the citizens of tomorrow do not repeat the mistakes of today.

16. Problems caused by *large concentrations of children* must be dealt with positively, not by imposing additional constraints, guards, locks, etc. . . . but by supplying creative alternatives to boredom, mischief-making and outlets for plain exuberance.

17. *Bold new solutions* that reflect children's real development needs must be found through experimentation, demonstration, adaptations of successful solutions, etc. Not only sewage needs recycling! Unused, poorly designed, static play environments must be recycled into living, learning, happy places to explore.

18. *The cost* of the proposed program can be met by decreasing the current expenditure on arms by 10 per cent.

19. We wish to fully endorse the International Year of the Child. Vitally needed is an advocacy for, and a focus on, the total needs of children and youth on our planet.

The statement endorsed the 1979 International Year of the Child

(IYC), which was later formally proclaimed by the United Nations in a
General Assembly Resolution of the 31st Session in December 1976.
Broadly speaking, IYC aims to provide an opportunity to emphasize the
intellectual, psychological, social and physical development of all
children in all countries — rich as well as poor. The Year differs from
other recent UN 'Years' in that there will be no UN world conference in
1979. This 'innovative' omission has been widely acclaimed by many
who feel that a year-long programme of activities and contributions by
people and countries throughout the world without a peak event would
better serve the aim of IYC than a jamboree of national delegations.
Rather, IYC will consist of a world-wide network of national activities
concerning and involving children.

Already committed to holding its triennial world conference in
Ottawa, Canada in 1978, IPA decided to adopt the title 'Play in Human
Settlements' as the theme of the conference using many of the issues
that were highlighted in the Habitat Statement as the organizing framework for the content of the conference. While some of the issues noted
in the statement were only dealt with peripherally at the IPA Congress
(e.g., pollution, nutrition), most of the issues became foci for papers
and discussion sessions at the congress and for contributions to these
volumes, including such topics as national policies for children, urban
planning, housing design, community involvement in planning, non-
traditional play environments, formal and non-formal educational
opportunities, environmental education and implementation strategies.
The congress was to serve as IPA's contribution to the preparations for
IYC.

This dedication to the aims of IYC was highlighted and reinforced by
IPA's 'Malta Declaration of the Child's Right to Play', formulated at a
Consultation in preparation for IYC held in Malta on 11 November
1977. The declaration stated:

> The Malta Consultation declares that play, along with the basic needs
> of nutrition, health, shelter and education, is vital for the develop-
> ment of the potential of all children.
>
> The child is the foundation for the world's future.
>
> Play is not the mere passing of time. Play is life.
>
> It is instinctive. It is voluntary. It is spontaneous. It is natural. It is
> exploratory. It is communication. It is expression. It combines action
> and thought. It gives satisfaction and a feeling of achievement.
>
> Play has occurred at all times throughout history and in all
> cultures. Play touches all aspects of life.

Through play the child develops physically, mentally, emotionally and socially.

Play is a means of learning to live.

The Consultation is extremely concerned by a number of alarming trends, such as:

1. Society's indifference to the importance of play.
2. The over-emphasis on academic studies in schools.
3. The dehumanising scale of settlements, inappropriate housing forms; such as high-rise, inadequate environmental planning and bad traffic management.
4. The increasing commercial exploitation of children through mass communication, mass production, leading to the deterioration of individual values and cultural tradition.
5. The inadequate preparation of children to live in a rapidly changing society.

Proposals for Action

Health. Play is essential for the physical and mental health of the child.

1. Establish programmes for professionals and parents about the benefits of play from birth onwards.
2. Incorporate play into community programmes designed to maintain the child's health.
3. Promote play as an integral part of the treatment plan for children in hospitals and other settings.
4. Provide opportunities for initiative, interaction, creativity and socialisation in the formal education system.
5. Include the study of the importance of play in the training of all professionals working with or for children.
6. Involve schools, colleges and public buildings in the life of the community and permit fuller use of these buildings and facilities.

Welfare. Play is an essential part of family and community welfare.

1. Promote measures that strengthen the close relationship between parent and child.
2. Ensure that play is accepted as an integral part of social development and social care.
3. Provide community-based services of which play is a part in order

to foster the acceptance of children with handicaps as full members of the community so that no child, whether for physical, mental or emotional reasons, shall be detained in an institution.

Leisure. The child needs time to play.

1. Provide the space and adequate free time for children to choose and develop individual and group interests.
2. Encourage more people from different backgrounds and ages to be involved with children.
3. Stop the commercial exploitation of children's play, e.g., manipulative advertising, war toys and violence in entertainment.

Planning. The child must have priority in the planning of human settlements.

1. Give priority to the child in existing and projected human settlements in view of the child's great vulnerability, small size and limited range of activity.
2. Ban immediately the building of all high-rise housing and take urgent steps to mitigate the effect of existing developments on children.
3. Take steps to enable the child to move about the community in safety by providing traffic segregation, improved public transportation and better traffic management.

The Malta Consultation

1. believing firmly that the International Year of the Child will provide opportunities to arouse world opinion for the improvement of the life of the child,
2. affirming its belief in the United Nations' Declaration of the Rights of the Child,
3. acknowledging that each country is responsible for preparing its own courses of action in the lights of its culture, climate and social, political and economic structure,
4. recognizing that the full participation of people is essential in planning and developing programmes and services for children to meet their needs, wishes and aspirations,
5. assuring its co-operation with other international and national organizations involved with children,

Appeals to all countries and organizations to consider seriously the implementation of measures to reverse the alarming trends, some of which are identified in this statement, and to place high on its list of priorities the development of long-term programmes to ensure for all time *the child's right to play*.

These three actions – the UN Habitat Statement, the Proclamation of IYC, and the IPA Malta Declaration – were, therefore, the impetus behind 'Play in Human Settlements', the Seventh World Congress of the International Playground Association. These two volumes, *In Celebration of Play* and *Innovation in Play Environments*, are a result of that Congress, with most of the papers being formal written versions of presentations made in Ottawa. It should be noted, however, that other papers were solicited by the editor to fill gaps recognized after the conference or to replace contributions from conference participants who were unable to submit formal papers. The volumes have been organized along the lines of the three sub-themes of the congress. *In Celebration of Play*, dealing with 'The Social Significance of Play', concentrates on the developmental aspects of play for the individual child and the importance of play in a social context. Topics explored include: the importance of play, development through play, leadership training, special groups, the role of play beyond the playground, and children and the future. *Innovation in Play Environments* concentrates on the planning and design of play programmes and play environments. It focuses on two of the sub-themes: 'Toward the Perfect Play Experience' deals with such topics as historical approaches to play, play in the home environment, play in institutional settings, handicapped children, planning for play in extreme climatic conditions, and play environments beyond the traditional playground; 'Urban Planning with the Child in Mind' focuses on the child and the urban environment, high-rise residential environments, and the street and the city.

In conclusion, these volumes, therefore, represent not only the personal contributions of the editors and authors to the International Year of the Child, but also the contributions of the International Playground Association, the Canadian Delegation to the International Playground Association, the Ontario Ministry of Culture and Recreation, and the Faculty of Environmental Studies, York University.

Notes

1. Membership in IPA is spread over 30 countries on 6 continents. In 1975, IPA was granted consultative status with the United Nations' Economic and Social

Council (ECOSOC) and Category B status, 'Information and Consultative Relations' status, with the United Nations' Education, Scientific and Cultural Organization (UNESCO) in 1976.

2. The other organizations were: Organization Mondiale pour l'Education Préscolaire (OMEP), United Nations' International Children's Emergency Fund (UNICEF), World Leisure and Recreation Association (WLRA), Foundation for Social Habilitation (FSH), Save the Children Federation Community Development (SCFCD), Rehabilitation International (RI), International Catholic Child Bureau (ICCB).

INTRODUCTION

Nearly twenty-five years ago, Riesman (1954, p. 333) exhorted social scientists to 'pay more attention to play, to study blockages in play in the way that they have studied blockages in work and sexuality'. Since that time, there has been increased interest in the study of play, leisure and recreation — three terms which are often confused. Perhaps the reason for the confusion underlying the use of these terms is that each has usually been examined in the light of the focus of interest of particular disciplines or areas of expertise, including psychology, sociology, geography, education, architecture, landscape architecture and so on. In terms of children and play, rarely has an attempt been made to bring together the concerns, biases and knowledge of the various 'experts'. Because such attempts are few and far between, no strong 'lobby' or organization has come to the fore to represent the interests of *all* persons interested in children and play, and to provide to the world a justification — if that is the proper word — for the importance of play and a set of guidelines suggesting possible approaches to providing opportunities for the development of the full potential of play for all children.

There is a great deal of confusion as to the meaning of the terms 'play', 'leisure' and 'recreation'. It is not the goal of these volumes to enter into this debate — the dialectical, semantical morass is simply too deep and foreboding. Indeed, within these volumes, one may find a number of interesting and often conflicting definitions of the one term that is of particular interest here, that is, play. To end the argument, once, if not for all, the editor uses his privileged position to state that children's play is the freely chosen activity of children; while from the point of view of adults play is a means and may serve several develop-mental functions, play is undertaken by children as an end unto itself. Play is what children want it to be; therefore, it manifests itself in a variety of forms, including arts and crafts, games, co-operative and solitary behaviour, reading, imitation, fantasy, sports and so on. The 'equipment required' for play ranges from such simple, common-place items as water, sand, sticks, stones and food to animals and trees to elaborate, self-built forts and houses constructed out of scrap materials. Given the choice, children would appear to prefer materials that are parts of their everyday lives rather than the mass-produced, expensive,

9

plastic toys and games that bombard them from the television screen. Indeed, adults are frequently dismayed to find that the expensive 'toy' is soon forgotten, to lie abandoned and often broken, in favour of the ball of string, the old wooden blocks and the home-made boat.

If play is so natural to children, why should society worry about it? Why not just let it happen? Will not children simply put what is available to good use? The answer to these questions is that play is too important — both to the individual child and to society as a whole — to let it just happen. It must be nurtured, encouraged and celebrated. Otherwise, it will suffer from benign neglect as it does today in many parts of the world — both rich and poor. An excellent justification for what they call the 'extraordinary power of play' is presented by Caplan and Caplan (1973, p. xi):

> We aim to present a hypothesis of such far-reaching implications that no parent, pediatrician, educator, sociologist, or politician can afford to ignore it. It is our intention . . . that the power of play is all-pervasive. We invite our readers to examine the power of play with us so that we might garner for child play the prestige and wholehearted public support it deserves and must have.
>
> We will set forth how play serves children, and even adults; how it can help to strengthen personality, encourage interpersonal relations, further creativity and the joy of living, and advance learning. We will trace the nature of play and playthings; how one can set the stage for creative play; how play is used to help the emotionally disturbed child; how it reveals the strengths and weaknesses of the child as well as his desires and satisfactions . . . we must take [the readers] through the various ages and stages of development in order adequately to illustrate the many basic facets of growing, learning, and living inherent in the play process.

They go on to provide a series of statements which describe the nature and importance of play:

> We believe the power of play to be extraordinary and supremely serious.
> Playtime aids growth.
> Play is a voluntary activity.
> Play offers a child freedom of action.
> Play provides an imaginary world a child can master.
> Play has elements of adventure in it.

Play provides a base for language building.

Play has unique power for building interpersonal relations.

Play offers opportunities for mastery of the physical self.

Play furthers interest and concentration.

Play is the way children investigate the material world.

Play is a way of learning adult roles.

Play is always a dynamic way of learning.

Play refines a child's judgements.

Academics can be structured into play.

Play is vitalizing.

   (Caplan and Caplan, 1973, pp. xii–xvii, *passim*)

(Various papers in these two volumes, and particularly in the first volume, will elaborate on many of these points.)

In addition to the confusion created by conflicting definitions and the entrenched positions of various disciplines as noted above, there are a number of other reasons why play has not been accorded high value in today's life schema. Perhaps the most all-pervasive reason is the dichotomy between play on the one hand and work and learning on the other hand. It is interesting that this distinction can be found in virtually all parts of the world. For example, Caplan and Caplan (p. xviii) note that in the United States,

> puritanical influence has dictated that play and learning are not synonymous. Play is placed at one end of the value scale, with learning and work at the other. Play and playthings have been called 'the companions of a lonely childhood', 'a way of keeping a child out of mischief', 'the discharge of a super-abundance of vital energy', 'the imitative instinct', 'the outlet for harmful impulses', and so on, in the same general vein.
>
> We have been conditioned to think of play and seriousness as antitheses. Most educators make a sharp distinction between academic work and play. . . . Few educators, even today, readily consider play as the art of learning.

Similarly, Hearn (1976–7, p. 145) notes that Marxist political thought has failed to examine the importance of play. In the Marxian perspective, and particularly in its more orthodox interpretations, the realm of freedom — the sphere of play — is contingent upon necessity. According to Marx, beyond necessity begins that development of human power, which is its own end, the true realm of freedom, which, however, can flourish only upon that realm of necessity as its basis. *The shortening of the working day is its fundamental premise.*[1] (Selsam and Martel, 1963, p. 269)

Hearn (1976–7, p. 145) goes on to note that, in Marxian terms, play is possible only after the productive forces have been sufficiently developed, when the time for necessary labour has been reduced:

Play as leisure, as free-time during which human capabilities are re-created, is important to the extent that it enhances the productive process. Severed from its instrumental relation to work, play tends to be regarded as inconsequential.

While Marx was apparently seeing play as being synonymous with recreation and leisure, and not speaking directly about children, the results of this philosophy and its implications for children are only too evident today. It is strange how capitalism and communism seem to have converged in theory at this point – the results for children throughout the world have often been disastrous.

This dichotomy between play and work has been carried over into the formal educational system. With the exception of recess time, the educational conspiracy seems to dictate that, after they have completed kindergarten, children are in school to learn and not to play. (Indeed, one may often conclude that the primary purpose of recess is to provide a coffee break for the teachers.)

The rigidity of the set curriculum demands that autonomy and decision-making be turned over to the authority of the teacher. Teaching replaces self-discovery, hatred of school replaces love of learning. The school supplants the environment of pre-school play – which the child can manipulate and affect – with a setting he can no longer control. School bells restrict personal research; stationary desks prevent gross motor exercise; large classes curtail freedom. Mastery of overwhelming and often unrelated subject matter replaces insightful experimenting. The reading of texts and recording of the conclusions of others are emphasized to the detriment of self-learning. The child who feels that he can no longer influence his environment soon loses interest. He ceases to be responsive to academic learning. As a result, he may often require expensive, intensive remedial attention. (Caplan and Caplan, 1973, pp. xviii–xix)

This attitude has developed largely because research has shown that the period of the most rapid increase in learning achievement and growth in certain personality traits occurs before the age of eight. On the other hand, there is no definitive research on the effects of play on the educative process. (There is research on the influence of play on monkeys, rodents and dogs, but the lack of funds available for research on play and humans seems to indicate a rather strange set of priorities.) One need only examine the curriculum of teacher-training institutions and see the lack of instruction on play and play leadership given to teachers to understand why little attempt has been made to break out of this vicious circle.

The argument presented above applies largely to the developed nations of the world. In Third World countries, it is usually not a matter of political, educational or social development philosophy that has resulted in the lack of emphasis on the provision of play opportunities; it is simply economics. Many countries are so poor that they are forced to concentrate on the provision of the basic necessities such as food, shelter and health. Play is simply not an issue for many countries. (Unfortunately, this state of affairs often results despite massive expenditures on such anti-human goods as military hardware by many 'poor' countries.)

This lack of money for play and recreation opportunities is not, however, limited solely to the Third World. In these times of inflation and economic uncertainty, most public agencies in the developed countries are sorely pressed for funds. They are constantly being required to justify programmes or facilities. One common result is that they are in effect forced into reinforcing their dependence on activities which have been traditionally successful (e.g., the Canadian penchant for ice hockey for young males). Quite simply, the economics of government do not encourage innovation. (This view is compounded by the complication that because of their very nature, bureaucracies are rarely innovative.) The problem is more severe for play and recreation facilities and programmes than for other government services (e.g., sewers, transportation) because play and recreation do not lend themselves to cost-benefit analysis.

Because of inflation, increasing taxes, high rates of unemployment, energy shortages and other assorted crises, it must be apparent to most planners and decision makers that the rules of the game of life are being changed. The phrase 'being changed' seems more appropriate than 'changing' because often the people directly involved in the changes have had no input into the process; the power of external forces is increasing. The implications of such a trend on the provision of social services — including the leisure services delivery system — are potentially great. The impacts are quite evident today. In the face of not-unexpected opposition to rapidly rising taxes, government agencies are drastically cutting back on expenditures on leisure services and even beginning to question the social value of existing services. For example, the Honourable D'Arcy McKeough (former Ontario Minister of Treasury, Economics and Intergovernmental Affairs) recently publicly questioned whether or not the Province of Ontario has devoted too much money to the acquisition of land for public recreation purposes. On another level, the parkland acquisition component of the budget of the Department of Parks and Recreation of the City of Toronto has lost ground to inflation over the last ten years. (More money is spent on replacing worn sidewalks in Toronto than is spent on acquiring new parkland.) But then, perhaps they are correct: what is needed is not more parkland, but a higher quality of recreation and play opportunities.

Planners and decision makers must recognize that the age of the 'Conserver Society' is imminent if it has not already arrived. In order to maintain the present level of services — to say nothing of increasing the level of services — it will be necessary completely to re-evaluate the present array of available resources and examine potential new resources. Quite simply, the probability is fairly high that recreation agencies, in the face of stiff competition from other social service agencies for a share of a finite resource base, will be forced to do more with less. Such a conclusion is reinforced by the following comment in a recent study of the attitude of elected municipal officials in the Canadian Province of Ontario toward culture and recreation (Zuzanek, 1977, p. 8):

> Generally, the survey revealed rather favourable attitudes of elected municipal officials toward culture and recreation, but when it comes down to decision-making, it appears that the support of culture and recreation is weighed against other social needs which are often perceived as more pressing.

Another major factor is that there is no identifiable profession which can be termed 'play planning' and no body of knowledge which can universally be defined as a 'theory of play'.[2] As a result, planning for play is usually done by professionals from collateral disciplines (urban planning, landscape architecture, social work, etc.). Often their knowledge of play is minimal. When people with an educational background in play are involved, their expertise is usually in the area of programming or research, not planning or design. Given the absence of a recognizable profession of play planning, it would appear appropriate to suggest that the only viable approach to play planning is either (a) an interdisciplinary team or (b) a person with an interdisciplinary education. The problems with the former are manifold, including the difficulty of working as a team and high cost. The problem with the latter is the rarity of such individuals (largely because of the small number of educational institutions that encourage interdisciplinary education and the difficulty involved in mastering and synthesizing all of the necessary fields of study).

Although the following quotation deals specifically with preschool children, it can be argued that its philosophy can be applied equally well to all children:

> Infants, toddlers and preschoolers are a vulnerable group with few past experiences to use as guides for dealing with their constantly expanding world. As well, they are in a period when the physical, mental and emotional patterns are formed which will ultimately influence their behaviour in later years. As such, they need an environment that nurtures, but does not frustrate, their total development. So precious and precarious is our charge as adults, that we must take seriously our responsibility of providing preschoolers with opportunities for healthy growth and learning through play that will give them satisfaction, a sense of competence and the joy of creativity. (Central Mortgage and Housing Corporation, 1976, p. 3)

Adults in general and public agencies in particular have a duty to provide constructive, creative play opportunities for children; out of necessity, they must be innovative. Such a duty has been emphasized in the United Nations Declaration of the Rights of the Child and at the United Nations Habitat Conference held in Vancouver in 1976. Despite the almost universal lip-service that is paid to this duty, Hill (1972, p. 1) notes that

> There is no country in the world, I truly believe, that has given proper priority to the needs of children in the modern city environment, in spite of the fact that the children comprise over 40 per cent of the population and are the biggest potential assets of any country. . . .

All the material gleaned from studies around the world cry out for designed, researched and legislated schemes of a positive, comprehensive nature, which have as their aim to enrich and stimulate the life of the young in mind, body and creative ability, thus preventing the ills that later need expensive remedies or soul-destroying custodial care.

The normal child is still in the majority, thank God, but it is the normal child that is most neglected.

She goes on to say that the reason for this short-sighted policy is that the child is not the paying client: the child has no power, political or financial, and no protest voice. The responsibility, therefore, must lie with adults; however, individuals are usually disorganized, unrecognized and often divided. Public agencies dealing with children, therefore, must accept a large proportion of the responsibility.

It would appear that, nominally at least, many public agencies have accepted their duty. One has only to examine the annual reports of such agencies to see the colourful maps that list all of the parks and playgrounds. Research, however, into the use of urban parks, for example, has shown that the basic characteristic of such facilities is non-use (e.g., Gold, 1972). Two questions arise, the answers to which are closely interwined: where do the children play; and why do they not play in the parks and playgrounds? The answer is that the children are playing everywhere — in their houses and private yards, on the streets, in vacant lots, in any area that even remotely resembles a 'natural' environment. In other words, they are playing in those environments which have all of the characteristics that most traditional parks and playgrounds do not have: complexity, variety, challenge, risk, flexibility, adaptability, etc. Quite simply, most traditional parks and playgrounds are boring for children. If they do use them, they spend most of their time playing in sandboxes and wading pools — i.e., those elements of the playground which have many of the characteristics noted above — or interacting with other children. The playground equipment is usually ignored, quickly abandoned, or merely incidental to the play experiences.

A basic reason for the continued dependence of most recreation agencies on traditional playgrounds with their static metal apparatus usually encased in asphalt or concrete is simply tradition. Another reason is the lack of sophisticated planning and design skills and a true understanding of the needs of children, characteristics which are particularly common for poorer countries. It would appear, however,

hat the basic reason is fear — fear on the part of planners and decision
makers (especially politicians) that playgrounds are dangerous. They
choose traditional playgrounds because they perceive that they are less
dangerous than creative or adventure playgrounds. In fact, however,
there is strong evidence that the number of accidents and fatalities
occurring as a result of the use of playground equipment has been
greatly exaggerated. Children do get hurt on playground equipment,
but then they can get hurt in many different places and in many
different ways. In addition, there is some evidence to suggest that
adventure and creative playgrounds are no more dangerous than traditional playgrounds (Wilkinson and Lockhart, 1976). Municipal
recreation agencies should be encouraged to go beyond the traditional
playground. As Lady Allen of Hurtwood (1968, p. 17) has stated,

> It is a rewarding experience for children to take and overcome risks,
> and to learn to use lethal tools with safety. Life demands courage,
> endurance and strength, but we continue to underestimate the
> capacity of children for taking risks, enjoying the stimulation of
> danger and finding things out for themselves. It is often difficult to
> permit children to take risks, but over-concern prevents them from
> growing up. This is all too clearly seen in the dull, 'safe' playgrounds
> that continue to be devised.

A *creative playground* — which appears to be a North American
phenomenon — is a formal playground characterized by apparatus that
is designed and created from materials which are more 'natural' (e.g.,
wood, stone, brick, hills). It is 'creative' in the sense of using more
natural materials while at the same time attempting to offer a wider
choice and range of alternatives by means of more abstract design.
Canadian cities now abound with creative playgrounds, but the
problem is that in many cases they are mere transformations of traditional playgrounds, with wood being substituted for metal. It is often
painfully obvious that there has been a lack of skilled planning and
design.

Adventure playgrounds have often been labelled 'junk' playgrounds,
in which children under supervision of trained play leaders are given
the opportunity to take part in a variety of self-directed activities (e.g.,
constructing huts and forts using materials and tools provided at the
playground, lighting fires and cooking, camping, keeping animals).
Adventure playgrounds are not a recent invention. In 1943 the
'Emdrup Junk Playground' was opened in German-occupied

Copenhagen. Now adventure playgrounds are widespread throughout Europe and Great Britain. Despite relatively extensive publicity, however, they have gained little acceptance in North America.

An even more interesting and innovative concept is that of the *playpark,* an integrated complex of activities and facilities which often includes an adventure playground, music and theatre programmes, the planting of fruits and vegetables, sports, outings, the keeping of animals, etc. Such playparks would require a fairly large area (approximately 7,500 m^2) and a year-round trained staff. In 1972, there were 157 such 'parkleken' in Stockholm, usually located adjacent to a residential complex. It would appear that such playparks have not spread beyond Scandinavia.

The above comments apply to both established and new parks and playgrounds. One other area of concern, however, should be noted. With the proliferation of high-rise residential areas and the development of new towns in Canada and many other countries, it would seem essential that research take place into the nature of the leisure service delivery system for such areas. The needs of children in such areas are different from those of children in older, single-family dwelling areas.

One could argue, however, that such facilities as creative or adventure playgrounds and playparks are merely marginal innovations, rather than substantive innovations. Chevalier *et al.* (1974) describe marginal innovation in terms of the management of established trends, which by definition means the reinforcement of the established pattern of interests. Substantial innovation is in terms of the management of new trends, which by definition means a realignment of interests. In effect, the first is within the existing institutional structure and the second is part of structural change.

> Marginal innovation and its consequent reinforcement of interests is a frequent occurrence — a matter of small-scale adjustment to the existing technology or organization of the system. And marginal innovation and reinforcement of interests can also result from the application of advanced technology. In fact, the application of new and highly advanced technology can cut down the possibility of substantial innovation by doing the old job just a little bit better — by making possible a marginal innovation, albeit often at much higher cost. Paradoxically, the higher cost can also have the tendency of reinforcing present interests.

> Neither marginal nor substantial innovation, then, is dependent solely on established or new technology, on one hand, or

institutional arrangements on the other. Each is derived from some appropriate new technological-institutional relationship or capacity. This is particularly true in relation to the incorporation of an environmental imperative into technological inventions and its adoption through environmental management procedures. (Chevalier *et al.*, 1974, p. 6)

It can be seen, therefore, that, except at a very basic level (i.e., established interests versus new trends), there is no simple, hard-and-fast distinction between marginal and substantive innovation. A further complication occurs when more than one decision-making unit is being discussed. For example, what is marginally innovative for one country (e.g., the extension of the concept of adventure playgrounds into playparks in Sweden) may be substantially innovative for another. Marginal innovation, then, is fine-tuning of an existing situation, without comment as to the present 'quality' of that situation. Substantial innovation is the creation of a new situation, which, it is hoped, is an improvement on the present situation.

Many countries — or, at least, parts of many countries — do already have a child-support system which goes a long way towards providing adequate play opportunities for all children. Such systems require only marginal innovation. Examples might include increased emphasis on play in hospitals; greater use of music, drama, games, arts and crafts; play training programmes for parents; etc. Other countries — and parts of even the 'richest' countries — have child-support systems which are woefully inadequate. They require substantial innovation. Examples might include teacher and play leader training; the provision of basic play opportunities; etc.

It is the purpose of these volumes to provide knowledge and incentive to planners, designers, researchers, politicians, parents and others involved with the upbringing of children that can lead to (1) increased awareness of the importance of play and (2) innovation — whether that be marginal or substantial innovation — in the provision of play opportunities within the context of their own culture. It must be noted that no hard-and-fast solutions, no definitive answers, no concrete plans or programmes are provided here, as each situation must be treated as being unique. Rather, a number of suggestions and possible alternative approaches are put forward which, with careful thought and research, may be applicable to other settings.

Finally, it must be repeated that the push for innovation rarely begins within an institution; it usually comes from an external force.

Quite simply, a lack of access to the planning and decision-making process is characteristic of most public agencies dealing with children. There are two broad levels on which public involvement is required. At the national or regional level, the public should be able to participate in the development of broad goals and objectives for their country or region as a whole. (This can be accomplished through the formulation of a national plan for child development.) At the local level, the public should have an opportunity to become involved in issues in the locality or neighbourhood. Such a process assumes an accurate data base of information on the supply of existing services by the recreation agencies and other agencies, on the nature of the population and its sub-populations, and the nature of their leisure patterns and requirements. It also requires means by which an interested and involved public can participate in decision making about their children and their future.

Notes

1. Emphasis added.
2. Even the work of Piaget is neither universally accepted nor widely known beyond the realm of developmental psychology. To prove this latter point, try asking a park planner or playground designer about Piaget.

References

Allen of Hurtwood, Lady Marjory. 1968. *Planning for Play*. London: Thames and Hudson.
Caplan, Frank and Theresa Caplan. 1973. *The Power of Play*. Garden City, New York: Anchor Books.
Central Mortgage and Housing Corporation. 1976. *Play Spaces for Preschoolers*. Ottawa: Central Mortgage and Housing Corporation.
Chevalier, Michel, David Morley and Don MacKay. 1974. 'Innovation in environmental management'. A working paper prepared for the Canadian Council for University Research on the Environment, Annual Meeting, Toronto, 27–8 May.
Gold, Seymour. 1972. *Urban Recreation Planning*. Philadelphia: Lea and Febiger.
Hearn, Francis. 1976–7. 'Towards a critical theory of play', *Telos*, 30, Winter, pp. 145–60.
Hill, Polly. 1972. *An Overview of the Needs of Children and Youth in the Urban Community*. Ottawa: Central Mortgage and Housing Corporation.
Riesman, David. 1954. *Individualism Reconsidered*. Glencoe, Illinois: Free Press.
Selsam, H. and H. Martel (eds). 1963. *Reader in Marxist Philosophy*. New York: International Publishers.
Wilkinson, Paul and Robert Lockhart. 1976. *Safety in Children's Formal Play Environments*. Toronto: Ontario Ministry of Culture and Recreation.
Zuzanek, Jiri. 1977. 'Attitudes of elected municipal officials toward culture and recreation', *Recreation Research Review*, 5, 3, pp. 7–11.

Part One

TOWARD THE PERFECT PLAY EXPERIENCE

1 TOWARD THE PERFECT PLAY EXPERIENCE

Polly Hill

Introduction

Many people involved in children's play share an ultimate goal, no matter what their discipline, their area of play work, or their relationship with children. The goal is to improve children's play environments and to increase the quantity and quality of children's play opportunities and positive play experiences. None — except a few dreamers — expects to reach the perfect solution. It is the striving toward that perfection that counts — and that is the topic of this paper.

What then are some basic principles or criteria that can be used to evaluate play experiences? What can be used to evaluate programmes, play environments and leadership techniques? One should start with the end-product: what kind of a human being or adult is desirable? What kind of Canadian, Swede, Britisher, Indian, African? Is there a common denominator? It is proposed that value systems, no matter how different, include the following elements:

1. physical fitness;
2. intelligence;
3. creativity and imagination;
4. emotional stability and initiative;
5. social assurance and co-operation;
6. self-confidence and competence;
7. individuality;
8. a sense of responsibility and integrity;
9. a non-sexist outlook;
10. a sense of humour.

Of course, the child's home and school are major influences in his/her development. There is ample evidence, however, to indicate that the out-of-school life — the play life — of the child is also a major influence on what he/she will become.

What then are the criteria for a perfect play experience? Several different sources, including instinct, personal experience, practitioners and researchers, have all contributed to the information on which these criteria are founded. Little need be said here about instinct and personal experience, but special note must be taken of practitioners and researchers. There are practitioners who share their philosophies and work experience through their writings — John Dewey, Susan Isaacs, Catherine Reed, Lady Allen of Hurtwood, Arvid Bengtsson, to mention only a few who have published in English. There are the researchers: Jean Piaget on how children learn; Michael Ellis on what play is; Hulme and Massie on where children play in the cities; and Robin Moore and Roger Hart on how children play when adults are not watching. As a practitioner, I have been interested in the Environmental Design Research Association's concern about the implementation of research. I am also delighted to see that researchers are working more and more with practitioners and in many cases involving the children themselves in the research process. But there are times when I worry about researchers. For example, I always knew someone, somewhere, would research children's use of mud. Well, somebody did. They put the data into a computer and came out with the astonishing finding that children preferred wet dirt to dry dirt. But will this well-documented, sensitively gathered evidence on children's love of mud and creative uses of mud convince recreation administrators and school janitors to put a mud hole in every playground? Or will this study instead collect dust? Dry dust?

We are in the computer age — an era of sophisticated research. We need these in-depth looks at what may be ignored or taken for granted, but, as one researcher said at the International Playground Association conference in 1972, practitioners must act, they cannot wait for us to prove that what they are doing is right or wrong.

Another example of research, which put forward recommendations that were acted upon and became government regulations, set play opportunities in council housing in England back 30 years, in my opinion. I am referring to *Children at Play*, a publication of the United Kingdom's Department of the Environment (1973). This study reported research based on existing playgrounds in council housing. It resulted in the Department of Environment Circular No. 79—12, which demanded a specific number of seesaws, swings, slides and roundabouts for each project; the bigger the project, the higher the number of each item required. What went wrong? The researchers were gathering the wrong data. They counted the times the children used the only equipment available to them, which happened to be traditional playground equipment. They must have had a computer code for seesaw, and none for mud. They did not consult the practitioners until the review copy stage. Eventually, the National Playfield Association managed to inject a chapter on adventure playgrounds, but too late to affect the Design Standards Circular.

It is the action criteria that I want to speak about: how to judge a good play experience, in order not to perpetuate the useless and meaningless; instead, how to create opportunities for play that nurture the child's total development. Figure 1.1 lists my criteria for judging the 'perfect' play experience. Other criteria may be added, or some of these omitted. First, each of the points will be explained and then used to rate five different environments or play programmes.

Physical Fitness

Physical fitness involves activities and equipment that develop the large muscles of the body in the arms, legs, neck, torso and heart. From birth, children stretch, pull, push, move from place to place and gain control from random action to purposeful action, all without anyone telling them how. As children grow older, adults have a tendency to instruct, to coach; however, there are a myriad of physical activities that children do that are not taught. They learn by doing. No one ever taught a child to climb a tree nor does a tree have built-in safety controls. In design terms, this means providing opportunities that require the use of the large muscles and present a challenge. Safety features should be designed for the unexpected slips, for being pushed, etc., but should not restrict the challenge. If there is no incentive to go higher, for instance, the child's physical development will not be stretched and he/she will soon get bored.

Intelligence and a Sense of Inquiry

The development of an inquiring mind requires as much exercise as developing the body muscles. Children need opportunities to explore, to experiment with cause and effect and with solving real problems. They need to work with things they can move and change. In design terms, it means an environment with a great deal of variety, with lots of loose materials and natural materials that can be studied and moulded. It also requires a leader who can act as a catalyst.

Creativity and Imagination

We know very well how to kill creativity, but little about how to nurture it and keep it alive. One still sees identical bunny rabbits on recreation centre and school walls, drawn to the model of the instructor. Children need practice and exercise in expressing themselves, in whatever media are available, or just with themselves and their imagination. There is a process that I call 'from mud pies to murals' or — to borrow from John Dewey — 'learning through experience', a process

Figure 1.1: Criteria for the Perfect Play Experience

Does the environment, or the programme develop and encourage:	T	N	P	C	A
1. Physical fitness	–	–	–	–	–
2. Intelligence and a sense of inquiry	–	–	–	–	–
3. Creativity and imagination	–	–	–	–	–
4. Emotional stability and initiative	–	–	–	–	–
5. Social interaction and co-operation	–	–	–	–	–
6. Self-confidence and competence	–	–	–	–	–
7. Individuality	–	–	–	–	–
8. A sense of responsibility and integrity	–	–	–	–	–
9. Equality between the sexes	–	–	–	–	–
10. A sense of humour	–	–	–	–	–
11.	–	–	–	–	–
12.	–	–	–	–	–
Totals	–	–	–	–	–

Note: For the purposes of this chart perfect means: toward perfect, good, positive, the opposite of bad, sterile, generating negative behaviour.

that continues throughout life. Creative adults are desperately needed, not ones who paint murals necessarily, but ones who can deal creatively with the world's ills. In design terms, the answer is the same as for developing intelligence: lots of variety, lots of loose material – lots of stimulation.

Emotional Stability and Initiative

How can emotional stability be fostered through play environments and play programmes? Perhaps here, more than anywhere else, a play worker can be the catalyst, intervening when children bully each other or ostracize one of their peers. Children take the initiative when they feel good about themselves. They search for new experiences and emotional satisfaction. (The need for a play worker to raise the quality of play experience for the individual child becomes more and more evident as this list proceeds.) In design terms, a play programme with a leader is required. In particular, a programme is needed which gives the leader time to know the children, to help them where needed, and which has the kind of environment that honours and encourages initiative.

Social Interaction and Co-operation

The primitive strivings of young children to share, to co-operate and to make friends must be recognized. Children need opportunities that bring them together, that give them something to do together, to laugh about, to exchange ideas about, and that will give them practice interacting on a social level. In design terms, social play can be encouraged by play houses; by materials to make their own huts; by blocks and boards for younger children to construct into houses, stores or spaceships; by places to meet and talk; by lots of loose materials with which to work — together.

Self-confidence and Competence

Doing well and knowing how to do things involves many things. It means experiencing and trying in an atmosphere that is uncritical and not too demanding. It means going at one's own pace, in one's own time. In design terms, this means a wide variety of choices and challenges.

Individuality

To conform without meaning to the dictates of a gang, to be afraid of being an individual, is a stage of development that sometimes needs the tender intervention of a parent or a play worker. Here again, play programmes that honour differences and do not ridicule them can do a great deal to help develop a child's individuality. In design terms, it means programmes which allow for a great deal of freedom and which have leadership that is not directive in nature.

A Sense of Responsibility and Integrity

Giving children responsibility — especially for something they love, such as an animal — helps them relate to the need to take responsibility for their own actions. Play programmes that foster responsibility taken positively, in a play situation, can have long-lasting effects. In design terms, it means places to house animals and freedom for a large degree of child control in the programme.

Equality Between the Sexes

Even though children in the middle years (7–12) tend to play separately and have gangs of their own sexes, programmes can do a lot to ensure that equality is maintained and not flaunted. In design terms, it means offering programmes that are of interest to both sexes and are not competitive between them or sexist in nature.

A Sense of Humour

Can a play programme develop a sense of humour? Possibly not. This seems to be basically the family role, starting at babyhood, but perhaps programmes can awaken the dormant sense that has not been stimulated, and recognize and cater to the natural gaiety of children.

If each play environment and play programme is evaluated according to these criteria, perhaps one will pause and not be content to go half-way, supplying only a physical play environment — as is happening so much here in Canada — with nothing for the mind or the development of creative power.

Return now to Figure 1.1 and score each type of play environment as described below. Score each type of play environment for each criterion from '0' (no value) to '10' (highest value). Then add the scores for each type of play environment.

T. Traditional Playground

Imagine a swing, slide and teeter-totter made of iron, or their modern equivalents made of wood, with rows of logs, stuck in the ground at different heights, usually in a semi-circle; a single culvert pipe on its side, and a 2 m x 2 m sand box with 5 cm of dry sand.

N. Natural Area

Imagine a wood and a small stream, a bog and some large rocks — accessible to the children, but unsupervized. Imagine your own ingredients.

P. A Preschool Play Centre

Visualize a preschool play centre modelled after the 'One O'clock Club' in England. It is open to all preschool children from 1.00 to 5.00 p.m. without charge. A parent or an adult accompanies them. An indoor room, equipped like a nursery school, with unit blocks, doll corner, book corner, dress-up corner, science centre. A large indoor climbing ladder with space around it for rainy days. Table toys and a place for parents to sit and watch, and have a cup of tea. An outdoor play-yard, a low containing fence to aid supervision, a 2-metre-high climbing-frame, some tyre swings, backed into a corner for safety. A small, simple play house with lots of old pots and pans. Two hundred large hollow blocks and boards and sturdy boxes to make your own house or store. A grass area, with wild flowers and sturdy bushes for hiding in, and for finding insects and tiny creatures. A large, well-drained sand area, the sand

50 cm deep, with a centre cake table. A play stream that you fill with a hose and empty like a bathtub near the sand area. Play leaders trained to work with young children, but able to handle more children, because a parent is there to deal with the child's bathroom and tear-producing problems. Open all year round, not just in summer.

C. Creative Playground

'Creative playground' is a term used in North America to differentiate it from an adventure playground. It is designed by adults; sometimes the children help in the design process and the building, but it is essentially adult-produced. Once it is built, it stays that way. This creative playground has a huge play structure with platforms, ladders upright and perpendicular to climb and hang from, apertures to crawl through, ropes to shinny up, gang swings made of tractor tyres, balancing beams, and wide slides at exciting inclines; places to perch, and also a variety of ways that each aspect of the structure can be used, including many ways the designer never dreamed of. The structure covers a large physical area. Make it any size, as long as it can accommodate a hundred 'monkeys' at one time. But everything is linked – it is all part of the same structure, carefully spaced to allow freedom of action. It stands on a large fine-sand surface to cushion falls. There is nothing else in the playground. There is no leader.

A. Adventure Playground

Imagine a 4000 m² of rough land surrounded by a high wooden fence with fast-growing willow trees planted around the outside. The fence has a wide gate for a truck and a regular door or gate for people. It can be locked when the leader is not there. A play hut containing one large playroom, a leader's office and sick bay, two bathrooms, and a storage area filled with creative materials, paint, clay, small wood-working tools, games, puzzles, musical instruments, slightly beaten-up but playable, innumerable treasures of mysterious origin, the cast-offs from the community – beautiful junk. Outside a large tool hut adjoins the building, with a large supply of hammers, saws, shovels, kegs full of nails. Near the gate there is a pile of lumber, scraps of wood, broken furniture, fence posts, wooden crates – the cast-offs of the building industry or wrecking company or junk dealer. Everywhere you look, huts of every description can be seen, arranged haphazardly covering the ground, grouped around an open space, where huge telephone-pole structures tower in the sky, and swinging acrobats fly overhead twenty feet up. A mud hole is found with an elaborate but temporary canal system. A bonfire consumes useless scraps and attracts fascinated onlookers. Close against the fence a series of original-looking rabbit hutches house an odd assortment of small animals. A small barn, obviously built by the children, houses two goats, one lamb and a very strange-looking dog. A slab of plywood resting on bricks serves as the editor's desk for the local newspaper. The playground has two trained workers and at least two volunteers at peak periods. It services a floating population of 30 to 150 children at any one time and is open all year round. Construction activities cease in winter because it is located in a cold climate, but the group still gathers after school and on holidays. Add your own embellishments. Perhaps you would like to turn this into a youth farm, with horses and open fields and trails nearby to ride them on, and the leader trained to help the child understand horses and how to handle them with care and love.

Now, sum the scores for each type of play space. There should be some differences. The higher the total, the more value has been attributed to the activities contained in the sample environment described. Of course, I have coloured my descriptions to persuade you to my bias — obviously towards those experiences that 'exercise' creativity, ingenuity and a sense of inquiry. I do hope that traditional playgrounds did not win! Someone asked me if, when I was a child, I had a bad bump on the behind from a teeter-totter because I seem to hate them so. No I did not, but yes I do! I hate them, not for what they are — that is harmless enough — but for what they displace. We cannot afford to clutter the landscape with sterile environments. Every bit of open space is precious and must be conserved for play — play that is meaningful and positive and attracts children away from the dangers of the street.

I also dislike the traditional playground because it serves the housing authorities, the developers, the recreation and school authorities as a way out, a scapegoat. Plunk down a few pieces of equipment and your conscience is clear. The fact that the play areas are put down on any old piece of land inappropriate for housing, but also inappropriate for play, and that the choice of equipment is inappropriate to the children it is supposed to serve, is not admitted. Somehow that does not count, because the user — the child — is not the client. I know of no other product on the market that continues sales when it is defunct, little-used and often dangerous. In Canada, a hopeful sign is that the biggest manufacturer of traditional equipment now offers an alternative line.

The alternatives for poor environments are many. They are examined in depth elsewhere in this book, but I would like to conclude with a few ɔmments on the other types of play spaces noted above.

If the natural area did not get your highest marks, perhaps it was cause there was not a leader, because your image of a natural area had me undesirable characters lurking in the bushes, or because you were inking that natural areas are just not available in some cities and to me children because of their handicaps. The natural areas that exist, t are not being used, can be made more available with a little forest eatment. The underbrush can be controlled, or a stream made more cessible for young children, by terracing the steep sides. Of course, a ɪder also will attract more children and more use means less abuse, wer undesirable characters. An important aspect that seems to be ɪored, however, is that, if a natural area for children is not available, e can be created. The Washington Environmental Yard in Berkeley, lifornia, is an example. Here, incidently, is where a researcher, Robin ɔore, had to 'make' a varied environment for play or 'cause it to ppen', before he could test the broad spectrum of play choices and ality of play that he knew existed.

I chose the preschool centre as one of many solutions because it is appropriate to North America, where a harsh climate restricts young ɪldren from outside play for long winter months. In spite of its propriateness, I know of none on this side of the Atlantic. The ʾedish Play Pens in Stockholm developed by Stina Wetland-Larsson ɛ open to all children without signing up. One can either drop a child ʾ while shopping, or going to the doctor, or come with him/her. The nciple behind these programmes is to provide for all preschool ɪldren, through the parks and recreation systems, what a few children ʋe in nursery school, day care, or organized preschool play groups. ese play centres operate all the year round and provide play oppor- ɪities on a community basis in all kinds of weather, cold or wet, by ɛluding indoor space.

The creative playground described above was of course a limited e, a huge play structure with nothing else, so common to North ɪerica. European creative playgrounds seem to be much more com- ʾhensive with a wider variety of play elements: go-cart trails down ɛp inclines, play streams, play houses, lots of loose materials, an ɛn space for ball games, and an adventure playground component ɪt could be closed off when the leader is not there. The creative part is rmally open at all hours and in all weather as there is usually indoor ɪce as well.

The adventure playground provides the maximum play potential for ɪividual development. It can take different forms, but as a concept it still has no equal. Nevertheless, it is hard to convince the paying clien of its importance. Children, however, do not need any convincing. Children are waiting!

I have not, on purpose, discussed perfect play experiences that happen in places other than formal play spaces. These are dealt with elsewhere in this book. Others have discussed the general topic of pla and described how cities can be designed to include play as an urban function. Many of the other papers address the subject of how childr can use the environment for play and education. Nor have I touched family interaction; indeed, I have spoken of leaders as if there were r parents. That is ridiculous, of course; doing things together as a fami is an essential ingredient in the enrichment of children's play experiences. On purpose, I did not talk about the handicapped child because I believe that our aims for them are exactly the same as for children without handicaps – only our expectations are different. Aiming for their full potential is the same. I have picked my samples where adult intervention in the environment and programme plannin can enrich play experiences for today's children.

I come fresh from a ten-day experience where eleven children, ranging in age from a retarded two-year-old to a gifted 15-year-old w a fair mix of boys and girls, used a perfect play environment to its fullest. It occurred on an island on a Canadian lake with a big sprawl cottage, where no one cares if you sit in a wet bathing suit on the liv room couch. The framework of rules was minimal, involving safety only. I watched as each age tested their skill and daring in swimming water skiing, climbing a ladder structure and high trees. I saw the litt two-year-old's plastic pool turned into a motor boat basin by three ∢ to 5-year-olds with accompanying noises, the loudest of which came joyfully from the squashed two-year-old. A volleyball net inspired games of all types, and served as a curtain for a dramatic production Card games, jokes, talent nights and building whole villages with floc blocks occupied the evening hours. Ten delightful parents acted as partners in play, catalysts and appreciative observers. They also had space and time to enjoy each other and play on their own level.

Perhaps what we are advocating is nothing new: we just want for children what only some children have now.

> I must laugh and dance and sing
> Youth is such a lovely thing
> Soon I shall be too old, stately
> I shall promenade sedately

Down a narrow pavement street
And the people that I meet
Will be stiff and narrow too
Careful what they say and do
It will be quite plain to see
They were never young like me
When I walk where flowers grow
I shall have to stoop down low
If I want one for a prize
Now I'm just the proper size
Let me laugh and dance and sing
Youth is such a lovely thing

Age 13

Reference

United Kingdom Department of the Environment. 1973. *Children at Play*.
　London: Her Majesty's Stationery Office.

2 'STANDARD' VERSUS 'ADVENTURE' PLAYGROUND

Brenda Fjeldsted[1]

Children did not need a 'special' place for playing in the years of yes
day. They had woods, fields, backyards and safe pathways in which
find adventure. They grew up in the midst of their elders in their sho
– the blacksmith shop, the grocery, the hardware store. As the adult
worked at his trade, the child was able to contemplate, imitate and
assimilate simply through play.

Today, the rural areas continue to be wealthy in this abundance o
ideal, natural places in which children can play. However, in the city
today the 'old' playgrounds have been taken over by traffic and hous
developments. Adults work in offices or factories. Thus the trend to
greater urbanization has created the new problem of providing specia
playgrounds for children. Because of this, the 'standard' playground
we know it came into being. This term refers to the conventional
neighbourhood playground with swings, slides, teeter-totters, swing-
boats, etc.

Tradition has decreed that this playground be designed to provide
opportunities for gross-motor activity through the use of standard st
apparatus (Ellis, 1973, p. 173). It has been assumed that it is possible
design and maintain a playground for its capital cost alone and that a
good playground is one requiring very little maintenance. However,
play is a process of consuming information. In the process, materials
and human resources are consumed and for playgrounds to continue
function, they require continual modification.

The neighbourhood playground's clientele are children who have
typically been there many times. As designed now, the standard play
ground cannot provide the appropriate interactions year-in and year-
to meet the changing needs of the developing neighbourhood childre
It is unfortunate that most of these 'standard' playgrounds are a disa
area for young children. Dramatic play and appropriate physical
explorations do not seem to flourish in this setting. The standard pla
ground seems designed to divert the child to gross-motor activity wh
there is nothing else to do. Boredom from doing the same thing
repeatedly often leads a child to try some dangerous variation. Instea
of being environments for pleasant physical play and social interactic

with one's peers, such playgrounds usually become battlegrounds where each child is on his own (Caplan and Caplan, 1973, p. 220).

Wade (1968) studied playgrounds in Philadelphia and noted that the average visit time to a playground was fifteen minutes and that, during times identified for peak usage, the non-manipulative items stood idle the majority (89–98 per cent) of the time. Dee and Liebman (1970) showed that attendance at a playground was inversely related to the existence of other activities provided by a neighbourhood.

Children have not had much influence on the development of playgrounds. There has been little evolution in the standard playground. Today's playgrounds look similar to those of fifty years ago. The most critical drag on their evolution seems to be the assumption that it is possible to sustain play over the early life of a child without there being any alteration in the play environment.

Playgrounds become unused because the child's interactions with its environment do not spiral upwards in complexity as the child revisits a playground. Once boring and redundant, the standard playground cannot function as a plaything (Ellis, 1973, pp. 137–8).

There have been some rumblings of new approaches to playground planning. Initiated in Sweden and other parts of Europe after World War II was the concept of the 'adventure' playground. Here children are provided with opportunities to explore, investigate, manipulate and engage in epistemic behaviour. There are interesting areas filled with bricks, lumber, dirt and scrap metal. After combining these materials with discreet leadership and supervision, the children can dig, build, change their environment and undertake co-operative projects. The setting is dynamic and manipulable, changing as the various children produce their effects and projects are progressively elaborated. Children use real materials to construct their own playthings and the play occurs during the process of their building as well as their use.

Ellis (p. 219) has noted that 'When children are in control of the equipment, they are in control of themselves as well'. For example, in the 'adventure' playground, when they want to test their balancing skill, they can put a plank on top of two low, hollow blocks and then gradually increase the height to that of a sawhorse or crate. They learn from experience how to avoid hurting themselves and others. Means of mastering potential danger can be incorporated into physical play equipment. A good playground should provide some calculated risk-taking that meets the needs of the adventurous. Ladders and slides without handrails will teach a child co-ordination and competence. The portable, manipulable materials also allow for imaginative play. The children can combine pieces in ingenious ways to create a large boat, a play house, etc., thus making the environment work for them. 'A good adventure playground is never static' (Bengtsson, 1974, p. 81). Construction and destruction go hand in hand. The one is as important as the other.

An important, indispensable factor in an 'adventure' playground is the play leader. Without a leader, the activities would soon stagnate and problems would arise. The experienced leader knows how to rekindle interest and to direct it into new channels when these periods of stagnation occur (Bengtsson, p. 87).

To explore the concept of the 'adventure' playground, comparisons were made between a 'standard' and an 'adventure' playground, using the play of the same group of four children as a basis. The 'adventure' playground was created by the writer on the rural farm where she lived and played as a child.

The group was comprised of two boys, Wade and Scott, respectively aged five and four years and two girls, Marla and Marie, three-and-a-half and two-and-a-half years. They were all from farm environments and none had been to a 'standard' playground before. The children were instructed only 'to play'.

The 'standard' playground was a grassy area of approximately 132 feet by 100 feet, located in the residential area of a town with a population of approximately 2,500. Its location was at one end of the town, having easy accessibility for the children in the neighbourhood. It was a fenced-in area with trees and bushes located near the fence. The equipment in the 'standard' playground consisted of two sets of toddler swings with crossbars to prevent falling out (six swings in each set), one set of big 'strap-like' swings (six swings in the set), one slide, three sets of teeter-totters (with two, two and four teeter-totters in each set), one swing-boat with six handles, one roundabout, and three benches. There was a large light standard with three garbage cans around its base. (See Figure 2.1.)

In building the 'adventure' playground, the natural terrain and structure were included as much as possible. Its area was approximately half the size of the 'standard' playground, measuring 66 feet by 50 feet. The area picked was relatively flat with short grass and was surrounded by some trees which formed somewhat of a 'border'. The bale and straw area, the tyre swing, and the obstacle course were incorporated into the trees that were naturally present in the site.

The materials used were readily accessible and had been present on the farm for some time. Their choice depended largely on their

Figure 2.1: Layout of the 'Standard' Playground

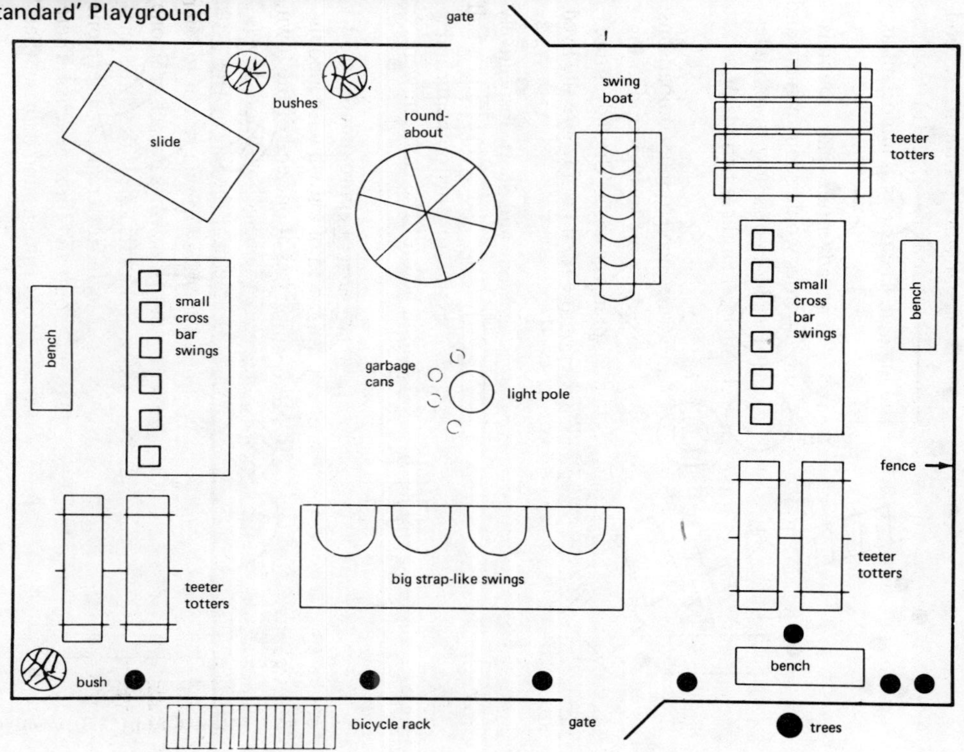

Figure 2.2: Layout of the 'Adventure' Playground

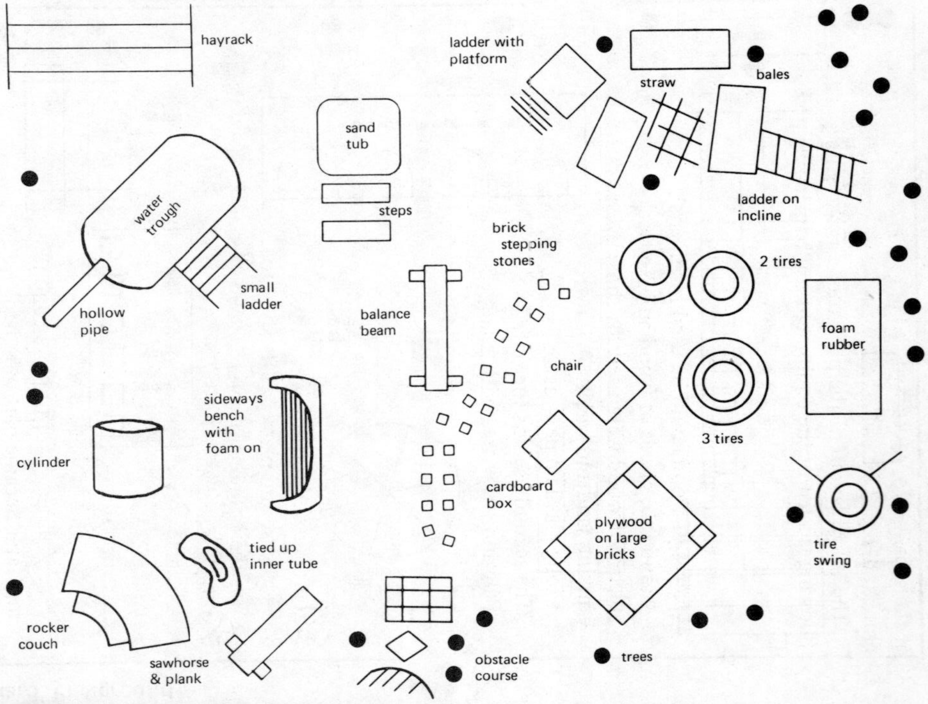

properties of ability to be manipulated and degree of versatility. Many of the gross-motor tasks involved in the 'standard' playground were simulated, e.g., tyre swing, plank and sawhorse 'slide'.

The actual layout of the playground is shown in Figure 2.2. The following is a list of the equipment used, including possible and actual uses:

1. 1 water trough and pieces of wood — used for water play and the pieces of wood could be used for 'boats'.
2. 1 sand tub, pieces of wood and 2 glasses — used for sand play, pieces of wood were used for shovels, and the glasses were used for mixing sand and water.
3. 1 long plastic pipe — as an 'echo chamber' and to run water down. The second use was the only one observed.
4. Bale and straw area with 2 ladders — for climbing and jumping in the straw.
5. Cylinder with one open end — for climbing into and over. Could be used as a 'horse'. The climbing use was observed.
6. Bench — intended for climbing, but during the observation it became a bed.
7. Turned-over couch — as a rocker.
8. Sawhorse and plank — as a slide and for climbing. The second use was the only one observed. Probable reason for not being used as a slide was because the plank's surface was too rough.
9. Obstacle course with grill, metal bed-back and chair — to climb over.
10. Boards and bricks — as a balance beam and to walk on the bricks as 'stepping stones'.
11. Foam rubber — for tumbling and jumping on. It was jumped on and later became part of a 'bed'.
12. Inner tube tied with a rope — as a 'horse'. In the observation, the inner tube was untied and put in the straw for use as a 'nest'.
13. Large piece of plywood with large bricks — to crawl under and on top of. It was observed to be used as part of one of the 'beds'.
14. Tyre and rope swing — to swing and climb on.
15. Chair — ?
16. Cardboard box — ?
17. 5 tyres — for stacking, balancing, rolling, etc. They were observed to be stacked on top of each other to be used as a 'well'.
18. A hayrack — This had not been in the playground plans but turned out to be a distraction that turned into an 'aeroplane'. It seemed to be

a natural climbing and balance beam device.

Results

The findings from the exposure of the children to the two different playgrounds have been summed up in table form for easy comparison.

Table 2.1: Analysis of Play Equipment

'Standard' Playground	'Adventure' Playground
Many pieces had only 'one use'.	Pieces were manipulable and had many versatile uses.
Seemed to involve only gross-motor activity.	Seemed to stimulate self-directed play of all the children, especially those of toddler age. Actual developmental stage in play was not as important.
Stimulated mostly onlooking, solitary, parallel and associative play.	Stimulated much associative and co-operative—imaginative play.

Table 2.2: Play Analysis Using Arousal-seeking Theory

Behaviours	'Standard' Playground	'Adventure' Playground
Exploration	Seemed to have a moment of visual exploration.	Had the same moment of visual exploration but seemed more anxious actually to get into the situation and play.
Investigation	Children went from object to object spending about 5 minutes with each until they had investigated all the objects.	First 10 minutes were spent exploring various objects; then they spent 35 minutes, 1 hour and longer playing with the sand and water before moving on to other objects.
Manipulation	Present.	Present. There seemed to be more actual learning through the manipulation.
Epistemic	Present, but seemed to stop at a point when there was nothing more to learn about an object. Pacer stimuli seemed to be used up.	Present. Each object seemed to provide a wealth of learning situations. Interactions with the environment seemed to spiral upwards.

Table 2.3: Play Analysis Using Social Quality of the Behaviours

Social Quality of Behaviours	'Standard' Playground	'Adventure' Playground
Onlooking	Evident in play of 2½-year-old.	Evident in play of 2½-year-old but seemed diminished because of the environment's provision of manipulable activities for her.
Solitary	Evident in all at some point.	Evident in all at some point but the total amount engaged in seemed less.
Parallel	Present.	Present.
Associative	Present.	Present, but to a greater extent.
Co-operative— imaginative	Only observed on one occasion.	Imaginative play occurred throughout the session with the 3 older children. Co-operative play occurred throughout session also with the imaginative — co-operative occurring at end. Children seemed able to transcend the immediate constraints of the reality of the situation with ease.

Table 2.4: Play Analysis Using Problem-solving Behaviour

Behaviour	'Standard' Playground	'Adventure' Playground
Problem-solving behaviour	Gross-motor problem solving.	Problem solving stemmed from gross-motor involvement and social interaction. Provided more 'real-life' situations.

Table 2.5: Length of Time of Sustained Interest

	'Standard' Playground	'Adventure' Playground
Total length of time of sustained interest of the group.[a]	1 hour, 40 minutes.	1 hour, 45 minutes.
Individual lengths of sustained interest:		
Wade (5-years-old)	55 minutes– 1 hour.	Group collectively decided to leave after 1 hour, 45 minutes.[b]
Scott (4-years-old)	1 hour, 15 minutes.	
Marla (3½-years-old)	1 hour, 10 minutes.	
Marie (2½-years-old)	1 hour, 25 minutes.	

Notes:
(a) There may be some reasons why these two figures are so close:
    1. All the children were experiencing first visits to a 'standard' playground.
    2. More visits to the different environments may have produced results more in keeping with that predicted by the literature, i.e. with less time being spent on the 'standard' playground and a fairly stable amount of time being spent at the 'adventure' playground.
(b) It was interesting to note that after this period of time and a break, the children returned to the 'adventure' playground and began building a 'fort'.

Conclusion

Results from the observation showed that the 'adventure' playground seemed to provide more effective play experiences and to be more stimulating than the 'standard' playground.

Arvid Bengtsson (1974) summed up the philosophy behind 'adventure' playgrounds beautifully in his statements:

> Play is where something turns up to move the imagination. This can be anything but preferably something that can be manipulated and influenced – a friend, a ball, or just a stone to kick about. (p. 49)

> Playgrounds should be community spaces and their social atmosphere is far more important than their mechanical equipment. (p. 63)

The 'adventure' playground seems to be a valuable tool for providing children with a repertoire of novel responses and a greater flexibility in everyday situations. On the other hand, the 'standard' playground teaches a set, rigid response repertoire mainly because of its properties of non-manipulability and inability to change with the changing needs of the child.

The rural area ideally fulfils the requirements of the 'adventure' playground, simply because its environment has safe open spaces, natural terrain and manipulable materials. It is acted and reacted upon continuously and in it children may easily transcend the immediate constraints of the reality of the situation in which they play.

The child who plays more vividly, and subsequently feels it was fun, has more optimism, more confidence and is better able to get on with his task of learning about man, society, culture and community. Apparatus such as swings and roundabouts do not help much in these developmental tasks. Of more value are the opportunities for exploring adult life and for access to facilities that allow children to experiment and become adventurous in meeting their needs and capabilities. What better way to prepare our next generation?

Note

1. This part originally appeared in the *Journal of the Canadian Association for Young Children* (May 1978) and is reprinted with the permission of the editors of the *Journal*.

References

Bengtsson, Arvid. 1974. *The Child's Right to Play*. Sheffield, England: International Playground Association.

Butler, George. 1960. *Playgrounds: Their Administration and Operation*. New York: The Round Press Company.

Caplan, Frank and Theresa Caplan. 1973. *The Power of Play*. Garden City, New York: Anchor Books.

Cohen, Dorothy H. 1973. *The Learning Child*. New York: Vintage Books.

Crowe, Brenda. 1975. *The Playground Movement*. London: George Allen and Unwin.

Dee, N. and J. C. Liebman. 1970. 'A statistical study of attendance at urban playgrounds', *Journal of Leisure Research*, 2, pp. 145–59.

Ellis, M. J. 1973. *Why People Play*. Englewood Cliffs, New Jersey: Prentice-Hall.

Longstreth, Langdon E. 1968. *Psychological Development of the Child*. New York: The Ronald Press.

Lucas, Joyce and Vivienne McKennell. 1974. *The Penguin Book of Playgroups*. Markham, Ontario: Penguin Books Canada.

Mabey, Richard. 1972. *Children in Primary School*. Baltimore, Maryland: Penguin Books.

McCord, Ivalee H. 1971. 'A creative playground', *Young Children*, August, pp. 342–7.

Passantino, Richard J. 1971. 'Swedish preschools: environments of sensitivity', *Childhood Education*, May, pp. 406–11.

Sponseller, Doris (ed.). 1974. *Play As a Learning Medium.* Washington, DC: National Association for the Education of Young Children.
Wade, G. R. 1968. 'A study of free play patterns of elementary school age children on playground equipment'. Unpublished Master's Thesis, Pennsylvania State University.

3 GENERATING RELEVANT URBAN CHILDHOOD PLACES: LEARNING FROM THE 'YARD'

Robin C. Moore

Play is the only way the highest intelligence of humankind can unfold.
>   Pearce (1977, p. 160)

Introduction

The Environmental Yard began in 1971 at Washington Primary School, Berkeley, California, as an urban school/neighbourhood involvement project focused on the conversion of a 1½-acre barren, asphalt 'playground' into a life-supporting childhood and community space.

In *Magical Child*, Pearce (1977, pp. 25–7) states that:

A fully developed intelligence is one designed to exchange energies with anything existing, without ever being overwhelmed. A mature intelligence should be able to interact on three levels . . . in the order arranged by the biological plan: developing a knowledge of the world itself, then a knowledge of the creative relations possible with that world, and then a knowledge of creative relations and possibilities themselves. . . . Any definition of intelligence that does not encompass these three categories of interaction is incomplete. Any development of intelligence that does not move through these three modalities falls short of the biological plan for intelligence and betrays nature's 3-billion-year investment and trust.

Any development can take place only on the foundation given by the child's actual bodily movements, making sensory contact with the world of things and processes. The growth of intelligence rests on a sensorimotor process, a coordination of the child's muscular system with his/her sensory system and general brain processes . . . . Intellectual growth is an increase in the ability to interact . . . that . . . can only grow from that which is known into that which is not yet known, from the predictable into the unpredictable.

These words closely mirror part of the beginning purpose of the Yard: to create a 'play-and-learning' place for the development of what Pearce calls the 'Earth matrix' — a necessity for the full development of creative intelligence and the future survival of planet/humankind.

The Evolution of the Yard

The Yard began with a simple notion (Figure 3.1) that people and place have a certain potential that stays at rest (Figure 3.2) until sufficient leadership is introduced to disrupt the inertia of the status quo and follow through to a point of higher-quality interaction (Figure 3.3).

As it currently exists, the Yard consists of three primary zones (percentage of site in parenthesis):

1. Natural Resource Area (33 per cent): vegetation, aquatic features, pathways, small meeting places;
2. Main Yard Systems (23 per cent): traditional metal play equipment, timber play structures, and 'edge' developments adjacent to fences and school building; and
3. Asphalt (44 per cent): ball play, games and circulation areas.

The Yard is used for informal play during and after school hours, and as a teaching/learning resource within the day-to-day educational curriculum.

Through direct experience, the playing child builds an intuitive connection between micro-scale and macro-scale realities: the child in the present moment interacts with a micro-earth, that accommodates the child's need to develop her/his genetic potential (Figure 3.4); simultaneously, the child assimilates the earth's knowledge, in order to maintain the natural-law relationships necessary for responsible decision-making adults.

Such a two-way flow relationship was inherent in traditional rural society. On-rushing technology has changed all that, to the point where the world faces an unprecedented responsibility to design its own future with a wide and only partly knowable spectrum of possibilities from which to select. The terrifying aspect is the lack of understanding of factors that control people—planet evolution. These factors should be imperative in early childhood education.

Pearce's work makes a uniquely successful intellectual integration between human development, physical environment and social relations. His many concepts, metaphors and warnings suggest alternative prognoses for the future and provide a type of creed to guide further efforts to create appropriate childhood conditions in the urban environment.

How can such a philosophy be translated into actual developments on the ground? It cannot be left to chance. The urban environment must be intentionally planned, designed and developed — especially where children are concerned. If not, they will suffer the results of conventional aesthetic thinking, resulting in surface appearances that have nothing to do with their deeper experiential needs.

The purpose of this paper is to share some of the guiding principles that helped to initiate the Yard or that have emerged as we have gone along. They arise from the perspective of intentional change — or 'design' — and in themselves represent a progression of Pearce's three levels of knowledge: direct 'phenomenological' experience; the application of creative, operational knowledge; and the evolution, manipulation and transfer of derived abstract models to entirely different contexts.

From the beginning, the Yard has evolved as a result of a community participation process (Figure 3.5) whereby site improvements stimulate new behaviour and awareness (feedback) which in turn modify subsequent cycles of site improvements (feed-forward), with progress of the whole being subject to the erratic flow of resource supports (money, materials, equipment, human energy, etc.). Beyond this ongoing cycle of events, the Yard has progressed through a series of distinct stages of development.

Initiation of the project began in 1971. Values of the constituent groups — children, teachers, parents, non-academic staff, neighbourhood residents and after-school users — were assessed systematically, using graphic simulation, interview, questionnaire (Figures 3.6 and 3.7) and observational techniques. Group process sessions — brain-storms, community clinics and environmental encounters — were held. Tentative proposals for changing the site were drawn up and hashed round by a 'core group' of leading participants at weekly workshop meetings, during 1971–2, to the point where people said 'let's stop talking and get on with it'.

Physical change to the site began at the first annual Yardfest held in February 1972, when a few square feet of asphalt were spontaneously torn up by people using their bare hands (Figure 3.8). Stimulated by this direct communication of community wishes, the remaining half-acre of asphalt covering the future Natural Resource Area was bulldozed-up and carted away before officialdom had time to realize what was happening.

Piecemeal development happened for the next two years conditioned by a slow trickle of funds, and punctuated by occasional

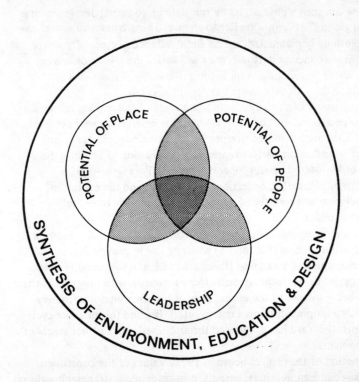

Figure 3.1 (left): The Potentials of People and Place are Activated by
Leadership Disrupting the Inertia of the Status Quo
Figure 3.2 (bottom left): Before: The Former, Asphalted, Monocultural
Yard (1971). Photo by author.
Figure 3.3 (below): After: The Environmental Yard (1978) as seen
from the school roof, showing edge developments, timber play
structures, remaining asphalt games areas, and the Natural Resource
Area in the rear. Photo: Roland Dare Graphics.

Figure 3.4: Direct Interaction with a Diversified Environment
Stimulates the Development of the Whole Person

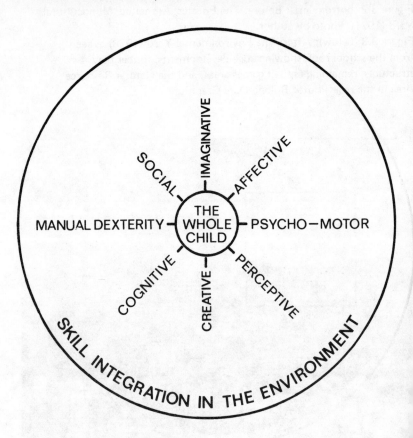

calls to defend the project against premature closure by the school
authorities — frustrating progress and sapping energy.

From 1972—4, progress was enormously stimulated by state, federal
and private sources of funding. The Yard began to bloom. People
appreciated the growth of softness in a 'hard' school (Barton, 1974;
Sommer, 1974). The demoralized community found new vigour, and,
as the 'greening' of the Yard progressed, many sceptical bystanders
began to realize there was something to it after all. It began to look and
feel like a place rather than a piece of urban wasteland.

Over the years, the Yardfest has become established as a crucial

Figure 3.5: Physical Change Stimulates New Experience and Awareness (Feedback), This in turn Helps Guide Future Development (Feed-forward) . . . always Subject to the Unpredictable Availability of Resources

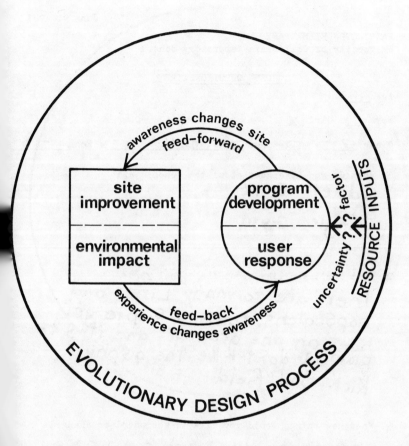

annual event in response to the tribal instincts of the wider scope of the community. The Yardfest has provided an opportunity for the many non-user participants in the Yard's evolution process (parents, city and school district officials, donators of resources, etc.) to interact with the everyday users (children, staff and local residents), to celebrate collectively the results of everyone's scattered efforts . . . in effect communicating the human essence of the demonstration model to a far broader community of interest (Figure 3.9) . . . including the readers of this book.

Figure 3.6: Eight-year-old's Completed Questionnaire (1971), Saying What She Liked and Didn't Like about the Yard, and What She Wanted Added or Changed

June 9, 1971

WASHINGTON ELEMENTARY
University of California Laboratory School

STUDENT QUESTIONNAIRE

Age **8**

Boy ____   Girl **X**

Grade **3**   Teacher **mr. cox**   Room **210**

1. What do you like most about the school yard?

   ladder Bars
   Jungle Gym

2. What don't you like about the school yard?

   ther are to many Lines and hopScotchs. to Many People get hurt on the ground. and it is to plain. I don't like the asphalt Kick Ball field

3. What new things would you like to see added or changed?

   trees Swings Slides grass tires and ropes long tunnel Bird Bath MaZe pond and Fish. Flower gavden

Figure 3.7: Part of the Questionnaire to Parents (1971), Asking What
They Thought of the Yard and How It Could be Improved

PARENTS

13. Do your children ever play on the yard at weekends?

seldom

14. What do you think the school yard should be used for?

*A relaxed place for playing. A
community Park after-hours.
Attraction for small animals*

15. What changes would you like to see made to the school yard?
(Imagine that money is no object!)

*Make "secluded" quiet areas TREES
bare EARTH and WATER ... A garden
area ... ropes to climb. Things built
by the kids. Grass and FLOWERS.
Picnic tables. HUMAN SPACE !*

16. Please use this space to say anything else you want about
the Washington School Grounds.

*This old style concrete, institutionalized
space limits educational experience.
Should be designed by the kids and
everyone else. Could improve
neighborhood greatly.*

Please return this questionnaire to school, to your child's teacher.
Thank you very much for your cooperation.

I would help work on construction.
           848-6874

Figure 3.8: At the First Environmental Yardfest (1972) People Began to Tear up the Asphalt with their Bare Hands, Giving a Clear Message that They Meant Business. Photo: Susan Mullally

Figure 3.9: The Community of the Yard

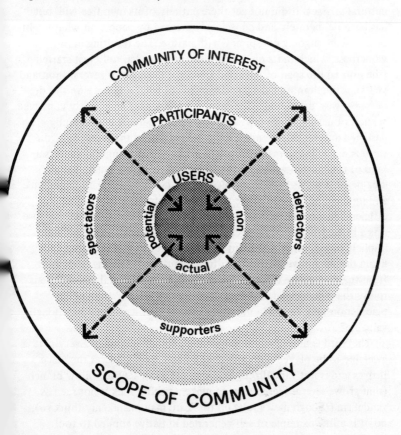

The 'community of the Yard' includes three primary, overlapping layers: the everyday 'users' (plus 'potential users' and 'non-users'); the 'participants' in the process (including 'supporters', 'detractors' and fence-sitting 'spectators'); and the broader 'community of interest' of many professions and types of folks, scattered far and wide.

As it exists today (1979), the Yard is by no means finished, and in some senses it never will be. Because of the strong emphasis on natural resources, originating from the desires of the community, the Yard daily becomes more self-sustaining as nature leads itself toward maturity. The important thing, however, is to look at the Yard as a cultural artifact. It did not get there entirely of its own free will, but has been deliberately and consciously created by people, in what might be called an ongoing conspiracy with nature. The resulting mini-wilderness, which in its own evolutionary terms has only just started (the normal life span of redwood trees, for example, is several thousand years), is much more than a replacement of what was once on the site before it was 'urbanized'. The Yard is a condensed and largely contrived version of nature in the raw. Just like a good park, it is a carefully designed and sensitively managed combination of the essences of the various natural systems appropriate to the surrounding region. It is a kind of museum in which all that is unique or significant about an area or culture has been assembled at one point to intensify experience and understanding — to make learning more feasible or, dare we say, efficient. It is not, however, a museum in the traditional sense, because it is a living environment, open to anyone 24 hours a day. The only implicit admission requirement is a respect for public property and living things. Above all, it has cultural depth and meaning, stemming from the co-creative efforts of many people over several years. Who is to say that the official elite 'big C' culture of 'others' from other places, normally found in museums, is more authentic or educationally valuable?

The Yard is devoid of 'look-but-don't touch' messages. Every part is available to be played with any time by anyone — and yet the place thrives and is not vandalized. Breaking off a few feet of willow branch (that grows several feet a year) to make a fishing stick is not seen as vandalism (though new adults on the Yard may mistakenly think so); no, it is a fine example of self-generated initiative applied to tool invention or problem solving. How does the child 'know' why not to demolish the whole willow tree 'for the fun of it'? Simply, because it would not be fun, because the 'culture of the place' tells her/him so. This culture, or implicit set of signals, that is now embedded in the community and lets newcomer young people know how to behave (mostly at a non-verbal level), forms the hoped-for values in an otherwise plural community.

Most newcomer adults present a much harder problem because of their need for labels and preconceptions about what the Yard is or is not or what it 'ought' to be. Adult mind-sets are terribly hard to change. How do people set themselves free from conventional epistemologies for a while, to take an open-minded trip, fully to sense something as it is, unconditionally? We have not found the answer and, perhaps, according to what Pearce (1977) has to say, there is not an answer; that is, a person's 'matrices' of response to the world were settled in childhood as a set of irreversible tendencies: either open to the learning possibilities of new interactions, or permanently stifled by anxiety. Perhaps intuitive knowledge of nature must be gained by direct experience in the first seven years or so, or it will be lost for ever.

A deep sense of human belongingness, learned through interactions with parents, must equally well be in place. How hard it is to find these two matrices (Earth and Humankind) firmly balanced and in place in the same individual. The split is no better signified than by the academic division of social and natural science. Perhaps there should be a new area of study: humankind/earth science. Conservationists are off in the woods, turning their backs on the dirty city. The urbanists occasionally get down to the neighbourhood, but are confined to sector-interests such as 'housing' or 'jobs' or 'open space'. Urban natural-systems do not attract sufficient interest or are shut out by assumptions of non-feasibility. The environmental needs of children are rarely considered by either group. Meanwhile, psychologists and teachers stay indoors, within the four-walled epistemology of laboratory and classroom.

The Yard began and continues to be a search for a new and radically different epistemology of education. At its core is a belief that education must begin to take the design of the future as a serious priority during the early years of a person's life. Appropriate settings are needed in which divisions between work and play can be overcome, and in which the direct experience of 3 billion years of evolution is available on an everyday basis.

Such experience must occur both during and after school hours, in a place that reduces the separations between childhood, education and community. Children must be reintegrated back into community life, with less emphasis on segregated child-only facilities like day-care centres and playgrounds. This is not to say that particular areas of community turf should not be geared toward the special needs of young people. They should, however, be integrated physically and philosophically into the community whole, so that geography and social experience can be mutually reinforcing. Clusters of public school/leisure life/education places need to be created, accessible to all age groups and life-styles, at the local level.

Application of cardinal ecological values (Figure 3.10) ensures that childhood-environmental quality arises from interaction between children and a sufficient diversity in their immediate surroundings.

Change is constant and is the primary stimulus for the process of learning, growth and development embodied in the continued adaptation of people and environment to each other.

Figure 3.11 illustrates the ideal conditions from which this ecological process must be generated. Since children can manipulate their environment, all relationships are potentially two-way (double-ended arrows). For example, if it rains or the wind blows, children can move to shelter or make one of their own (if materials are available). Since adult society ultimately controls resources, 'institutions' has a one-way connection to all other factors (broken lines), although individual 'people' carry responsibility for extending or inhibiting children's contact and understanding of all the items around the circumference of the diagram. Factors also have independent interactions with each other (not shown by the diagram), which can be modified by design, with good or bad effects, e.g., high buildings can blot out the sun, starving vegetation of light and limiting children's contact with nature. The social processes of play are represented by a link to 'children' and 'people'.

The time factor is present in many forms. All types of development — cultural, physical and individual — are a cumulative, sequential affair . . . a process of maturing through a series of stages and transitions. Other changes are cyclical and to an extent repetitive, e.g., seasons, day and night, the contrasting dynamics of schoolday and weekend. Space and time are interwoven in the experience of movement and speed, so much so for some children that the factors are better considered as a fluid — space-time — in contrast to the way they are chopped up and divorced from each other in adult life.

A child's pace is entirely different from an adult's. This gives leisure planning the primary task of ensuring that children have an opportunity to live in their own space-time, separate from tightly scheduled adult life-styles. It is critically important for children to have escape places of their own, where worldly time can be suspended, so that the nature of their surroundings can be fully explored and they themselves can be protected from the premature effects of 'functional rationality' which Berger *et al.* (1973, p. 202) contend is 'imposed by technology upon everyday life . . . which youth culture has singled out as a principal foil against which to define itself'.

Making Places

The task of design is to bring all that has been discussed up until now down to earth — figuratively and literally. It has much to do with

Figure 3.10: The Development of High-quality Adaptations between Children and their Surroundings can be seen as a Continuing Ecological Process

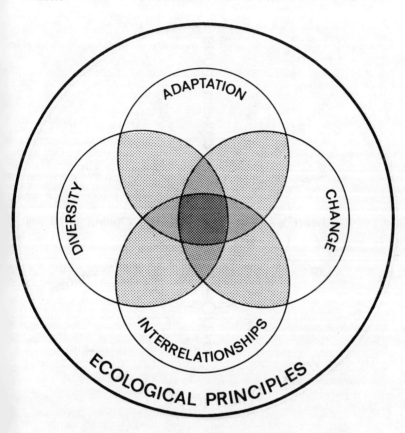

making places, or, rather, creating appropriate support conditions so that places can evolve. What is 'place'? To me, it is a means for integrating knowledge of the world into human relationships. It is the currency of belonging — a hierarchy of intersecting social and physical geographies. Different writers have used different terms: 'topophilia' (Tuan, 1974), 'rootedness' (Lynch, 1976), and 'placeness' (Relph, 1976). Figure 3.12 gives a sense of what it means in physical design terms, involving four basic classes of place-making variables:

Figure 3.11: Access to a Broad Diversity of Resources is Essential to Stimulate Adequate Play and Learning Behaviour. The responsibility for Access and Diversity rests squarely with adult institutions.

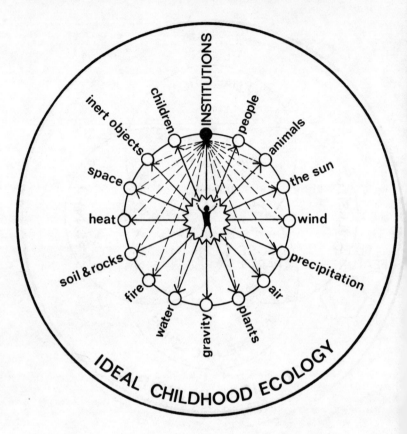

Fixed features:	spaces and permanent accoutrements.
Loose parts:	objects, materials and general 'stuff' that can be manipulated or moved around.
Natural phenomena:	manifest properties of the environment, e.g., the weather.
Populations:	groups of human and non-human inhabitants from the surrounding community.

The meaning of fixed features is self-evident; however, it is

Figure 3.12: Design Includes the Choice and Assembly of Elements, the Provision of Access to Loose Parts and Populations, plus their Interactions with Natural Phenomena, to Enable People to Acquire a Sense of Place

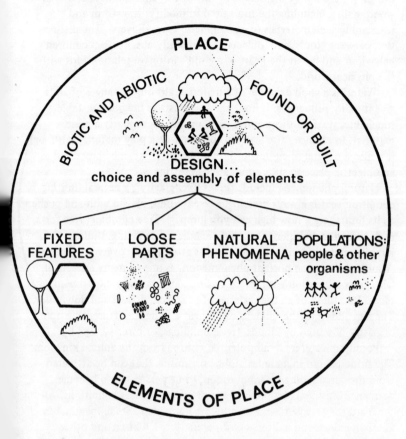

important to remember that most permanent accoutrements of places occupied by children should be considered potential play resources, e.g., benches, rubbish cans, fences and gates, retaining walls, steps, utility poles, trees, etc.

The concept of loose parts was originally described by Nicholson (1971). Two distinct sub-groups are included: objects and materials.

Objects often seem largely to comprise the child's universe. Plants, animals and other natural resources are things that children respond to directly. A child's behaviour, and presumably his/her perception of the world, appears very often to be 'object-oriented'. The 'inert object' category in Figure 3.12 is the rubric for a multitude of 'people-made things' (e.g., empty cans, scraps of cardboard, aluminium foil, bits of wood, nails), including the tools used to modify, transform and reassemble such materials (e.g., hammers, saws, shovels). The distinction between 'tools' and 'objects' is frequently absent from children's behaviour and lies at the heart of a child's intuitive relationships with the physical world.

'Water' is a good example of a material, although changes of state give it many properties. It none the less exists as tangible, tastable, touchable, stuff-on-the-ground. 'Soil' or 'dirt' is similarly a basic material. In essence, 'fire' can also be 'used' as a play material (although it is also a natural phenomenon). In addition, fire can be perceived as an object: a place to sit around, a social setting.

Natural phenomena include things like 'gravity', a natural limiting condition that is always present to be explored, played with and pushed to its limits (e.g., 'how high can you jump?'). Tree climbing, tree forts, rock throwing, ball playing, and all manner of swinging, sliding, jumping and climbing activities express attempts to 'overcome' gravity. 'Wind' is another important phenomenon, as one of many aspects of 'air'. In combination with 'precipitation', air has many experimental faces. Just think of all the varieties of mist, fog, drizzle and downpour. The sun adds a further dimension of heat and light; diffused, scattered, or partly obscured by clouds, trees, buildings, or birds passing by.

Populations refers to all potential visitors from the animal kingdom. The principal group includes mobile organisms that can be attracted from the surrounding neighbourhood, to be persuaded to become permanent residents by providing appropriate habitat conditions. At the Yard they range from ants and leaf-hoppers, to small mammals such as salamanders, and a diverse bird population. Children and other members of the human community are also of course included. Some organisms must be initially transported by hand; the pond inhabitants (fish, tadpoles, frogs, water snakes, turtles, etc.) are a clear example. Occasional short-term visits (a few weeks, usually) of larger farmyard animals (ducks, chickens, rabbits, goats and pigs) have also been organized at the Yard.

Scale — a sense of the relative size of things — is an implicit yet crucial consideration in the design of childhood places. It is conditioned in three ways: inherent limitations of the site (size, shape, topography, climate), natural properties of materials used in construction (sawn timbers, trees, water, asphalt, rocks, wire ropes, etc.), and the scale of the pattern of behaviour to be accommodated (from wide-ranging chase games and ball-play to intimate social activity). The aim of the Yard design was to provide for the maximum feasible diversity of inter-actions. The participatory process and the recollection of my own childhood 'Earth matrix' (in the south of England) irresistibly emphasized the intimate scale of simple structures mixed with natural resources in much of the area. The need for ball-play and large-muscle activity elsewhere was also recognized.

User Response

Between 1975 and 1978, a number of research studies were carried out to make an *ex post facto* assessment of the children's response to the evolving Yard. Figure 3.13 shows the results of the 'behaviour-mapping' study, separated by sex to show marked differences in the way girls and boys use the space. Girls' behaviour seems clustered in more intimate place-relationships; boys' behaviour is more wide-ranging, especially across the asphalt, with less deep involvement in specific locations. There is a feeling of transition from depth to breadth between girls and boys. Obviously such findings give rise to considerable speculation concerning the sex-accommodating versus sex-differentia-tion role of play environments. Hopefully other researchers will make contributions before hasty conclusions are drawn.

From the behaviour maps, 58 'activity places' were identified by visual inspection, relating patterns of behaviour to the physical boundaries accommodating it (Figure 3.14). To conduct a useful analysis, the 58 places were grouped into 10 'Behaviour' Environment Ecosystems' (BEEs) (Figure 3.15); these in turn were subdivided into the three primary zones or tertiary place-systems of the Yard: the Natural Resource Area (NRA), the Main Yard Systems and the Asphalt. Figure 3.16 shows the conceptual structure of the Yard in diagram-matic form. The number of activity places, percentage of use and percentage of space occupied, are shown for each primary zone and BEE.

If the values for use are divided by space occupied, a key measure of space utilization is derived (Use/Space Ratio (USR), shown along the bottom line of Figure 3.16). A USR value of 1.0 indicates a use level in exact proportion to the space occupied. Rather obviously, both Asphalt BEES are under-utilized, compared to the play structures, which seem 'over-utilized'. In fact, this latter result matches a design objective of attracting a larger amount of behaviour to the play

Figure 3.13: Behaviour Maps of the Yard for Girls (left) and Boys (right), Composed of Eighteen Observation Cycles at Noon-time Recess (Spring 1977)

Distinct differences in the use of space are clearly visible. Girls' behaviour is more clustered, boys' is more spread out.

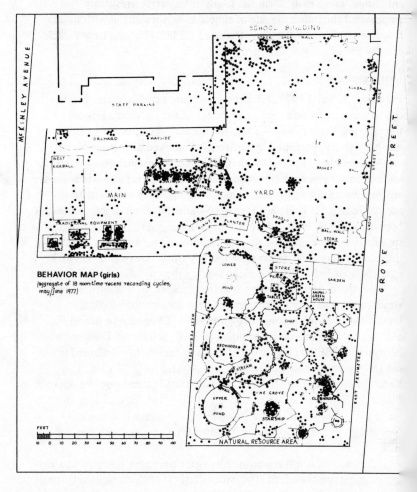

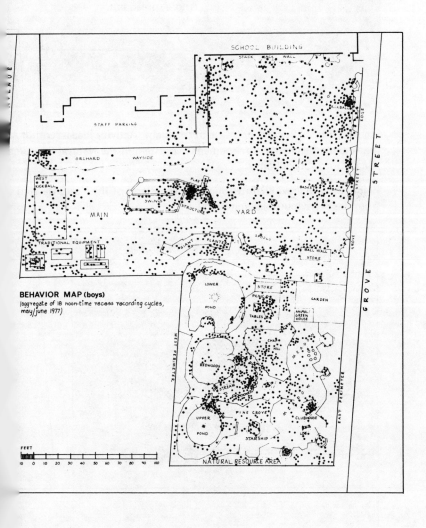

BEHAVIOR MAP (boys)
(aggregate of 18 noon-time recess recording cycles,
may/june 1977)

Figure 3.14: 'Willow Island'. One of the Eight 'Activity Places' within the Aquatic Behaviour/Environment Ecosystem of the Natural Resource Area. Photo: Steve Bailey.

Figure 3.15: Behaviour/Environment Ecosystems of the Yard, Derived from the Behaviour-Mapping Study

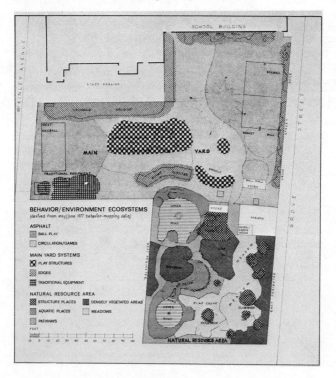

Figure 3.16: Eco-conceptual Structure of the Yard, Derived from the
Behaviour-Mapping Study, Comparing Space Occupied with Actual
Use for Primary Zones and Behaviour/Environment
Ecosystems

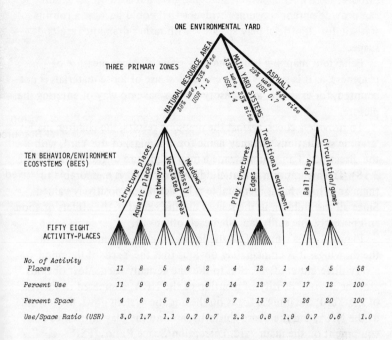

No. of Activity Places	11	8	5	6	2	4	12	1	4	5	58
Percent Use	11	9	6	6	6	14	12	7	17	12	100
Percent Space	4	6	5	8	8	7	13	3	26	20	100
Use/Space Ratio (USR)	3.0	1.7	1.1	0.7	0.7	2.2	0.8	1.9	0.7	0.6	1.0

structures and equipment to encourage social interaction and to ensure
that the more expensive elements had the highest level of use. The same
result and justification applies to the NRA structure places (small
meeting/working structures). An added aim here was to reduce impact
on sensitive vegetated areas by attracting higher use to structure places.
This turned out very successfully, as indicated by their USR of 3.0
(the highest in the Yard). Correspondingly, USR values for the densely
planted areas and meadows are satisfactorily low (0.7 in each case). The
high attraction of aquatic places, compared to the other vegetated
BEES, is clearly indicated by differences in the USR values.

Comparison of USR values for the three primary zones clearly
indicates that the Asphalt (USR 0.7) was under-used, suggesting that
an additional area be turned over to natural resource development; this

is now in hand (1979) – note substantial tree planting in asphalt areas and around play structures in updated layout (Figure 3.17).

The preceding represents a very small part of the kind of analysis made possible by behaviour-mapping studies. Details of the method and fuller discussion of the results can be found in a research report (Moore, 1978). As behaviour mapping gives a record of 'actual use', it can provide potent consumer evidence that could become a routine statistic for all official play spaces – with rather dramatic results, I suspect.

Behaviour mapping is not the only or a sufficient measure of placeness, as it is subject to several biases: use of loose materials is not counted, for example, and sensory factors have no way of entering the picture.

To provide a check against the mapping results, the children made 'graphic simulations' (a fancy name for drawings) of the Yard, with the direction: 'Can you draw me a map or picture of the Yard' (Figure 3.18). The assumption is that children draw what is memorable to them and that what is memorable is by definition positively valued. Since all the children in the school did the exercise, the effects of good and poor graphic skills cancelled each other out.

Figure 3.19 is a map of all site-locatable elements mentioned in the drawings. It is immediately obvious that the Yard 'of the mind' has a very different configuration to the one actually used. Most obvious are: the over-all density of mention of the NRA, compared to the rest of the Yard; the intense focus on the aquatic system down the left side of the NRA; and the dense clustering around the play structures and equipment on the main yard. Perception/Space Ratios (PSR – similar to USR), calculated for the three primary zones, substantiate the visual impression:

Natural Resource Area	1.9
Main Yard Systems	1.6
Asphalt	0.1

Perception/Space Ratio is a rather crude but direct indicator of 'thereness' in the play environment. Just consider the contrast between natural resources and asphalt shown by these figures: one provides the most powerful image of the Yard, the other seems sensorily non-existent. The high value for the Main Yard Systems is attributable to the play structures (PSR = 2.3), and play equipment (PSR = 1.1), indicating their important role already suggested by the behaviour-

Figure 3.17: Layout of the Existing Yard, Showing Current (1979) Tree Planting in Under-used Asphalt Areas

Also note the 'yet-to-be' development of a neighbourhood 'common' by closing the street to the left of the Yard.

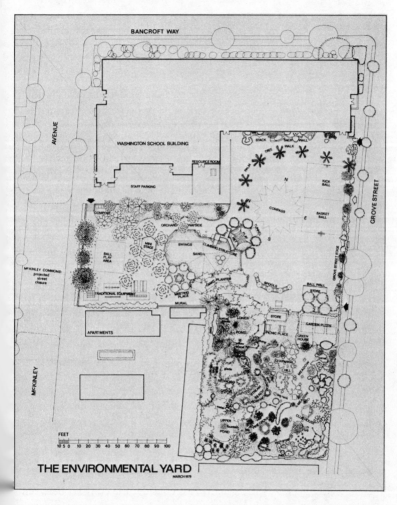

Figure 3.18: Example of a
'Graphic Simulation' by a Nine-
year-old Boy, when Asked to
'Draw a Map or Picture of the
Yard' (1976)

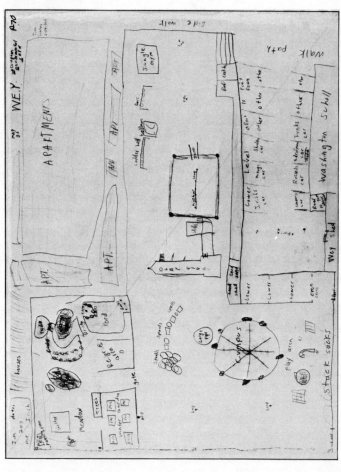

Figure 3.19: The Yard 'of the Mind' Constructed from the 1976
Graphic Simulations

Each dot represents a spatially locatable element mentioned in the
drawings.

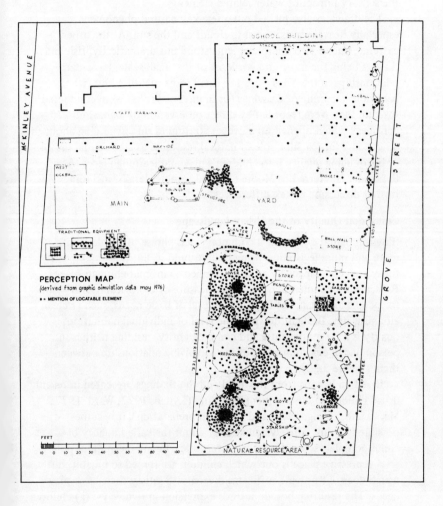

mapping results. Perception and use do not always coincide, however. It is interesting to note that the two most frequently drawn elements, the fountain in the upper pond and the island in the lower pond, were unfeasible to use (without getting very wet) — a powerful indicator of the sensory impact of water-related elements.

The drawings also picked out a few key natural phenomena, especially heavenwards: the sky, clouds and the sun. At the other extreme, one or two micro-elements stood out dramatically, fish and flowers being the most intense. Most of the small-scale, loose-part relationships in the Yard were too small to be identified by either behaviour mapping or drawings (or in interviews that were conducted). Instead, they were recorded by direct observation of 'behaviour episodes', which opened up a deeper stratum of understanding about the unique and far-reaching role of natural resources as an essential means of introducing quality into children's play and learning places. Again, the reader is referred to Moore (1978) for more details, including further discussion of sex differences.

Childhood Quality of the Urban Landscape

'Environmental quality' is a common catch-phrase of the day, with more and more legislation being built around it, but it is an extremely fuzzy concept, especially so when applied to intimate human spaces. Big-scale environmental quality is a measure of biological health, good for people and planet at large at the level of basic needs, such as clean air and water. Brought down to the level of individual habitation, quality is a far more subtle and complex entity, residing neither in person nor in environment, but in an evolving relationship between them (Figure 3.20).

Based on lessons from the Yard and the findings presented in recent urban childhood/environment literature (Lynch, 1977; Ward, 1977; Moore and Young, 1978; and Moore in preparation), it becomes possible to think more systematically about the varied quality of childhood places, as a first step towards developing meaningful policy.

A repressive place is one which children are forced to inhabit, but which does not provide sufficient diversity to satisfy their basic play needs. The resulting boredom finds expression in two ways: (a) children use each other and available adults as play objects — as things rather than people — a peculiarly alienating relationship that inevitably results in social conflict; and (b) so-called 'vandalism' which in most cases represents children's vain attempts to manipulate their surroundings, even though it is illegitimate in adult eyes. Low-quality environments,

Figure 3.20: People/Environment Quality can be Seen as an Evolving
Relationship between Place and Person, Beginning with Initial
Disruption of the Status Quo, Leading to the Development of a
Deliberate Process of 'Educated' Change

An eventual state of total awareness and integration between people
and planet remains an unreachable ideal. . .

in a sense, turn against and abuse their users, inducing the pathological
effects of unfulfilled environmental needs. The most common example
by far is the asphalted schoolyard — surely the spawning ground of
much urban violence.

An urban non-place does not provide sufficient diversity, nor are
children obliged to use it. Non-use is the common result. There would

not be much of an issue, except that the amount of space involved is so large, including parking lots, plaza paving, corporate landscaping, over-lawned parks, under-used sports fields, etc. By any reasonable measure the 'social opportunity costs' are vast.

Neither repressive nor non-place categories contain sufficient educational potential, except in the hands of the most innovative and rare teachers.

Possessive places can be colonized by children on their own terms. In theory, official childhood places (such as playgrounds and school-yards) should fall within this category. In practice this is rarely the case, because of their insufficient diversity. The best examples of possessive places are unkempt pieces of vacant rough ground and abandoned places which are relatively inaccessible and unattractive to adults. As a result, such places are usually located outside immediate residential areas and are only accessible to older children — more frequently boys than girls — with understanding parents providing freedom for the young mind and body to flourish. Possessive places provide considerable educational potential for the more intrepid teacher, who must be mindful of the privilege of sharing children's private world.

Accommodative places fulfil community social purposes, ideally, for all age groups. In practice, children's presence is tolerated to a greater or lesser extent by adults, depending on circumstances. Whether controls are tight or loose, adults call the behavioural tune and children face the threat of censure or exclusion if codes are transgressed. None the less, many public places, especially mature urban parks, provide reasonably accommodative settings and excellent opportunities for educational activity away from school, either with teachers or with other adult leaders.

Syndetic places represent the highest level of quality normally obtainable and are a rare occurrence in the urban scene. In syndetic ('connected') places, possessive and accommodative aspects are combined, opening up a sense of ownership to the whole community. The Yard seems at, or near, this evolutionary state.

Beyond the syndetic state lies a possible, yet so far unreachable, state of true anarchy, of completely self-regulated community-place evolution, where arbitrary distinctions between place and person, childhood and society, work and play, education and recreation would cease to have significance.

Children may occasionally create this state for themselves in possessive places. Adventure playgrounds seem to be the only contemporary institution where high quality is inherently built-in, although, interestingly enough, they are rarely looked upon as possibly the most advanced educational institution yet invented.

Meanwhile, functionary, low-quality, repressive/non-place landscapes abound, mixed with varied proportions of more accommodative quality. The challenge for the future, for education (Wong, 1977), leisure planning and urban policy, is to find ways of advancing the quality of people—environment relations for everyone, everywhere.

References

Barton, Anthony. 1974. 'The hard-soft school', in Gary Coates (ed.), *Alternative Learning Environments.* Stroudsburg, Pennsylvania: Dowden, Hutchinson and Ross.

Berger, Peter, Brigitte Berger and Hansfried Kellner. 1973. *The Homeless Mind: Modernization and Consciousness.* New York: Vintage Books.

Lynch, Kevin. 1976. *Managing the Sense of Region.* Cambridge, Mass.: MIT Press.

—— (ed.). 1977. *Growing Up in Cities: Studies of the Spatial Environment of Adolescence in Cracow, Melbourne, Mexico City, Salta, Toluca and Warsaw.* Cambridge, Mass.: MIT Press.

Moore, Robin C. 1978. 'Meanings and measures of children/environment quality: some findings from Washington Environmental Yard', in Walter E. Rogers and William H. Ittelson (eds), *New Directions in Environmental Design Research*, EDRA 9. Washington, DC: Environmental Design Research Association.

—— Forthcoming. *Landscapes of Play.* London: Croom Helm.

—— and Donald Young. 1978. 'Childhood outdoors: toward a social ecology of the landscape', in Irwin Altman and Joachim F. Wohlwill (eds), *Children and the Environment.* New York: Plenum Publishing.

Nicholson, Simon. 1971. 'The theory of loose parts', *Landscape Architecture*, 62, 1, pp. 30–4.

Pearce, Joseph Chilton. 1977. *Magical Child: Rediscovering Nature's Plan for Our Children.* New York: E. P. Dutton.

Relph, E. 1976. *Place and Placelessness.* London: Pion.

Sommer, Robert. 1974. *Tight Spaces: Hard Architecture and How to Humanize It.* Englewoods Cliffs, NJ: Prentice-Hall.

Tuan, Yi-Fu. 1974. *Topophilia: A Study of Environmental Perception, Attitudes and Values.* Englewood Cliffs, NJ: Prentice-Hall.

Ward, Colin. 1977. *The Child in the City.* London: The Architectural Press.

Wong, Herbert H. 1977. 'Muses, monitors and millennia: a celebration of children/environment relations and transitional environmental education curricula', in Robert H. McCabe (ed.), *Current Issues in Environmental Education – III.* Columbus, Ohio: The ERIC Center for Science, Mathematics and Environmental Education, Ohio State University.

4 YOUTH FARMS

Edgar Boehm

It's a hot summer day. Children in jeans and T-shirts arrive on bikes carrying plastic bags full of greens for their animals. They hurry straight to the newly-painted animal house. Soon one can hear eager discussions, calls, noises. Dirty straw is carried off. Struppi, the pony, well-loved by all, is led out and heads straight for the large bathtub for a drink. The chickens dash for the corn brought by Isolde, the playground supervisor. Three rabbits have just given birth — this brings fresh problems for their owner and the supervisor. The goats are taken from their stall and proceed to range over the playground. Otto, the he-goat, draws attention to himself through his joyful jumping.

A few children have started a fire and soon a large number of them are sitting around it and eating bread that they have made themselves.

Huts are being extended and painted, for painting is in fashion. Even the walls of the big playground house are being decorated in many colours.

In the playhouse itself, Isolde has unlocked the tool room. The children fetch their hammers, nails, pliers, paint pots and brushes, boards for painting, and old wallpaper. It is a hive of activity.

Alexander — one could almost call him the playground's mascot — together with Jurgen, is doing what he likes best — squirting water in the 'swimming pool', skidding down the plastic slide into the pool, and splashing happily in the water. Cooling down is something quite exquisite in this heat. The children themselves supply the drinks; in the well equipped kitchen of the playground house, several girls and boys are preparing tea which is taken out in large jugs and handed round. A pancake is quickly made of fresh eggs from their own chickens for a guest who has just arrived.

A Volkswagen bus arrives full of pallets and wood. The children help unload it and pile the wood along the wall of the animal house.

At 3.00 p.m., the playground meeting, which takes place every two weeks, is held. The 'Mayor' reminds them that wastes must be brought to the container, and that there will be no more sporting events because a 'Trimmy' was not elected at the last meeting. In other words, no 'Trimmy', no sports. A hasty election is held. Later in the afternoon, soccer is being played again. The zoo director tells them that the veterinarian is coming next week to advise them about feeding the animals.

The awareness of human companionship is put in a better light through association with the animals. The young people clean the stables and the paddock, and construct dung-heaps. After a year these will have turned into crumbly, light, black humus which they can take in carts to their borders, and the following summer they will be able to pick large sweet, juicy strawberries, crisp radishes or sweet smelling flowers. The children assist at the birth of a lamb. They experience the problems and joys of rearing, seeing how the thick silky coat grows, shearing, and the marvellous fleece that is then carefully washed in rainwater. The children are allowed to pick it into loose 'clouds' and then help with spinning the wool. A pullover knitted from this wool feels quite different from one bought in a department store.

In the afternoon other groups of visitors can be seen on the playground — some foreigners are among them. They are looking for information, taking pictures, gathering experiences.

Bietigheim Adventure Playground

Introduction

The Federation of Youth Farms and Activity Playgrounds (a registered society) is the central organization for playground initiatives in Germany. Its aim is to provide youth farms or other playgrounds, in or near densely populated urban areas, which will help children and young people, no matter what their economic and social backgrounds, by giving free rein to their creative and manual abilities, by developing their capacity for living together through playing and working in groups, and by developing a healthy relationship with their natural environment through responsible association with animals and nature. Their activities vary, depending on their locality, what assistance is available, the attitude of the parents and the financial position of the associated societies. They affect changes and use their resources accordingly.

At the start there is always a question of finding space — not always an easy problem to solve. Another problem is getting help and finance. In Stuttgart the municipal government bears the cost for full-time staff and 50 per cent of the operating costs. The youth office, social welfare office, real-estate offices, horticultural landscape offices and others are well disposed toward the venture and are extremely helpful. Other official bodies which have less directly to do with children sometimes create difficulties. The most frequent problem, however, consists of the difficulties caused by neighbours. The reaction of parents, and the citizens in general, to the youth farms and adventure playgrounds varies from violent opposition, to indifference, to being well disposed toward them and giving objective recognition and support.

All playgrounds belonging to the central organization are supervised throughout their opening hours, and are run as public utilities; that is, they are not reserved for members only, but are open to all children and young people. Users simply pay a minimal insurance premium against third-party liability and accidents.

Play Leader Training

The full-time helpers are qualified either through educational experience or training. The voluntary helpers and other assistants (conscientious objectors, craftsmen, farmers, mothers, gardeners, pensioners) have opportunities for further training using the farm library, in discussions with colleagues, exchange meetings, weekend conferences, and through courses offered by several institutions, in education, psychology, sociology, riding therapy, etc.

Since 1977, the Federation of Youth Farms can achieve what it has been working toward since its foundation: youth farm supervisors can now complete their academic education as social pedagogues on the farms close to practical reality. Theory and practice are united by two major structural features. Fifty per cent of the training takes place on the farm in the middle of its regular activity; the other 50 per cent takes place at the vocational academy in Stuttgart (State Educational Academy of Baden-Württemberg). Every twelve weeks, the students change their training place: trainees at the Academy go to the farms and vice versa. During these twelve weeks, theory and practice, experience and requirements (both for teachers and students) are changed continuously. After two years, the examination for 'Educator (BA)' is held and after three years the 'Social Pedagogue (BA)' examination. This is believed to be an ideal combination which could produce model supervisors, not biased in any way, not permanently with their noses in the dirt, but versatile, schooled and experienced youth farmers.

Children's Play Activities

Children live in a world mainly conceived by grown-ups for grown-ups.

Home, school and environment form much too narrow limits for the needs of young people. Existing demands for performance and general education to a great extent neglect the actual needs of children, withhold experiences from them, hem in their demand for personal experiences. Sports facilities, the 'Kindergarten' and youth clubs are important and necessary, but many young people need contact with nature and animals as well. Who is going to protect the environment later on if today's children can no longer obtain personal experience with nature? This healthy instinct still lives in many children. The goal of the Federation of Youth Farms is to create places in all districts of the cities where every child can go every day — to play, to roam about, to build, to help others or just to dream.

Children want to move, run around and be noisy. They want to play and chat with others; yet, at the same time, be taken seriously as partners and see their abilities confirmed. Children wish to show and receive physical affection. They enjoy changing things, and do not want to be always told what to do. They need a climate for playing that is not determined by unnecessary restrictions. Surroundings are needed in which they have both the space and the material to be able to play on their own and with other children in a creative way. To do this, they need the understanding of adults who stand up for the interests of the children and strive for sufficient playing possibilities.

When young people do not get what they need, they are inhibited in their physical, emotional, mental and social development. The pedagogic aim of the work carried out at the playgrounds, therefore, is the development of the following qualities and abilities:

1. physical skills and manual abilities, self-motivation (to be active themselves, set themselves a task, and seize the initiative themselves);
2. creativity (to plan, carry out, change, experiment, discover and invent);
3. sensitivity (intense social perception and experience, open-minded to everything going on);
4. self-assurance (to experience success increases self-confidence; dealing with risk increases self-assurance);
5. reduction of excessive aggressiveness (in play, using materials in discussion with peers and supervisors; to be understood);
6. making contact with individuals and groups at play (with the playground as a meeting point, to practise co-operation, partnership, carrying out joint projects and adapting to the group);
7. handling of social pressures (girls—boys, adults—children);

8. overcoming social barriers (breaking down prejudices, getting to know other groups);
9. behaving democratically (coming to terms with other opinions and interests, arguing, acting in solidarity, taking a critical point of view, defending one's own interests, influencing others and accepting responsibility).

Far too much today occurs in an unseen manner by pressing a button. In contrast, youth farmers shear their sheep by hand, work their potter's wheel by foot, spin with spindle and spinning wheel, fertilize their borders with their home-made humus, experience the birth and death of their animals. They literally grow into life's secrets without the need of explanations; they will know them instinctively all their lives, long after they have outgrown the youth farm.

Children at youth farms are not forced into doctrinal, ideological or pedagogic principles. They find an opportunity to test their own skills and abilities, to exercise and prove them. They can romp about without supervision or verbose instructions and can enjoy getting back to nature with the elements — with earth, fire, water, with animals and tools, and with each other. For here the helpers do not have to think up 'campaigns'. The farm itself is alive and offers an ideal variety of pleasures which leaves room for their own investigations and inventions on the one hand, and hard work in farm life on the other — simple, understandable, necessary work with which they can lend a hand of their own free will. Many of the activities help form partnerships. Anyone who is planting a border, mending a fence or building a hut does so together with others. It is more fun and the work is easier. With animals, one becomes less selfish when gradually realizing what another being wants or feels. This transfers itself to companionship. One learns to talk with others, to gain the confidence of others and to express one's feelings. The social stratum from which one comes, the amount of pocket money or the type of school attended lose their separating effect. Even the only child soon finds company. Children from socially deprived or problem families are offered a chance of developing and making up for what they lack.

Spheres of work on the youth farms which interlock and overlap include play such as party games, lighting fires, playing with water, music, dancing, theatre, charades, festivals and celebrations. There is a myriad of handicrafts: wood (carpentry, joinery and carving), earth and clay (dabbling, modelling and pottery), paper, cardboard, rope, farm-grown sheep's wool, textiles (painting, batik work, pleating, plaiting, spinning, weaving, knotting, sewing, etc.). Technical work such as filming, photography, tape recording, working on vehicles and the like is normally for the benefit of the whole farm only. Building involves both private buildings (huts, cabins and caves) and public buildings (stables, fences, cages, bridges and towers). Individual border gardens or the whole playground may be planted; and the horses, donkeys, sheep, goats, dogs, cats, rabbits, guinea pigs, poultry and pigeons are all raised and cared for.

Work with the handicapped, which will be discussed later, includes therapeutic riding, and including the handicapped in all the above-mentioned activities.

Individual dialogues and group conferences, discussions with parents, supervising homework, and comprehensive assistance for the juvenile courts all provide help with special problems. On holidays, games are organized or excursions, partly on horseback, may be taken. Weekend leisure is often spent with youngsters from other farms or playgrounds. In addition to this, the helpers themselves are involved through holiday camping, international youth meetings, and workshops. Building up and managing one's own farm and helping other farms require certain skills, as do the joint campaigns that must often be undertaken to obtain helpers and procure materials. So, both to do all this and as a result of it, organizational skills are developed.

The effect of the variety of activity on the children ranges from simple relaxation or, at the beginning, even running wild, to the development of their own abilities, an increase in self-confidence, experience, practice and proving their own worth, discovery and further development of social relationships, and finding a vocation, because here varied talents can be tried out quite spontaneously during play. This applies to the able-bodied, as well as to the handicapped and the fringe groups.

Extensive sociological studies have been carried out on how children who do not use these facilities spend their spare time after school, and take into account among other things their varying interests, their milieu and what facilities are offered in the city districts. A large number of these children spend their free time watching television, at the cinema, wandering about the streets, etc.

Handicapped Children

The potential for special assistance to handicapped children has been widely recognized. To quote Professor Margarete Erpelt-Sauer:

In my opinion, youth farms, with their many specific central
elements, have to fulfil urgent pedagogic tasks. These are:
a) the healthy development of the child. (They provide, in their
function as activity playgrounds, inner and outer freedom of movement, both alone and with others; they offer the chance of a
'natural life', from the point of view of 'lebensraum', animals and
plants; they stimulate healthy curiosity, the desire to do something
oneself, to share experiences, to observe, to reflect).
b) children with emotional, mental, physical or social handicaps.
(In addition to the above, they are also of therapeutic value, e.g.,
therapeutic riding, and fields for social experience).

It is my view that the work of the youth farms is now an integral
part of pedagogics and of pedagogic prophylaxis and therapy.
Because this work requires in particular socio-pedagogic specialists
in increasing numbers, I have spoken up for the youth farms as
bases for students studying at the specialized institute for social
welfare in Stuttgart-Esslingen. Youth farms are further fields of
experience for students, because they can experience direct contact
with children doing what they like best, planning both creatively
and experimentally, in a social field which, for example, always
provides new impulses through friendships, conflicts, and the
encounter with new values and valuations.

Multiple sclerosis patients have been coming to the youth farm in
Mohringen on Wednesdays for several years. For many of them it is one
of the very few chances they have of actually leaving the wheel-chair
and of being able to enjoy nature on the back of a pony, at the same
time carrying out respiratory exercises and gymnastics. Of almost equal
importance is the contact with other handicapped and healthy persons.
All patients come at the express wish of their doctors. One must, of
course, know the patient and the cause of the illness as well as possible
in order to be able correctly to calculate the permitted physical strain.

In the early 1960s, ponies were being used in Elsental for the
benefit of handicapped children; Traudi and Iduna — 'patient and
therapeut' — began the necessary and natural integration of handicapped children into farm life using Gladur, the patient Icelander.
Under medical supervision, wherever there are suitable ponies and
skilled help available, it is possible to carry out this sort of therapy for
the benefit of both healthy and handicapped children.

Dr E. Mack, head of the Medical Department in the Centre for
Treatment of Children with Motor Disturbances in the Victor Kochel
Pediatric Hospital, feels:

Therapeutic riding for children has proved to be very satisfactory. Not only is their motoricity improved (control of head and trunk), their balance, use of arms and hands, the adapting of the legs, and muscle tone, but it has also resulted in successful treatment of pedagogically difficult children. This mainly concerns spastic diplegia, ataxia, athetosis, mixed forms and minimal forms, among others.

Mr Hublow, the head of a special school for educationally backward children and young people, noted that 'We were able to observe an emotional stabilization and favourable change of social behaviour in all those children taking part'. In particular, he noted improvement of responsiveness, surmounting of anxiety, improvement of drive and will-power, and improvement of body control.

The report of the Carl Schubert School for Children requiring mental care notes that some of their mentally handicapped children accompanied by teachers and helpers visited the youth farm in Elsental. Observations established that there had been a definite improvement in the obvious behavioural disorders, as well as a positive influence on their social attitude. At the same time, an activation of their sensory perception occurred.

The Goals of Youth Farms

In the late summer of 1975, for the first time, the Youth Farms presented themselves internationally at the Sixth World Conference of the IPA (International Playground Association). In an exhibition special emphasis was placed on the following techniques.

The objects used by the young people in their activities are not prefabricated toys nor do they derive from modern techniques; rather they are what nature offers, materials such as fire, water, earth, and activities such as gardening and agriculture, pottery, spinning, weaving and keeping animals. The simple jobs involved mean constant, intensive work and help the young get used to real life.

While nowadays children's play is crammed into a sort of ghetto outside the adult's world, the youth farm blends in with what adults are doing with animals and nature. This way, young people feel they are participating in actual life processes: 'We are not just playing, we're doing some real work'.

Occupying themselves with strong animals strengthens courage, makes young people considerate, gives them self-confidence, and brings some of the youngsters with unrealistic TV-consumers' attitudes back to earth again.

With youth farms, the fact that differences in the adult world remain outside and all the handicapped and fringe groups are drawn in aids personal identification. Additional benefits include the low operating costs of the youth farms. Despite many a disappointment, the youth farms strengthen and cultivate anew the over-all atmosphere of mutual trust, which helps mould the social behaviour for the future.

5 SAFETY IN CHILDREN'S FORMAL PLAY ENVIRONMENTS

Paul F. Wilkinson and Robert S. Lockhart[1]

Introduction

There is evidence to suggest that many recreation and education personnel and parents believe that large numbers of children are being seriously injured in formal play environments. The purpose of this study is to investigate children's formal play environments in public settings in an attempt to answer a basic question: are children's formal play environments safe?

A number of problems were evident from the beginning of the project. First was the meaning of 'safety' and the unit of measurement of safety. It was decided that safety would be described in terms of accidents (as defined by morbidity and mortality data). Second, there was a problem in separating playground-related accidents (i.e., those related to the design of the apparatus, siting, surface materials, the interaction of users and equipment, etc.) from non-playground-related accidents (i.e., those accidents occurring on playgrounds, but which are not related to either the design or the use of playground equipment). The latter included accidents related to sports, vandalism, poor main-tenance (e.g., broken glass), bicycles, etc. Third, there was the problem of unavailability, incompleteness or unreliability of much of the necessary data. Fourth, there is no common format for gathering or reporting data. For example, often little information is available on the nature of accidents (e.g., location, type of environment, causes). Fifth, obviously data are available only for those accidents which are recorded by either playground or hospital personnel. Many minor accidents are never recorded and probably some serious accidents are not attributed in recording to playgrounds.

Despite these problems, however, enough data were available to arrive at a number of conclusions and to make some recommendations. Data were gathered by means of personal and telephone interviews, literature review and examination of accident records.

The Issues of Safety

There are two prime factors in accident prevention in any setting:

85

protection and education. There is an obvious reciprocal relationship between these two. As the effectiveness of user education increases, the necessity for protection decreases. It is important to note, however, that some degree of protection is always necessary; the problem is the degree of protection. When dealing with children and their play environments, emphasis must be placed on protection. Safety education is also important, but it decreases in effectiveness the younger the child.

It is possible to create an environment which is almost perfectly safe simply by avoiding risk. The problem is, however, that such a setting would not make a good play environment because it would lack many of those elements necessary for meaningful play: variety, complexity, challenge, risk, flexibility, adaptability, etc. Quite simply, such a playground would go largely unused. Indeed, this is the case with many of the traditional playgrounds now in existence. They are not being heavily used because children do not like them; they are neither fun nor challenging. Incidentally, this also gives them the appearance of being safe. Few accidents are reported because few children use them. As a result, no meaningful or definitive statements can be made about accident rates.

There are two goals in any safety programme: (1) to eliminate serious types of injuries, e.g., strangulations, skull fractures, concussions, and causes of death or dismemberment; and (2) to minimize other minor types of injuries, e.g., broken bones, abrasions, lacerations, punctures, etc. There are a number of ways to meet these goals: (1) eliminate obvious sources of danger, e.g., sharp edges, protrusions and hard surface materials; (2) construct equipment from safe, durable, materials; (3) maintain and install the equipment properly; (4) educate the children about safety and supervise them where necessary; (5) adopt performance standards which apply to all playground equipment. The emphasis should be placed on performance rather than design standards so that the focus is on hazards rather than specific pieces of equipment. In this way, once a safety requirement (e.g., abrasive qualities) is established, it can apply to any given situation (National Recreation and Park Association, 1976a, p. 1).

Such standards must be aimed at both normal use patterns and anticipated misuse patterns. Examples of anticipated misuse include the following: user overload, pushing, shoving and general 'horseplay', running up slides, climbing on top of guard rails, supports, etc., head-first sliding, hanging by the feet from climbing equipment, penetrating openings, etc. (National Recreation and Park Association, 1976a, p. 20).

There has not been a great deal of research on use patterns and it is an area which merits further study.

Causes of Accidents

The two major categories of causative factors for playground-related accidents are falls, bumps and blows. At the Toronto Hospital for Sick Children in 1973 and 1974 (Haffey, 1974, 1975), there were no deaths as a result of accidents on playground equipment in either year. Playground equipment accidents represented 1.5 per cent or less of the total cases and 2.0 per cent or less of admissions for all causes in each of the two years and very low percentages of falls, bumps and blows and other causes.

Therefore, accidents related to playground equipment in total (i.e., in both public and private settings) represent only a small percentage of all children's accidents. From an over-all safety point of view, therefore, children's play equipment is not a major problem. Every attempt, however, should be made to understand the causes of those playground accidents that do occur and to minimize them.

Location of Accidents

Bongers (1975) found that of 122 cases of playground equipment accidents there were 21 (17.2 per cent) in which the equipment was or may have been a causative factor. More accidents (57.1 per cent) occurred on private property than on public property, a trend supported by the results of other studies (e.g., United States Consumer Product Safety Commission, 1975; Mahajan, 1974; McConnell *et al.*, 1973).

Care must be taken in interpreting some of the available data on 'playground accidents' as to location. For example, detailed analysis of all accidents from the playground programme of the City of Winnipeg for the summer of 1975 indicates that only about one-quarter of the accidents were actually related to playgrounds *per se*. The rest were related to swimming pools (where broken glass is a serious problem), sports and excursions. To confuse the picture even more, the 'swimming pool' accidents took place at supervised swimming pools and, therefore, do not include accidents occurring at wading pools in playgrounds.

Adventure and Creative Playgrounds versus Traditional Playgrounds

It is not possible, however, to give any detailed statistics on the type of public playground in which the accidents take place. On one hand, the data do not exist in such detail, while on the other hand there are few creative playgrounds and very few adventure playgrounds in comparison to traditional playgrounds so that comparison would be difficult even if the data did exist. A number of qualitative reports on comparative safety have, however, been found (e.g., Anonymous, 'Adventure Playground Proves Great Success', 1975; Rhind, 1974; Ontario Ministry of Community and Social Services, 1972; Reid, 1971) which suggest that the difference in danger between creative and adventure playgrounds and traditional playgrounds is not significant.

Seriousness of Accidents

A serious injury may be defined as follows:

> Any injury in which, based on medical experience, there is a reasonable chance of prolonged disability or permanent physical damage to the injured party. *Some* examples of injuries considered 'serious' under this definition would be brain damage, fractures, deep laceration, amputation, impalement, loss of eyesight or hearing, and of course any injury leading to death. (National Recreation and Park Association, 1976b, p. 6)

The question arises, however, as to whether the issue is the seriousness of individual accidents or the rate of serious accidents. To construct a serious accident rate would obviously require a great deal of data: the exact nature of the accidents, numbers of children served by the playgrounds, average frequency of use, use patterns, etc. Basically, then, all that can be discussed are raw numbers of accidents. The question arises as to how meaningful such numbers are.

As indicated above, the most common causes of playground accidents are falls and bumps and blows. It is not easy to answer the question as to how serious these accidents are. Playground accident reports usually only record those accidents occurring during times when supervision is present and very rarely contain follow-up information. Some reports deal with 'accidents', no matter how trivial (e.g., minor scrapes), while others deal with 'non-accidents' (e.g., illness).

The United States Consumer Product Safety Commission (1975) analyzed an estimated sample of 117,951 playground equipment-associated injuries as reported by the National Electronic Injury Surveillance System during 1974. The following is a summary of their findings. Most accidents (78 per cent) occurred to children less than ten years of age, with just over half all persons injured being males. The older the child, the greater was the probability that the accident occurred on public equipment. Lacerations and contusions/abrasions were the dominant diagnosis (75 per cent) for children under 5 years of age; with older children the proportion of fractures and strains/sprains almost equalled lacerations and contusions/abrasions. In terms of parts of the body, injuries occurred most often to the head (46 per cent), then upper extremities (30 per cent), lower extremities (15 per cent) and trunk (9 per cent). The rate of hospitalization was 5 per cent. There were 24 deaths from playground equipment injuries, 15 occurring on home equipment and 9 on public equipment. Of the victims, 7 were under 5 years of age and 13 between 5 and 9 years. Thirteen of the injuries were to the head, 9 to the neck, 1 to the trunk and 1 unknown.

The available data, therefore, simply do not give a comprehensive picture of either morbidity or mortality, largely because of the complexity of the problem. Accidents do happen, but it would appear that most are not serious and that the mortality rate is very low.

In summary, the part of the body most frequently injured (approximately one-half) is the head, face or neck area; the most frequent type of injury (approximately one-half) is laceration or abrasion; and the most common contributing factor (again, approximately one-half) to the injury is that the child has fallen for one reason or another.

No research has been done to deal with the causes of particular accidents on a comprehensive basis. Past research that is of relevance to this study falls into three basic categories: maintenance/manufacturing/construction; types of equipment; and surface materials.

Types of Hazards

Maintenance/Manufacturing/Construction. The National Recreation and Park Association (1976a, pp. 15 and 18) makes two interesting observations:

> There is very little evidence of hazards or injury resulting from equipment failure in public playground apparatus. At least to date, this equipment has been well constructed and is durable. . . The incidence of injury relating to maintenance and/or installation . . . is infrequent.

Two warnings are, however, necessary. First, the statement on construction relates only to public playground apparatus; there is considerable evidence that home playground apparatus is much more dangerous (Mahajan, 1974). Second, these statements deal with equipment and not surfacing or general maintenance. For example, the number of accidents which are a result of falling on broken glass is very great; obviously, this is a major maintenance issue, but it has little to do with playground equipment or design. This is not to say that playground equipment is generally in good condition; not enough data exist on the condition of equipment to make a meaningful statement.

Types of Equipment. The actual design of individual pieces of equipment is obviously a factor in accidents and is currently receiving a great deal of attention, particularly in terms of design and performance standards.

Although every effort should be made to reduce the likelihood of hazard as a result of design, the following statements are worth noting:

> . . . there does not appear to be a high incidence of injury relating to edges, protrusions and crush points. And when they do occur they tend to be less severe. For this reason, there may be considerably more injuries of this type that occur on the playground that do not get reported . . . there does not appear to be a high incidence of entrapment-related injury. When it (sic) does occur, entrapment injuries tend to be serious. (National Recreation and Park Association, 1976a, pp. 15 and 16)

These statements are borne out by several sets of data. For example, data from both the National Recreation and Park Association (1975) and the Toronto Hospital for Sick Children (Haffey, 1974, 1975) indicate that falls and moving impact (i.e., bumps and blows) are the major causes of accidents on all types of equipment. Obviously, design does create hazards in terms of entrapment, protrusions and the nature of the materials themselves.

The most serious causes of accidents relate to the use of equipment rather than its design *per se.* The National Park and Recreation Association (1976a, pp. 15 and 16) notes as follows:

> Other than falling from the equipment, injuries resulting from either moving elements striking the user or the user striking another part of the equipment, are the most common cause (sic) of accidents. They also result in some of the most serious types of injury. . . The most common type of injury results from falling from equipment — regardless of the reason for the fall. The usual injury

agent is the surface under the equipment or another part of the equipment.

There is a great deal of data on the types of equipment on which accidents occur. One issue that must be emphasized, however, is the difference between public and private equipment. For example, McConnell *et al.* (1973) found that swings account for 50 per cent of the accidents on home equipment, with climbing apparatus second (32 per cent), slides third (16 per cent), and seesaws fourth (2 per cent). For public equipment the distribution is quite different: climbing apparatus first (43 per cent), then slides (38 per cent), swings (9.5 per cent), and seesaws (9.5 per cent). In comparing accidents of home versus public equipment for specific pieces of equipment, it can be seen that home swings account for 83 per cent of all swing accidents; Mahajan's (1974) work shows that a safety standard for home swing equipment is desperately needed. Conversely, public slides account for 77 per cent of all slide accidents; perhaps home slides, which are generally smaller, lower and fewer in number, are also less attractive than longer and higher public slides. Similar reasons probably account for the fact that 63 per cent of all climbing accidents occurred on public equipment.

There is some evidence to suggest trends in accidents from various types of equipment (National Recreation and Park Association, 1976a, p. 13). The number of injuries associated with swinging elements has become significantly lower, perhaps as a result of an increase in the number of rubber belt-type seats on the market or the use of tyres as seats. The number associated with climbing apparatus has significantly increased, perhaps as a result of the greater number and variety of such equipment on the market. There have been no significant changes for sliding equipment, seesaws and other non-specific equipment.

The type of injury also varies with the type of equipment. For example, there is a higher incidence of fractures and strains/sprains on climbing equipment and of lacerations on swings and slides.

The major question, however, is whether or not the fault for the accident can be laid on the nature of the equipment itself. The extent to which the operator (i.e., the child) or other children were at fault is a major issue. Obviously, there will be a combination of factors in many cases. A number of sets of data provide some insight into this problem.

Bongers (1975) found that the large majority of accidents for all products, for all playground and sports equipment in general, and individual types of playground equipment in particular, were not the fault of product failure. Blame could be put on the operator in most cases.

With other data, it is possible to subdivide further the root cause into people-related (i.e., the direct fault of the operator or another person), product-related (i.e., the direct fault of the product), or people- and product-related (i.e., a combination). Examples of these three types would be, respectively, as follows: a child unexpectedly getting off a seesaw, thereby injuring another child; a piece of equipment breaking, having sharp edges, protrusions, etc.; and a child 'horsing around' on a climbing platform and falling over a railing that was too low to stop his fall. Such studies (e.g., National Recreation and Park Association, 1976a; United States Consumer Product Safety Commission, 1975) indicate that very few accidents are directly related to the equipment itself. Most are the fault of people directly or a combination of people and product.

Surface Materials. McConnell *et al.* (1973, pp. 9–10) state that in 60 per cent of the public playground equipment accidents they investigated in depth the injury agent was the area beneath the equipment.

In a study of surface materials, the National Recreation and Park Association (1976b) reached a number of important conclusions. The following materials were rated unacceptable in safe public playgrounds no matter how low the equipment (i.e., minimization of maximum height of fall): packed earth, grass, concrete, asphalt, and Kempf mat combination (corrugated rubber mat with vinyl cover). Sand was marginally acceptable. Both cocoa shell and pine bark show excellent energy-absorbing qualities, but are not conducive to walking or durability. They could be considered for high injury rate locations. Wood chips are good energy absorbers but get wet, rot and are easily dislodged. Pea gravel is a good energy absorber, provides excellent drainage, is an all-weather surface and, although it is relatively easy to walk on, is difficult to run on and impossible to ride a bicycle on. It does, however, require daily raking and can easily be thrown about. Rubber mats, in double thickness, showed acceptable impact characteristics but to date they have not been manufactured in double thicknesses. Pea gravel and rubber mats are presented as the most viable solutions as energy-absorbing surfaces, considering safety, durability and ability to withstand the environment.

Impact of the Issue of Safety

It is quite obvious that the issue of safety has had observable impacts on a number of areas with which agencies involved in children's formal play environments are concerned: planning and provision; maintenance; and programming and supervision. Too often, inadequate formal play environments for children are provided because good design, plans and equipment are modified or rejected based on an over-reaction to or misconceptions about what is needed to provide a safe environment, and how safe a playground should be to provide sufficient value to children.

In terms of planning and provision, there have been a number of obvious impacts. First, there seems to be a widespread belief that creative and adventure playgrounds are more dangerous than traditional playgrounds. Quite simply, there is no evidence to support this view, but there is still a tendency for agencies to prefer traditional playgrounds. Second, there has been an impact on location. There has been a tendency to locate playgrounds away from busy streets or other conflicting uses within a larger park. Such actions are understandable, but there is no evidence to suggest that there have been effects on accident rates. Third, safety considerations have often prohibited or restricted the development of one or more of the developmental functions — physical, social, cognitive and emotional — of play environments. Fourth, the layout of activity zones and functional areas has been affected. Activity zones or apparatus should be located far enough apart to ensure that activity in one zone will not interfere with activity in an adjacent zone. Similarly, circulation patterns should be planned so that dangerous flow patterns of children do not exist. Often, this concept is taken to its extreme: the equipment is so widely separated that functional linkages between pieces of equipment are disrupted. Finally, there have been many important effects on the selection and design of apparatus. These include: modification of some well-established types of equipment (e.g., rubber seats for swings, lower slides); continued reliance on steel equipment; the tendency to choose established and time-tested equipment; improved installation techniques; avoidance of high equipment; avoidance of moving equipment; avoidance of overhead linkage or circulation systems; avoidance of hard surface materials; avoidance of enclosed structures; avoidance of water and fire as aids to play; avoidance of certain types of equipment found to be related to accidents (e.g., teeter-totters, high slides, etc.); and discouragement of multi-seasonal use. It must be emphasized, however, that not all of these effects are based on factual safety data (e.g., avoidance of overhead linkage or circulation systems, innovative equipment, etc., or the acceptance of steel equipment). Such decisions are based to a large degree on a desire for safe environments, but are at best opinions based on personal beliefs and are seldom founded on fact.

The effects on maintenance are great. Regular maintenance schedules are usually strictly enforced by the agencies involved. There is also a tendency to discourage winter use of many playgrounds in the belief that there is then an increased danger. While some equipment has been designed so that winter use is not possible, there is no evidence to suggest that accidents increase during winter months.

In terms of programming and supervision, concerns for safety have resulted in restrictions being placed on use: the lack of integration of playgrounds into children's recreation and education programmes, the limiting of the numbers of users, and the restricting of types of activities. Re-evaluation of these actions should be made in the light of the data presented on safety in this report.

In the light of these findings, it is strongly suggested that performance standards for playground equipment be adopted. Performance standards are preferable to design standards because the focus is on hazards rather than specific pieces of equipment. Once a safety requirement is established based on performance, it can apply to any given piece of equipment. Such standards would depend on a number of testing factors: surface material, impact, abrasion, durability, function, costs, supervision, age grouping, labelling and use area. The safety requirements themselves would deal with the following: materials of manufacture and construction; edges, protrusions and crush points; moving impact; entrapment; falls from equipment; surfaces under equipment; and maintenance, installation and identification. Research currently being conducted by the National Recreation and Park Association will be of immense importance in this area.

The Issue of Liability

Finally, a major area of concern for agencies planning and providing children's formal play environments is the issue of legal liability. There is some degree of uncertainty, however, because of the few legal precedents with respect to play environments. A number of concepts can be applied from liability cases in general and those dealing with other recreation settings in particular. The points are as follows:

1. the duty of the supervisor of children is considered to be that of a careful parent;
2. facilities must be maintained in a reasonably safe condition;
3. a regular maintenance system is important;
4. a facility operator is not responsible for all injuries within his facility, but only those in which he has shown a lack of care;
5. competent supervision must be provided for sports in which there is a foreseeable danger as a result of lack of competence;
6. signs limiting liability must be clear and specific;
7. a facility operator is not responsible for faulty equipment if his equipment checks correspond with approved practices;
8. the long safe use of equipment is not a guarantee that it is legally safe;
9. hidden or unusual dangers must be avoided.

The following recommendations are made:

1. that participants do not assume that the facility operator is responsible for all accidents;
2. new equipment should be professionally approved; and
3. increased emphasis be placed on safety education.

It is important to note that, despite the number of playground accidents that have occurred, there have been relatively few lawsuits and few of these have been won.

Conclusion

In summary, it seems fair to suggest that, in terms of the over-all picture of children's accidents, playgrounds are not a major safety concern. Accidents, however, do occur and will continue to occur, but most accidents are caused by the operator of the equipment and are not a result of product or design failure. There is a variety of means by which the number and seriousness of accidents can be reduced (e.g., changes in surface material, performance standards, safety education, supervision, improved planning), but some accidents will always occur in playgrounds. The question arises, however, as to how many more accidents would occur elsewhere (e.g., on the streets) if there were no playgrounds.

Note

1. This research was conducted for the Creative Play Committee of the Ontario Recreation Society and for the Ontario Ministry of Culture and Recreation. The full report, entitled *Safety in Children's Formal Play Environments*, has been published by the Special Services Branch, Ontario Ministry of Culture and Recreation, 400 University Avenue, 23rd Floor, Toronto, Ontario, Canada.

References

Anonymous. 1975. 'Adventure Playground Proves Great Success', *California Parks and Recreation*, June, pp. 19–21.

Bongers, Mickey. 1975. 'Consumer product accident report 1975.' Report prepared for the Consumer Standards Directorate, Product Safety Branch, Canada Ministry of Consumer and Corporate Affairs, Ottawa.

Haffey, Helen. 1974. 'Causes of Injury – 1973.' Report prepared for Toronto Hospital for Sick Children, Toronto.

——1975. 'Causes of Injury – 1974.' Report prepared for Toronto Hospital for Sick Children, Toronto.

McConnell, William H., Jerry T. Parks and L. W. Knapp, Jr. 1973. 'Public playground equipment.' Product Investigation Report Contract No. FDA 73–6. Iowa City, Iowa: Institute of Agriculture Medicine, University of Iowa.

Mahajan, Bal J. 1974. 'Recommendations for a safety standard for home playground equipment – swing sets.' Interim Report NBSIP 74–563, prepared for the Consumer Product Safety Commission, United States Bureau of Standards, Bethesda, Maryland.

National Recreation and Park Association, 1975. 'Summary of in-depth accident studies received from 1–9–74 to 6–17–75.' Mimeo. paper. Arlington, Virginia: National Recreation and Park Association.

——1976a. 'Background and rationale for proposed public playground equipment safety standards.' Working Draft (20 January 1976) developed for the Consumer Product Safety Commission by the National Recreation and Park Association, Arlington, Va.

——1976b. 'Proposed safety standards for public playground equipment.' Working Draft No. 5 (20 January 1976) developed for the Consumer Product Safety Commission by the National Recreation and Park Association, Arlington, Va.

Ontario Ministry of Community and Social Services. 1972. 'Case Studies', in *Creative Play Resources Bank.* Toronto: Youth and Recreation Branch, Ontario Ministry of Community and Social Services.

Reid, Marilyn J. 1971. 'An Evaluation of creative/adventure playgrounds and their use by pupils of elementary schools.' Research Report 71–10, prepared for the Dept. of Planning and Evaluation, Board of School Trustees, Vancouver.

Rhind, Susan. 1974. 'Does dirt really hurt?' *Pools, Parks and Rinks*, XVII, October, pp. 18–21.

United States Consumer Product Safety Commission. 1975. *Hazard Analysis – Playground Equipment.* Washington, DC: US Consumer Product Safety Commission, Bureau of Epidemiology.

6 PLAY ENVIRONMENTS IN ARID LANDS

William B. Watkins

Introduction

The research described in this paper deals with play equipment and materials for children in arid environments. It demonstrates that many types of play equipment are incorrectly placed on such playgrounds. It also suggests some alternative play materials.

A study of the research literature, as it pertains to materials most often used in construction of play-yard apparatus, revealed little information. The academic disciplines searched were architecture, engineering, physical education, recreation and geographic climatology. Based on the literature review, the eight basic materials selected for research purposes were aluminium, natural grass, artificial grass, concrete, rubber, sand, steel and wood. These materials were found to be the most commonly used on most playgrounds in Arizona.

Nearly one-third of the area and one-eighth of the population of the world is within the climatic zone of arid and semi-arid regions. Statistics indicate that there is a long-term shift in population occurring in the United States. Americans are moving to the Sun Belt states. The Sonoran Desert provides the major climatic condition for the states in the southwest. In the city of Tucson, Arizona, 3,000 people per month, or 36,000 per year, become new permanent residents. The city has grown from 260,000 in 1970 to 500,000 in 1978. This is a growth of nearly double in less than 10 years. Any community that experiences this type of rapid growth faces great problems not only of roads, services, education, but also in recreational spaces. In Tucson there is no winter, just three seasons: spring, summer and autumn. There is an average of 354 days of sunshine per year. Yearly average temperature during the day is 28°C (82°F). To emphasize the arid climate, Tucson has an average of 139 days per year over 32°C (90°F). Average relative humidity is less than 15 per cent. Average annual rainfall is 17.9 cm (7.05 inches) per year. All these statistics demonstrate an arid and condition but, more importantly, ideal outside conditions for play for children for most of the year.

Little reported research, however, has been conducted to demonstrate the usability of equipment on play-yards in this climate.

97

Two independent studies were, therefore, conducted during the summers of 1976 and 1977 in Arizona, aimed at identifying what materials are being used now, and what materials should be used in consideration of the high ambient temperatures. It is argued that the results of these studies are applicable to any climate with high temperatures in any season.

Types of Materials in Present Use

The results of the study on the types of materials being used now will be discussed first. One hundred and sixty-eight licensed day-care centres were randomly sampled to be participants in this study. Of the 168 centres, 73 responded to the three-page questionnaire, for a 43 per cent return rate.

The major findings were as follows: on average, 50 per cent of the school site is devoted to outdoor play, with 30 per cent of that area shaded from noon till 5.00 p.m. (It was found that the most common times children usually go outdoors to play was between 2.00 and 5.00 p.m.) Sixty-seven per cent said they noticed that in summer children used metal slides less; 54 per cent said tyres; 50 per cent said swings; 35 per cent specified jungle gyms; and 22 per cent said sunny areas. There were, again on average, four shady trees taller than 4m (12 feet) in the playground. In addition, 90 per cent had water and concrete available within reach of the children; 89 per cent had sand and/or wood; 78 per cent had rubber; 60 per cent had bricks and/or aluminium; other materials included steel (56 per cent), natural grass (44 per cent), glass (33 per cent), adobe (23 per cent), artificial grass (20 per cent). The playground itself had been designed in a variety of ways — 50 per cent said it had just evolved; others thought it had been designed by no one (20 per cent), a consultant (20 per cent), Centre Director (30 per cent), parents (20 per cent), and other (20 per cent). Interestingly, 89 per cent responded favourably to the adventure playground in their school area.

The Effect of Temperature on Surface Materials

Based on information on types of material now in use, eight basic materials generally used in playground apparatus were selected. Temperature experiments were conducted on all eight materials, recording 12.00 noon sun and 12.00 noon shade temperatures, and 8.00 p.m. light and 8.00 p.m. shade temperatures for each material.

The eight materials selected were:

1. unpainted aluminium;
2. 3-inch thick concrete;
3. 2-inch high grass – natural;
4. 2-inch high grass – artificial;
5. black rubber;
6. sand;
7. painted steel;
8. unpainted pine wood.

From the day-care survey, it appears that most of the children play outdoors in the afternoon. Using the official United States Weather Bureau temperature as the base figure, on-site temperatures were recorded for each of the above materials at 12.00 noon and 8.00 p.m. These data, then, give a range of temperatures as a control. More importantly, they provide for a 'cooling' effect for each material as evening comes on.

Some of the statistical results are presented in Table 6.1. The basic conclusions that can be drawn from these data are:

1. The most common material used in play-yards is metal.
2. Shade brings a lowering of at least 15°C (59°F) for most materials used.
3. At noon in the sun, steel is the hottest, with black rubber, concrete and aluminium next in descending order.
4. Cooling is greatest in black rubber, concrete and artificial grass in descending order.
5. Sand and artificial grass are virtually the same temperature in sun and shade as well as having the same cooling rate.
6. Concrete is the coolest hard surface if it can be in shade.
7. The more air in the soil or surface material, the lower will be its ability to hold or conduct heat.
8. Temperatures will rise and fall more quickly over a dry sand than over a more moist loam or clay soil.

Conclusions

The results of the research presented here indicate that some materials commonly used in the construction of play equipment are totally inappropriate for use in arid environments (and, indeed, by extension in playgrounds in any climate in which temperatures reach relatively high levels in any season). Some of these materials are acceptable, however, if they are located in the shade.

Table 6.1: Average Surface Temperatures

Material	12.00 Noon Sun		12.00 Noon Shade		12.00 Noon Sun to Shade Difference		8.00 p.m. Sun		8.00 p.m. Shade		8.00 p.m. Sun to Shade Difference	
	Rank	Temp (°C)	Rank	Temp (°C)	Rank	Temp (°C)	Rank	Temp (°C)	Rank	Temp (°C)	Rank	Temp (°C)
Painted steel	1	53.7	1	51.2	5.5	2.5	1	49.8	1	47.0	8	2.8
Black rubber	2	52.8	7	31.9	1	20.9	2	47.6	5	28.2	1	19.4
Concrete (8 cm thick)	3	48.2	8	29.0	2	19.2	3	45.0	7	26.5	2	18.5
Unpainted aluminium	4	45.2	4	34.1	3	11.1	4	41.6	2	32.0	4	9.6
Wood (unpainted pine)	5	38.5	2	36.1	7.5	2.4	5	34.7	3	31.3	6	3.4
Artificial grass	6	37.4	3	35.0	7.5	2.4	6.5	33.6	8	20.8	3	12.8
Sand	7	37.3	5	33.0	4	4.3	6.5	33.6	4	29.1	5	4.5
Grass (5 cm high)	8	34.5	6	32.0	5.5	2.5	8	30.6	6	27.3	7	3.3

It is suggested that grass, sand, artificial grass and (unpainted) wood are the most appropriate materials for play equipment. Consideration should also be given to the use of such natural materials as shaded bowers made of branches (and other materials such as adobe) under which equipment can be located.

References

Allen of Hurtwood, Lady Marjory. 1968. *Planning for Play.* Cambridge, Mass.: MIT Press.

Aitken, Margaret H. 1972. *Play Environments for Children.* Bellingham, Washington: Educational Designs.

Baker, Katherine Read. 1966. *Let's Play Outdoors.* Washington, DC: National Association for the Education of Young Children.

Battey, Charles. 1976. *Specialization Study -- On Playgrounds.* Washington, DC: American Alliance for Health, Physical Education and Recreation.

Block, Susan Dimond. 1977. *Me and I'm Great: Physical Education for Children Three through Eight.* Minneapolis, Minnesota: Burgess.

Butler, George D. 1958. *Recreation Areas, Their Design and Equipment* (second edition). New York: National Recreation Association and the Ronald Press.

Cratty, Bryant J. 1970. *Perceptual and Motor Development in Infants and Children.* London: Macmillan.

Educational Facilities Laboratories, Inc. 1971. *Patterns for Designing Children's Centers.* New York: Educational Facilities Laboratories, Inc.

Friedberg, M. Paul. 1969. *Playgrounds for City Children.* Washington, DC: Association for Childhood Education International.

Hill, Dorothy M. 1977. *Mud, Sand, and Water.* Washington, DC: National Association for the Education of Young Children.

Hole, V. 1966. *Children's Play on Housing Estates.* London: National Building Studies Research Paper No. 39, Her Majesty's Stationery Office.

Kritchevsky, Sybil and Elizabeth Prescott with Lee Walling. 1969. *Planning Environments for Young Children.* Washington, DC: National Association for the Education of Young Children.

Ledermann, Alfred and Alfred Trachsel. 1968. *Creative Playgrounds and Recreation Centers* (second edition). New York and Washington: Praeger.

Leeper, S. H., R. J. Dales, D. S. Shipper and R. Witherspoon. 1968. *Good Schools for Young Children: A Guide for Working with Three-, Four-, and Five-Year-Old Children.* Philadelphia: Macmillan.

Millar, Susanna. 1968. *The Psychology of Play.* Middlesex, England: Penguin Books.

Moore, R. 1966. 'An experiment in playground design.' Unpublished Master's thesis, Department of City and Regional Planning, Massachusetts Institute of Technology.

National Association for College Women and the National College Physical Education Association for Men. 1976. *Quest: Learning How to Play.* Monograph No. 26, Brattleboro, Vermont.

Quail Roost Conference. 1965. *Planning the Environment for Early Childhood Education.* New York: Educational Facilities Laboratories.

Sellers, William D. and Richard H. Hill (eds). 1974. *Arizona Climate 1931–1972* (second edition). Tucson, Arizona: University of Arizona Press.

Stone, Jeannette G. 1970. *Play and Playgrounds.* Washington, DC: National Association for the Education of Young Children.

Van der Smissen, Betty. 1968. *Legal Liability of Cities and Schools for Injuries in Recreation and Parks.* Cincinnati: W. H. Anderson Company.

Ward, Roger. 1972. *Children's Access to Environmental Resources.* Toronto: University of Toronto Press.

Werner, Peter H. and Richard A. Simmons. 1976. *Inexpensive Physical Education Equipment for Children.* Minneapolis, Minnesota: Burgess.

Williams, Wayne. 1958. *Recreation Places.* New York: Reinhold.

7   THE WINTER USE OF PLAYGROUNDS

Paul F. Wilkinson, Robert S. Lockhart and
Ethel M. Luhtanen

Introduction

In the past ten to fifteen years, a great deal of research has been
undertaken on the topic of the use of playgrounds, but little study has
been focused on the use of playgrounds during the winter months in
temperate climates. There would appear, however, to be a growing
trend for the winter use of playgrounds.

Until recently, it was the policy of many municipalities virtually to
close down many parks in the winter months, or at least to cease
provision of services. These patterns, however, seem to be changing.
Winter use is being encouraged, but little is known about the patterns
of use, its potential and its problems. This paper will, therefore examine
current patterns of use (both traditional and innovative), demand,
programming, resource availability, the issues of demand and facilities,
and trends for potential use, and will make recommendations for
future planning design and policy.

Literature Search

Although the results were not unexpected, the literature search was
disappointing. Virtually no research has been conducted on the
winter use of playgrounds. The occasional general interest article was
discovered and a number of studies did mention that winter use was a
subject which warranted extensive research. Studies on the use of
urban parks either referred only to summer use or the data were not
provided broken down by season.

It is suggested that this lack of research is a function largely of the
concentration in the past on two basic areas: the summer use of urban
parks; and organized sports. It has only been during the last few years
that there has been a visible shift towards year-round use and non-
organized sport activities (e.g., cross-country skiing, physical fitness,
family activities).

Physical Factors Affecting the Winter Use of Playgrounds

Local Topography and Vegetative Cover

There would appear to be two major physical factors affecting winter outdoor recreation: local topography and vegetative cover; and climate. The major factors in terms of local topography and vegetative cover are: elevation above surrounding land, slope, variation in local topography, vegetative ground cover, tree cover, and groundwater and surface water. These factors have a great influence on many winter activities, such as (downhill and cross-country) skiing, snowmobiling, snowshoeing, skating, tobogganing, etc. In general, however, they are of lesser concern when examining playgrounds because the land on which playgrounds are constructed has certain basic characteristics: generally flat, but often with some variation in surface topography as a result of berms; either grass, sand or a hard surface; either no trees or isolated, large trees; and dry.

Climate, therefore, is the major physical factor affecting the winter use of playgrounds.

Climate[1]

Suitable Weather as a Supply Factor. In a certain sense, it would appear that the climatic conditions amenable to such activities as skiing and snowmobiling are quite different from those for playground activities. The contrary is the case, however. All activities are precluded if temperatures are too low, wind chill too high, or snow too heavy. Similarly, winter activities are hindered if conditions are at the opposite end of the scale: too much rain, melting snow resulting in surface water or mud, etc.

It would appear that the basic parameters defining the winter season with respect to outdoor recreation activities are the presence of snow and of ice cover; however, snow is the major parameter when considering playgrounds. Crowe *et al.* (1973b) state that winter begins on the median date of the first 2.5 cm (1 inch) of snow cover and ends on the median date of the last 2.5 cm (1 inch) of snow cover. Even if there is technically a snow cover, however, snow conditions may be far from ideal in terms of particular winter activities.

While such elements as sunshine, daylight, cloudiness, fog, and wind speed do influence the winter use of playgrounds, their effects are secondary in comparison with temperature, wind chill, precipitation and snow cover.

Temperature. Winter outdoor recreation requires air temperatures within a very specific range. Excessively low temperatures are a handicap to all outdoor activities because of their adverse effect upon human comfort levels. On the other hand, high air temperatures may result in melting, which spoils snow surfaces, weakens ice and may produce wet surfaces and flooding. In general, temperatures decrease rapidly during the early winter and increase quickly during the late winter, the coldest month usually being January. Over the long term, the average spread between maximum and minimum temperatures varies from 5–17°C (10–30°F). The daily (or diurnal) range is greatest in mid-winter and at inland locations away from the Great Lakes.

Obviously, low temperatures necessitate closing many facilities which have not been constructed for winter use (e.g., washrooms, drinking fountains). Many activities, however, will require warming huts, changing rooms, washrooms, etc. Such facilities are expensive and retrofitting existing facilities to winter standards may not be feasible. The implications of this problem will be discussed later.

Wind Chill. The most serious limitation to the pursuit of outdoor winter recreation as far as comfort is concerned is not low temperature *per se*, but rather wind chill. Wind chill is an approximation of the rate of loss of heat from exposed flesh. The combination of high winds and low temperatures causes serious discomfort and at times presents the danger of frostbite or even death. Wind chill is generally a serious problem only in (late) December, January and February and is most serious in central and northern Ontario. Warming huts and shelters would be useful for many activities to overcome this problem, particularly when young children are involved.

Precipitation. Winter recreation may be hindered in varying degrees by many types of winter precipitation (e.g., rain, snow, freezing rain, ice pellets), with light snow being the least disruptive. In fact, some light snow may enhance the recreational experience, from both physical and aesthetic points of view. Other forms of precipitation, however, can affect the nature of the recreation experience itself, visibility, transportation, comfort, etc.

Significant snowfalls usually occur as early as September in northern Ontario and October over southern Ontario, with appreciable amounts as late as May in the north and April in the south. Over southern Ontario, most of the snow falls in mid-winter, but in the north there is a tendency for heavier amounts in the early part of the season. The higher values at stations in the lee of the Great Lakes are notable features, the snowfall diminishing as waterways become ice-covered.

Rainfall can adversely affect both the snow surface and the base snow. This is a major factor in much of the south during the winter months. A suitable measure of the problem is the percentage of total precipitation falling as snow cover during the winter months. Rainfall has serious implications for the maintenance of suitable conditions for most winter activities. For those activities dependent on snow *per se*, there is little that can be done in a preventive or remedial way.

Snow Cover. The presence of a snow cover is essential for many winter pursuits. Also, the snow cover must have acceptable physical characteristics and be of sufficient depth.

Meteorological data give the median value of snow depth; however, the data usually refer to airport sites which may be more windswept than could normally be expected in areas where recreation activities occur. For example, wooded areas would usually have greater snow depth. Average winter maximum values of less than 30 cm (1 foot) of snow cover are common over most of central and eastern Ontario at some time during a normal winter and 90 cm (3 feet) or more over northern Ontario. Again, increased snow depth in the lee of the Great Lakes is a notable feature. It should be emphasized that the variation in snow depth from day to day and from one year to another is great, and that great spatial variations may also occur at any specified time.

Snow conditions can be inferred from rainfall data for winter months. In general, the greater the rainfall in these months, the greater the probability of poor snow conditions, because rains and thaws tend to compress and melt the snow cover. Moreover, those parts of Ontario having the lowest average snow depth generally have the lowest probability of good snow surface conditions. Much of southern and southwestern Ontario receives considerable rain in January and, therefore, crusty and wet snow conditions are frequently encountered.

Satisfaction. To date, there has been no research on children and satisfaction in terms of climate. There are a great number of factors involved: physical parameters of the climate; type and level of activity; clothing; individual physical and psychological differences; etc. The only major work done to date (Crowe *et al.*, 1973b) concerns adults and activities of skiing and snowmobiling; therefore, only its general conclusions are of interest here. It is argued, however, that this research gives an initial indication of the issues involved.

Crowe *et al.* provide an interesting attempt at measuring the quality of the adult recreation experience through analysis of satisfaction in terms of comfort, weather and snow cover suitability. Comfort is largely dependent on wind chill, which is a function of wind speed and temperature. Obviously, this is a major constraint to outdoor winter activities, particularly in northern Ontario. As noted above, the effect of weather is a function of such factors as precipitation, fog, cloudiness, etc. and may vary greatly among different activities. Suitable snow cover, in terms of skiing and snowmobiling, depends on a minimum snow depth, good tractionability and a snow surface that is not crusty or wet. The exact parameters and limits are not known, but the following criteria are suggested for a day suitable for several activities, including cross-country skiing, downhill skiing and snowmobiling:

1. snow cover of 5 cm (2 inches) or more at 7.00 a.m.;
2. no measurable liquid precipitation (rain, drizzle, freezing rain or freezing drizzle) during the 24-hour period;
3. maximum temperature for the day less than 4°C (40°F).

The choice of these criteria was based on a combination of the availability of data (e.g., snow depth data are available on a daily basis only for 7.00 a.m. EST) and discussions with individuals, organizations and agencies associated with winter activities. They must be treated, therefore, as being highly tentative.

Using these parameters, Crowe *et al.* go on to analyse the suitability of snow cover for skiing and snowmobiling in Ontario. Table 7.1 summarizes by regions the mean percentages of time when conditions are too cold and completely comfortable for skiing and snowmobiling at the end of January, the approximate mid-point of winter. There would appear to be three major parameters in determining the suitability of snow cover for these activities:

1. Mean maximum temperature: the lower the temperature, the higher the probability of having a suitable snow cover; however, the relationship is not linear.
2. Total precipitation: at reasonably low temperatures, the greater the precipitation, the greater the snowfall and, therefore, the higher the probability of suitable snow cover.
3. Time of the year: the probability of suitable snow cover increases throughout the winter season for a given mean temperature (largely because of accumulating amounts of snow on the ground).

Table 7.1: Summary by Regions of Mean Percentages of Time that
Conditions are too Cold and Completely Comfortable for Skiing and
Snowmobiling at the end of January

	Skiing		Snowmobiling	
Station	Too cold Max <−3 °F	Completely comfortable Max >20 °F	Too cold Max <−9 °F	Completely comfortable Max >8 °F
SOUTHWESTERN ONTARIO				
Leamington	0	88−89	0	99−100
Kent and Essex	0	86−87	0	99−100
Lake Erie Counties Inland	0−1	80−89	0	95−99
Lake Erie Shore	0	86−89	0	99−100
SOUTHERN ONTARIO				
Toronton-Burlington	1	77−79	0	96−97
Niagara Fruit Belt	0−1	79−86	0	96−99
South Slopes-West	0−1	74−80	0	95−98
South Slopes-East	1	70−75	0	92−95
Lake Ontario Shore	1	75−77	0	94−96
Prince Edward County	1	74−76	0	93−95
Lake Huron Shore	0−1	78−84	0	98−99
Bruce Peninsula	0−1	75−77	0	96−98
Southern Georgian Bay	1	69−74	0	94−97
Huron Slopes	1	70−81	0	91−98
Dundalk Upland	1	65−74	0	93−96
Simcoe	1	67−74	0	93−95
Kawartha Lakes	1−2	62−73	0−1	90−95
EASTERN ONTARIO				
Eastern Counties	2−3	51−69	1	82−91
Renfrew	4−6	43−50	1−2	74−81
CENTRAL ONTARIO				
Muskoka	1−2	58−68	0−1	90−93
Haliburton Slopes-West	1−2	56−66	0−1	86−91
Haliburton Slopes-East	1−6	43−61	1−2	74−88
Algonquin Park	1−5	55−59	1−2	79−90
Manitoulin	1	62−65	0	91−94
Sudbury-East	2−7	41−59	1−2	74−89
Sudbury-West	2−3	49−61	0−2	83−91
Sault Ste. Marie	1−2	56−60	0−1	88−91
Timiskaming	7−8	38−41	2−3	72−74

Table 7.1: (continued)

Station	Skiing		Snowmobiling	
	Too cold Max <-3 °F	Completely comfortable Max >20 °F	Too cold Max <-9 °F	Completely comfortable Max >8 °F
NORTHEASTERN ONTARIO				
Superior Shore	3–10	39–55	2–3	69–87
Superior Inland	3–11	36–55	2–4	68–87
Height of Land-East	4–17	26–48	3–11	58–82
Northern Clay Belt	10–18	25–35	4–9	53–69
NORTHWESTERN ONTARIO				
Height of Land-West	11–16	26–35	4–11	59–67
Thunder Bay	4–5	44–46	2–3	74–77
Kakabeka	5–10	36–46	2–4	68–77
Rainy River	11–16	26–35	3–8	61–67
English River	16–24	20–25	9–13	50 60
FAR NORTHERN ONTARIO				
Albany-West	17–40	10–25	12–22	35–58
Albany-East	19–30	15–25	10–17	39–52
Patricia	31–52	6–14	18–39	21–38
Hudson Bay Shore	53–57	3–5	40–43	17–20

Source: R. B. Crowe, G. A. McKay and W. M. Baker, *The Toursit and Outdoor Recreation Climate of Ontario*, Vol. II: 'The Winter Season' (1973), p. 76.

The basic conclusion is that winter conditions for skiing and snowmobiling generally improve to the north and away from the moderating influence of the Great Lakes.

While these data relate to adults and to skiing and snowmobiling, it is argued that the results can be applied in general to the consideration of children and playgrounds. In geographical terms, a large part of Ontario has a winter climate highly suited to winter outdoor recreation, but the problem is that those areas where the snow cover is not very reliable contain the largest proportion of the population. The impact of this fact on municipal recreation agencies is great. Those municipalities located in areas of reliable winter conditions are not under very great pressure to provide winter recreation programmes and facilities within the urban area for two reasons: the populations are relatively small and the resources (e.g., snow, forests, lakes, hills) are readily available in close proximity to the municipalities. Such is obviously the case in northern Ontario. The southern parts of Ontario, however, have exactly the opposite problem: large populations, unreliable winter conditions and few alternatives for winter outdoor recreation activities nearby. The question then arises as to whether these southern municipalities should de-emphasize winter outdoor activities and concentrate on other seasons and/or indoor activities or whether they are obligated by the very nature of the situation to provide basic winter outdoor recreation activities when their populations have no alternative outside the municipality in nearby areas, and/or alternative activities.

Winter Outdoor Recreation in Ontario Urban Centres

The major thrust of this project was to examine the current situation with respect to winter outdoor recreation in urban centres in Ontario. Consequently, information was gathered from 36 municipal parks and/or recreation agencies with respect to five basic areas:

1. perceptions of the nature of the winter season;
2. available resources;
3. activities;
4. policies, by-laws, regulations and philosophy;
5. future trends.

An attempt was made to get as wide a range as possible of different sizes of municipalities spread throughout the province's different climatological regions, with distribution being roughly proportional to regional population distribution. Interviews were conducted with senior management personnel in the municipal parks and/or recreation agency.

Thirty-six muncipalities were included in the sample, accounting for a total (1973) population of 4,142,929 (or 69.5 per cent of the total population of all municipalities in Ontario with a population of 5,000 or more). The minimum size of a municipality to be considered for inclusion in the sample was 5,000. Population totals for the municipalities sampled in each region are roughly proportional to the total urban population in each region.

The most common resources for winter outdoor recreation were:

1. unstructured areas;
2. sliding/tobogganing slopes or undesignated downhill skiing slopes;

3. outdoor natural ice surfaces;
4. trails for cross-country skiing, walking, hiking and, to a lesser extent, snowmobiling;
5. children's playgrounds.

The most popular activities, in order, were (see Table 7.2):

1. tobogganing;
2. pleasure skating;
3. outdoor shinny (unorganized hockey);
4. cross-country skiing;
5. use of children's playgrounds.

There was a great deal of variation by region in most activities. In particular, participation in southwestern Ontario was usually lower than the other regions because of the lack of variations in local topography and because of an inadequate and inconsistent climate. Playground activities formed the exception; participation was generally higher in southwestern Ontario, a trend which is related to a combination of milder climate and perhaps the lack of other opportunities (see Table 7.3). Participation in most other winter-oriented activities generally increased to the north, as did a tendency towards more traditional attitudes about recreation on the part of municipal agencies.

There did not appear to be any significant relationship between the availability of playgrounds for winter use and the size of the municipality or the region in which it was located. The exception was the southwestern region; the municipalities of this region had placed less emphasis on the provision of facilities and resources that were dependent to a great extent on climate. Nor did there seem to be a very strong relationship between the number of facilities of a particular type and the population of the municipality.

A number of local practices can be cited as influencing the availability of resources.

Land Acquisition Practices

Land acquisition practices varied greatly among the municipalities. A major influence was the geographical situation of the particular municipality. For example, municipalities in northern areas were surrounded by vast areas of non-urbanized land, often in the form of Crown Land. Because their residents could easily and quickly take

Table 7.2: Most Popular Winter Outdoor Recreation Activities in the Sample Municipalities, 1977

Activity	Number of Municipalities with participation rated high, moderate and limited (n = 36)		
	High	Moderate	Limited
Tobogganing	20	8	2
Pleasure skating	18	16	2
Shinny (unorganized hockey)	14	22	0
Cross-country skiing	14	17	2
Use of children's playgrounds	1	17	9

advantage of these resources, these municipalities were reluctant to acquire land within their boundaries for recreation. In southern areas and particularly in large urban areas, the municipalities were usually very concerned about acquiring available land. A major influence in these areas was, of course, the extremely high cost of urban land. Because land acquisition budgets were usually small, municipalities were often forced to seek special grants from the provincial government when large blocks of urban land were put on the market. Regardless of such distinctions, however, many municipalities were simply not taking advantage of available land. Others owned the land, but were not making great efforts to make it usable or accessible to the public. Budget deficiencies were often the basic problem.

Quality of Planning

The most obvious trend throughout all regions and sizes of municipalities was the lack of adequate site planning. The need to use urban recreation areas and the inherent potential of these resources was often overlooked or, at best, treated superficially and in a non-comprehensive manner.

Quality of Site Design

Although not examined in great detail, site design would also seem to be a major area of deficiency. Many municipalities appeared to take a very traditional approach to site design, placing emphasis on such facilities and features as grass and trees. Playground equipment was usually of the very traditional metal, mass-produced variety. The majority of changes involved the use of some railroad ties or a few concrete sewer pipes for climbing through. Creative playgrounds were rare, especially in the smaller municipalities, and adventure playgrounds virtually non-existent. Basically, playgrounds were designed with only one season in mind — summer.

Regulations

It would appear that many policies and regulations that encourage or discourage particular uses or users were quite unique as no trends could be seen.

Equipment

An important example of great differences among the municipalities was the policy towards equipment in children's play areas. Most respondents described their children's play areas as being usable in the winter season, despite the fact that over half of the municipalities dismantled and stored the key elements of play apparatus (e.g., swing seats, teeter-totter seats, slides, picnic tables, benches). A number of respondents mentioned potential safety problems in winter use of such equipment. Research has shown, however, that there is little evidence to support the belief that play areas are more dangerous in the winter (Wilkinson and Lockhart, 1976). Others said that the equipment was removed as a matter of course for regular painting and maintenance, but many said that it was simply not returned until the spring. It was surprising, however, that a few respondents did not know why the equipment was removed, other than that it was a traditional practice; most of them assumed that all municipalities removed all equipment. (As a result of being interviewed for this study at least one municipality has reversed its policy and has stopped removing the equipment.) There would appear to be a trend towards leaving the equipment intact all year and only removing temporarily those pieces of equipment that are in need of repair. The cost savings would be significant. Of course, there is the additional factor that use will probably increase if the equipment is left out. (Observation has shown that playgrounds will be used in the winter if the equipment is available.)

The range of activities was extensive and much greater than originally imagined by the researchers. Of particular interest were a number of innovative activities:

a variety of field sports (snowshoe softball, snowball, snowshoe soccer, snowshoe football);
snolf (winter golf);

Table 7.3: Playground and Winter Use

Municipality (By Climatic Regions)	Population (1973)	Area (Sq. Mile)	Climatological Data[1]			Winter playground activities	Playground equipment removed in winter
			Weeks of snow cover marginally reliable or better	Weeks of total winter season	Number of playgrounds usable in winter		
SOUTHWESTERN							
Windsor	199,250	46	0	17	73	●	
Sarnia	54,782	13	0*	18*	35	●	
Welland	43,767	31	2*	17*	15		L
Leamington	10,576	3	0*	16*	11		
SOUTHERN							
Metropolitan Toronto	2,081,724	243	6	17	S	●	
City of Toronto	676,363	38	6	17	N	●	
North York	527,564	68	6	17	N	●	●
Scarborough	348,266	72	6	17	S	●	●
Etobicoke	282,998	48	6	17	N	●	
York	141,193	9	6	17	O	●	●
East York	105,340	8	6	17	S	●	●
Hamilton	303,794	47	0	17	O	●	●
London	232,660	62	9	18	N	L	
Kitchener	121,441	52	8*	20*	N	●	●
Kingston	59,289	11	11	18	O	?	
Peterborough	56,349	21	10*	19*	N		
Belleville	34,812	9	10*	17*	O		●
Halton Hills	32,160	107	8*	20*	S	●	
Barrie	28,678	11	12*	21*	S	L	●

	Population						
Stratford	24,048	8	12	20	N	L	•
Orillia	21,698	9	12	21	S	L	• •
Port Colborne	20,522	47	2*	17*	O	L	
Milton	15,667	105	8*	20*	S	L	
EASTERN							
Ottawa	292,983	43	15	19	120		• • •
Cornwall	44,672	24	13	18	15		
Pembroke	15,064	4	15	21	4		•
CENTRAL							
Sudbury	95,094	102	17	22	S	L	•
Sault Ste. Marie	77,501	86	15	22	S	L	
North Bay	46,409	108	17	22	18	L	• • •
Huntsville	9,363	271	16	23	2		
NORTHEASTERN							
Timmins	41,957	912	19	26	35		•
Kapuskasing	12,526	32	20	28	0		
NORTHWESTERN							
Thunder Bay	105,954	125	16	23	N	L	• • •
Dryden	6,810	7	16*	24*	4	L	
Total Population	4,142,929						

? Not known.

* Estimate based on data from nearest climatological station.

N Numerous.

S Some.

• Yes.

L Limited

¹ Source: R. B. Crowe, G. A. McKay and W. M. Baker, *The Tourist and Outdoor Recreation Climate of Ontario*, Vol. II: 'The Winter Season' (1973) p. 76.

3. winter children's playground programmes.

One example of an innovative playground programme took place in Ottawa. The Ottawa Recreation Department, during the winter of 1977—8, acted in accordance with its philosophy that there are winter activities other than ice skating than can take place in urban parks. In addition to the usual rink attendants, part-time programmers were hired to conduct activities for all ages, primarily after school and on weekends. Each programmer rotated among an assigned set of parks, directing events that ranged from inter-park hockey competitions to family barbecues, skating parties, etc. The experience was such that participation was relatively high if the rink attendants provided continuity to the programme (depending also upon factors such as weather and structure of the community). In the absence of such continuity, however, participation dwindled.

At the time of the writing of this report, the recreation department was in the process of debating the programming issue and establishing some directions for next winter. The following are some of the considerations in this debate:

1. an emphasis on specialized programmes;
2. programming in fewer parks;
3. the programmer spending more time per location;
4. a survey of the demography of each community;
5. greater emphasis on education regarding winter activities.

Planning and Design of Playgrounds for Winter Use

It appears, from all available research, that children's playgrounds will be used if the equipment is not removed during the winter months. Although it is not possible at this time to compare the amount and type of winter use that playgrounds receive in relation to the summer season, the data that are available suggest that winter use is significant. It is recommended, therefore, that playground equipment be left in place during the winter. Maintenance programmes should be designed so that necessary repairs, repainting, etc., can be conducted when necessary and the equipment should be removed for as short a time as possible. A small extra supply of high-repair items would allow damaged equipment to be replaced with no loss of service. Stock could then be repaired and rotated.

Many municipalities still maintain a very traditional approach to planning and providing for children. It is recommended that there be a shift away from traditional playground design towards creative and adventure playgrounds. At the very least, a move should be made towards introducing more natural materials and designs which encourage a wider variety and a greater value of play experiences.

A number of detailed guidelines have been developed to assist with the planning and design of playgrounds for winter use. They are not intended to be all-inclusive but, rather, they should cover many of the most significant principles that underlie the provision of good recreation areas. The focus is not just on planning and design for winter use, because playgrounds should function well in all seasons, although some playgrounds, usually because of their physical character, can offer more for one season than the others.

1. Design should be for people.
2. Parks should be planned, designed and maintained for year-round use.
3. The design of all equipment, apparatus and facilities should be properly scaled to meet the requirements of the intended users (i.e., children), rather than to allay the fears of non-users (i.e., adults).
4. A park plan should accommodate the needs and preferences of as many people as possible, especially local residents when dealing with a neighbourhood recreation area.
5. The park plan should relate to the surrounding physical area. The plan should encourage resident interaction between the park and adjacent complementary land uses (e.g., school, houses, library, etc.), and restrict interaction between the park users and incompatible land uses (e.g., busy street, dangerous industrial area, parking lot, etc.). The character of the built forms (i.e., buildings and landscaping) should not strongly contradict the type of development in the immediate area, such that local residents would not be able to identify with the site as being suitable to their neighbourhood.
6. Everything should have a purpose. Function should be considered before form or design. A park is a complex of many parts. The location of every park unit affects the workability of another.
7. Demand for site development (related to user demand and need) should be matched to the potential of the site for development. Use areas should fit naturally on the site. Natural features (slopes, hills, level ground), soil (carrying capacity, drainage), vegetation (grass, trees) and orientation (sun, wind, shade) should all be considered carefully.

8. The site plan and facility design should be flexible and should relate to function, changing requirements for use, and available resources.

9. When planning, designing and administering each site, regular evaluation and subsequent modification should be allowed for in order to help ensure an adequate maintenance and improvement programme.

10. When making decisions about land acquisition, the physical and locational features that permit certain recreational uses should be taken into account. Hills and slopes, sheltered areas, linear spaces, a quiet pond that will freeze safely for skating, coniferous trees, access for all seasons and other features are important for winter use.

11. The most important considerations of climate that centre on micro-environments are wind protection and exposure to the sun. Effective design of outdoor space can counteract undesirable conditions and encourage desirable ones. For example, sitting areas, useful in early spring or late fall, or on calm days in winter, should be oriented to the sun and baffled against driving snow. Study of localized wind patterns is essential in each individual case to prevent snow build-up and the consequent unusability of such spaces at these times.

12. In order to compensate for climatic conditions to some degree, care should be taken when siting the playground. Coniferous trees, shrubs and mounds should be provided to the northwest, north and east to shelter the playground from cold winds and trap the sun in winter. When designing individual components and laying out the various activity areas throughout the playground, the effect of snow cover and icing should be carefully considered. The base of the playground will usually be raised a foot or more by packed snow cover, and protruding and overhanging hardware, etc., could become dangerous as clearance is reduced and children could come unexpectedly in contact with these structures. Icing on equipment and underfoot can be reduced through thoughtful design. Also, the flow pattern established for summer use of the playground may change in the winter and care should be taken in design to avoid potentially dangerous patterns. Monitoring of the winter use of each playground should become mandatory to improve the potential for winter use and to reduce dangerous features.

13. The effect desired from the sun varies depending on the activity.

With some activities, it may be desirable to trap the sun from the east, south or west and to reflect the heat back into the activity area. This would be the case for a sitting area or perhaps parts of a children's playground area.

14. Sun glare into interior spaces from which people look out may be a problem in winter. Coniferous trees can be used to filter the glare to reduce this effect, while at the same time not blocking views completely.

15. Enclosure of space is a fundamental requirement, and can be achieved by building form or by major trees, or both.

16. Large open spaces require shelter belts of coniferous trees (particularly pines) to provide protection against prevailing winds. Not only is wind chill reduced, but there is also an effect on snow drop and retention.

17. Large open courtyards and other activity areas are subject to wind eddies and should be either made small or planted with trees as borders for protection.

18. Snow build-up and drifting can be reduced in areas where that is desirable and encouraged in other areas by correctly locating barriers against prevailing winds.

19. Walks associated with large open areas that are exposed to winds should be protected by high shrubbery, trees, walls or screens. Pine trees are particularly suitable for buffers, as are poplar, aspen and willow.

20. It should be recognized that buildings can create both good and bad conditions. For example, they can be used to shelter an activity area from the prevailing wind. On the other hand, they can also cast unwanted shadows on an activity area and, if large enough, can create wind-tunnel effects.

21. The maintenance and servicing needs of the area should be accommodated. Winter conditions should be carefully considered in order to ensure adequate access to activity areas and indoor facilities for both park users and staff. The over-all recreational and aesthetic value of the site should not, however, be significantly compromised by maintenance considerations.

22. Facilities, spaces and fixtures should be safe, yet over-reaction to the issue of safety can destroy the inherent value of children's play areas.

23. Structural materials appropriate for the intended use should be selected, taking into account durability, availability, appearance and maintenance.

24. The border and entrance and exit of a recreation area are usually not considered as activity areas, but are certainly functional areas. The border or boundary provides an 'edge' to 'frame' activities and can provide an appealing atmosphere of human scale and, in some cases, protection for the user.
25. A significant portion of the perimeter of the area should be directly exposed to the street in order to permit the recreation area to add aesthetically to the surrounding community, to encourage use through awareness and improved access, to reduce negative impact on surrounding residences and to permit a wider range of uses.
26. Playgrounds, especially those in major parks, should be located so that they are visible to major vehicular and pedestrian routes, in order to improve both access and visibility. Care should be taken, however, not to locate a playground too close to an outdoor ice rink in order to discourage children from using playground equipment while they are still wearing skates. At the least, some form of winter barrier such as snow-fencing should be used temporarily to impede direct access between incompatible areas.
27. Physical structures (buildings, parking lots, fixtures, playgrounds, etc.) should be arranged around the perimeter of the site in order to leave the largest possible open area.
28. The organization of use areas on the site should provide for supervision needs. For example, sitting areas should be close to the children's play area.
29. Circulation and traffic systems between various areas should be planned to encourage interaction, promote safety and support an aesthetic environment.
30. The site and facilities should be aesthetically pleasing, yet appropriate for intended use.

Activities and Programming

Perhaps the most important trend that has been noted throughout this project is the shift in interest away from organized activities — particularly competitive team sports aimed at certain limited sectors of the population — towards more spontaneous, individual and family-oriented activities. Recreation practitioners should be prepared not necessarily to cut out all such competitive team sports, but to reassess them in the light of the over-all population and the leisure delivery system as a whole. A further incentive to the adoption of such activities as winter playground use is their relatively low cost in terms of capital, operating and maintenance expenses.

Recreation practitioners should also be prepared to break out of the confines of the limited set of traditional activities that are usually considered in programme planning. Such a reliance is to a large degree understandable, since it is only natural to want to continue with successful and proven activities. The adoption of new activities will, however, have two benefits: it will broaden the proportion of the population participating in the recreation programme; and it will broaden the range of possibilities for those already participating.

Such activities, however, will not be successful unless the potential client is aware of them, understands what they are and learns how to take part in them. There are two functions necessary here: promotion and education. In terms of promotion, the potential clients should be made aware of the range of activities available, costs if any, equipment required, rules of any games, and so on. Education in turn can be broken down into two parts. The first is general leisure education, i.e., the necessity to explain the importance of leisure, the role of recreation, fitness, participation, etc. The second is education in terms of the specific activity, whether it be physical skills or rules. For many of these activities, it is necessary only to provide enough information to get people started; after that, they should be left alone, the only function of the practitioner being to maintain the facility, safety, etc. The mix of activities provided by any agency should allow both for people who want the entire programme 'laid on' for them and for people who merely want the opportunity provided so that they can do their own thing when they want to, rather than in groups or at specific times or locations.

Such a mix of activities and a search for new activities emphasize the importance of the relationship between the roles of the planner/ designer and of the programmer. Each must know what the other is doing and needing. Neither one should be the supreme determinant of the nature of the programme; rather, they must operate as integral, interacting elements in the leisure delivery system.

Above all, it should be recognized that the philosophy for the winter use of urban parks noted above applies directly to activities and programming:

. Think winter.
. Promote winter.
. Quality over quantity.
. Know your client.

5. Do more with what you have.
6. Be innovative.

Note

1. The authors gratefully acknowledge the importance of Crowe *et al.* (1973a, 1973b) in the writing of this report.

References

Auliciems, A., C. R. De Frietas and F. K. Hare. 1973. 'Winter clothing requirements for Canada', *Climatological Studies Number 22.* Toronto: Atmospheric Environment Service, Environment Canada.

Crowe, R. B., G. A. McKay and W. M. Baker. 1973a. *The Tourist and Outdoor Recreation Climate of Ontario.* Volume I: 'Objectives and definitions of seasons.' Toronto: Meteorological Applications Branch, Atmospheric Environment Service, Environment Canada.

———, ———, ———. 1973b. *The Tourist and Outdoor Recreation Climate of Ontario.* Volume II: 'The winter season.' Toronto: Meteorological Applications Branch, Atmospheric Environment Service, Environment Canada.

Wilkinson, P. F. and R. S. Lockhart. 1976. *Safety in Children's Formal Play Environments.* Toronto: Ontario Ministry of Culture and Recreation.

———, ———. 1977. *The Winter Use of Urban Parks.* Toronto: Ontario Ministry of Culture and Recreation.

———, ——— and E. M. Luhtanen. 1978. *The Joy of Winter: Winter in Ontario's Urban Parks.* Toronto: Ontario Ministry of Culture and Recreation.

8 PLAY IN A COLD CLIMATE

Harvey A. Scott[1]

Introduction

The cold regions of the world provide some unique play opportunities and challenges to children and adults and to those who wish to develop play settings and programmes. The Northwest Territories, that vast third of Canada of over 3,100,000 sq. km (1,200,000 sq. miles) lying north of the 60th parallel north latitude, provides many interesting examples of the expression of man's basic urge to play in an environment of both great climatic contrasts and diverse cultures. This paper will share a few observations and possible implications of this environment for planners and programmers of play.

The approach of the author — someone primarily involved in the professional preparation of play leader-programmers — tends to be general and programme-oriented rather than providing facility design detail. Additionally, due to an active concern with encouraging the recognition and redevelopment of Inuit and Dené play culture, the cultural aspects of play have been emphasized as much or more than the climatic. There is much to learn from these people who have adapted their work and play so well to this harsh environment.

The Organization of Play in the North

Before examining seasonal play involvements in the north, it is useful to outline who is responsible for planning and programming play activities. Traditionally, and to a great extent today, play in the transitional settlement is organized in an informal, relaxed manner. Usually no one had to be overtly designated as the 'recreation director'. As with other aspects of their integrated culture and life-style, an elder or another person who had demonstrated leadership or abilities in singing, drumming, dance, games, etc. was expected to initiate things. This was particularly true with games and dance programmes held as part of feasts or celebrations. Often the headman or chief actually presided over the ceremony itself. It is important to note that individual initiative and quiet, covert planning and preparation took place without the formal assignment of roles. Play was seen as an integral part of the culture seemingly without the clear-cut conceptual

123

distinctions that southern cultures make between work and play, between serious and non-serious, and most importantly between the religious and non-religious. Play activities and religious activities were difficult to separate. The co-operative values and the respect for the natural environment and all its non-human beings were all celebrated in the play of their games and dance.

The new Euro-Canadian northern town takes the kind of formal, institutionalized approach to planning and programming play found in southern Canada and elsewhere. Most towns have a part- or full-time paid recreation director who answers to an elected community board. He/she liaises with and is funded in part through the Territorial Recreation Division. The mandate generally encompasses all aspects of play facilitation, setting design and development, programme organization and administration, and even activity operation and instruction. He/she encourages and assists volunteers. Play or its institutionalized pseudonym 'recreation' is seen as dichotomous from work, as non-serious (but important), and as secular and non-sacred in much the same way most southerners would see it. In short, it is a separate sphere of human activity calling for a separate bureaucracy and if possible specially prepared and designated leaders.

The Northwest Territories Government Recreation Division has the mandate to encourage and facilitate recreation in all its forms in the Territories. Through a programme of capital, travel, outdoor facilities and operating grants, it helps communities and groups to develop facilities and programmes. Consultants are available to assist with the planning process.

Parks Canada, in liaison with the Territorial Recreational Division and Travel Arctic, is also involved in encouraging the development and use of parks in the Territories, most notably the new Baffin Island Park. In the Yukon Territory, Kluane and Nahanni Parks are directed through a similar process.

The transitional settlement, arising as it did from groups of nomadic hunting families settling near their children's school or the mission, has until recently had very little formal organization for planning, designing and programming play. In the case of the smaller settlements where one or several strong and willing initiators exist, play programmes have been quite active. Generally, however, the unaccustomed large size of the settlements and the unfamiliarity with the need of and techniques for planning play opportunities have resulted in limited programmes in these communities. Fort Franklin is an exception to this situation. Here a strong continuing commitment to traditional values and informal modes of organization results in strong, apparently spontaneous play programmes utilizing both traditional activities and imported activities such as cross-country skiing. Most other settlements are being forced to form community clubs which have as their prime responsibility the planning and programming of play. Several of these have hired part-time recreation directors who build on existing informal play organization. Unfortunately, as happens elsewhere, the designation of a paid recreation director sometimes results in loss of volunteer enthusiasm.

Types of Play Activities

What types of play activities occur in a climate that has been fairly accurately described as 'nine months of winter and three months of tough sledding'? This paper will look at the special challenges, problems and advantages; some unique settings, facilities, activities and programmes; and a few possible implications related to play in a polar or sub-polar climate found in Canada's Northwest Territories. It begins with a brief, generalized overview of the annual seasonal cycle. It then looks at play settings, activities and programmes season-by-season in the context of their particular type of northern human settlement in the traditional nomadic group on the land, in the transitional native settlement, in the new northern town or city and in the new northern national parks. While technically the last category is not a human settlement in any permanent sense, it is used to designate a place where humans — typically non-northerners — gather to live and travel together.

The Northern Seasonal Cycle

While temperatures vary somewhat from south to north and from marine to continental areas, the entire area experiences long, cold winters and short but warm summers. While most non-northerners expect the cold winters, they are often surprised by the almost sudden arrival of an 'instant' warm summer.

At Inuvik in the Western Arctic some 80 miles up the Mackenzie River from the Arctic Ocean, a week of $-45°C$ ($-50°F$) weather in January or February is not uncommon. Similarly a week of 27°C (80°F) weather and regular 15—27°C (60—80°F) weather would be normal in July. Such summer temperatures spread over a 24-hour growing day can compensate beautifully for a very short frost-free growing period. The result can be unexpectedly beautiful gardens, well inside the Arctic circle, despite a perma-frost that hovers just below the plant roots.

Wind is a major factor in winter, particularly on the coasts and barrens where wind chill effects can be dangerous even in only 'cool' weather. Generally speaking, precipitation is not heavy in the Arctic although somewhat more may fall in the Subarctic Boreal Forests farther south. As a rule, the north is considered semi-arid although the myriad of potholes, lakes, muskeg and rivers, blooming with greenery during the short Arctic summer, would suggest otherwise.

A final, pronounced effect of the extreme latitude is that of quantity of daylight. At Inuvik for example, the sun is never seen above the horizon for a six-week period from late November to early January. A comparable period of continuous sunlight is experienced in summer. The effects these dark and light periods can have on the human psyche and the sense of time can be quite profound.

The yearly cycle and the temperate zone conception of time and seasons necessarily undergo some major revisions in the north. With the return of a daily dark period night in late July, the days become rapidly shorter and cooler. By mid-August, autumn has begun. Frost is to be expected again and the clouds of insects are gone.

Occasional snow showers begin by early September. Freezing and associated temporary travel problems follow in early October with temperatures dropping steadily until the darkness and cold establishes itself in mid-November. Now the northern outdoor player is truly at the mercy of the environment.

While the sun returns in January, the intense cold continues. If the wind is still or if in the shelter of the spruce woods, the player may be able to carry on. Generally, however, he/she cannot expect to be able to play outside regularly until March when daytime temperatures will usually climb above -23°C (-10°F). Mid-March to early May sees cool, long, sunny days with a dependable snow cover that affords a variety of play opportunities.

Suddenly in mid-May the combination of hot sun and long days are too much for the snow. Seemingly overnight it disappears. A few weeks later, the river ice breaks up and summer is on. Aside from a week or two of mud caused by the thawing surface frost and the temporary inconvenience of the river's change from ice road to barge canal, spring as experienced in the south is almost non-existent. Suddenly the plants seem to be in full bloom. Hard on their tracks come their friends the blackflies, the sandfleas, no-see-ems, mosquitoes, and bulldogs — final proof that northern summer has arrived.

Traditional Play in the Seasonal Round

Long before the whalers, the traders, the missionaries and other new northerners ever saw this land 'north of 60', two well-adapted cultures – the Dené and the Inuit – existed and played in this harsh seasonal cycle. In the Boreal Forests the various Athapaskan Indian or Dené peoples moved seasonally to intercept and harvest the plants and animals they depended upon for their living. For the Hareskin and Bear people living around Great Bear Lake, this meant travelling by dog-sledge to places such as Hottah Lake in winter to intercept vast caribou herds on their annual migrations. There and elsewhere, the people lived and played in their portable caribou-skin tents. Here they might meet their Dogrib friends from Rae far to the south. Then, after a successful hunt, they would play their favourite indoor game, the hand game or stick gambling, to the sound of the drum.

Here also men and women would dance the simple communal circle dance to the sound of the drum and chanting. Winter was a time to play indoor games – games of fun, clowning, friendly deception and sharing. It was also a time for stories by the old-timers.

On good days the outdoors might be a place for children to roll and slide and tumble, but generally the winter outdoors was a place for hunting. As the days got longer and the sun warmer, the people might begin to move along the Great Bear Lake to places where the beaver might be caught. At this time, and at the summer fish camp, outdoor games became the focus.

By far the most popular game was the moose-skin handball game. Here a moose-skin ball about the size of a tennis ball, stuffed with moss, was volleyed or pushed into the air with one hand. The idea was to keep the ball in the air. Everyone played – men, women and children. Generally women and girls formed one very loosely knit team, and men and boys the other. A friendly but rough and tumble game of 'keep-away' ensued with the female side inevitably pushing the males down to steal the ball away. Although potentially competitive in structure, in line with the culture's values the game was one of fun, involvement and sharing.

The Loucheux or Kutchin living on the Peel and Mackenzie River Deltas demonstrated a somewhat similar annual cycle adapted to their unique ecological niche. Their play culture was quite similar to that of the Hare. One game illustrates how play and religion were inseparable in this integrated traditional culture. When a winter hunting party had suffered several consecutive days of bitterly cold weather and wished to seek a break in the cold they set up the 'bouncing game'.

To do this, they folded a tough moose-hide sled cover into a thick, strong bouncing mat about 0.5 metres square. To each corner of this they lashed a tough piece of rawhide rope. A place was found where four spring spruce trees stood roughly in a 6 metre square. One of the ropes was firmly tied to each of the trees such that the bouncing mat was suspended very tightly about 2 metres from the ground. One person climbed up on the mat and found his/her standing balance. Each rope was assigned a puller. As the women in the group sang the song calling for warm weather, the pullers pulled the ropes and mat down in unison bouncing the rider well up. This they repeated until the rider was unseated. Warm weather was the intended outcome.

Outdoor games of great variety were played in later winter and throughout the year — Loucheux football, stick-pull, foot races and hoop-and-pole. Again the games were essentially friendly and co-operative.

The Eskimo or Inuit followed a comparable kind of seasonal cycle and demonstrated some unique play adaptations to this climate. Traditionally the people would spend the winter housed in the igloo or sod house while hunting seal or caribou. The dark days were a time when it was important for people to get together and play. Often a larger central snow house was constructed where several families would meet. Elders would tell stories. Men would test their strength and endurance in friendly pulls and jumps. Women would test their dexterity with various games like bone-and -pin. The Inuit indoor games and tests of strength, endurance and agility are unique in that they require no equipment or very simple equipment made from readily available bones and other materials. Their games also utilized the very small indoor facilities available, yet involved some dynamic and demanding abilities. No Inuit gathering was complete without the highly interpretative dances. All these forms of Inuit play served multiple functions, one of which was the alleviation of some of the tensions of the long, cold, dark period.

Like his Dené counterpart, the adult Inuit probably saw the winter outdoors as a place for hunting, and indoors as the place to play. Except for very severe weather, however, Inuit children seem to have spent a lot of winter-time outdoors in creative tumbling and sledging, a phenomenon persisting until this day.

As the days lengthened into spring and summer, the family moved from caribou or seal hunt to fishing and whaling. In the case of the Mackenzie Inuit, this might mean joining with many other families at the whaling station at Kitigazuit. Here, while father watched for the beluga whale and mother made dry fish and muktuk, the children played the traditional games, imitated the harpoon throw and other hunting skills or played cat's cradles.

In summary then, despite the differences in their cultures, Dené and Inuit had somewhat comparable seasonal cycles and interesting commonalities in play adaptations. Both expressed the dominant sharing and co-operative values one nation of people would need to struggle for survival in a hostile environment. The dead of winter was an important time for play but primarily indoors. Spring, summer and autumn lent themselves more readily to outdoor pursuits. Both peoples' play implements and activities demonstrated ability to make use of existing materials and to develop activities well suited to small play spaces.

Seasonal Play in the Transitional Native Settlement

While traditionally the indigenous peoples did not establish any permanent settlements, most now live in communities of 200–900 people usually called 'settlements'. They have 'settled' for a number of reasons, voluntary and involuntary.

Settlement life and social organization was a new existence for most and one to which they did not easily adapt. This change was only one of many rapid social and cultural changes facing the aboriginal northerner. The need for play opportunities in this troubled period would seem to be doubly strong. The Northwest Territories Government has begun to recognize the importance of recreational opportunities through the programmes of its recreational division.

What kind of play settings exist in these transitional settlements? What kinds of activities and programmes utilize these facilities? As the long, cold, dark days of winter arrive, the community hall or school gymnasium becomes the focal point for play activity. While some of these community halls are well insulated and adapted to the north, many are not. Consequently many settlements literally spend the bulk of their recreation budget on heating the outdoors. Along the Arctic Coast the community hall is often a poorly insulated corrugated steel warehouse abandoned by the DEW line establishment. None the less, these halls do provide a much-needed communal play space.

Typically the community winter recreation programme is composed of one or two movie nights a week, a bingo night and a dance. Visiting and playing cards in friends' homes are perhaps the most important cold weather pastimes. With the advent of satellite-delivered television, visiting seems likely to become a lost art, just as it did in the south. In a few traditionally oriented settlements such as Fort Franklin, regular feasts with hand games and traditional dancing are still held. Although most communities had dropped this kind of traditional play programme, there appears to be a considerable upswing in interest in traditional culture.

The outdoors is generally little used for play during the extreme part of winter. Late autumn and late winter, however, see the outdoors used for a variety of outdoor pursuits. Perhaps the most striking is the omnipresent creative sledging and tumbling play of children. As indicated above, this was frequently seen even during the dark cold days of mid-winter. Whether the onslaught of television eliminates this primal expression of the play urge remains to be seen.

Many settlements develop outdoor hockey and skating rinks, but volunteer manpower shortages seem to be a perennial problem. Typically rinks are developed and used with great enthusiasm until the first bitter cold spell, then generally abandoned. Shinny or broomball variants often seem to be more popular than ice hockey. Whether this is the result of shortage of skates, one cannot say. Late winter and early spring see young people in most settlements in the Mackenzie District training for competitive cross-country ski racing. Regional meets are held followed by a Territorial Championship. The Territorial Ski Association selects a territorial team to represent it at the National Championships. Skiing got its main impetus from the Territorial Experimental Ski Training Programme in the mid-1960s. TEST was a federally funded project aimed at giving native northern youth an opportunity to compete and excel in a medium well suited to their environment. A large number of TEST skiers have gone on to become national champions. Recently, a small recreational and touring element has developed in some settlements. Spring touring and picnicking are becoming quite popular. Despite its popularity in the Boreal Forest Area, skiing has not taken root to any large extent in barrens settlements because of the hard-packed snow conditions and wind chill. Many Mackenzie District communities have cut excellent ski trail circuits of various lengths. These are used by competitive and recreational skier alike.

Late winter and early spring also signal a time for spring 'break-up' festivals complete with snowmobile races and/or dog team races. The snowmobile is a good example of how old play forms are adapted to new technology and vice versa. While primarily seen as a hunting implement, it is also seen as a vehicle for thrills and play.

Summer is a time for outdoor play of all kinds, traditional and
adopted. Swimming or at least wading has always been a popular
activity in most settlements. Unfortunately relatively few ever learned
to swim with any confidence. An inordinate number of drownings
seems to have been the result. An interesting and innovative step was
begun during the early 1960s by the Red Cross Water Safety Section
to remedy this situation. A pool was placed on a barge and towed from
settlement to settlement complete with operational and instructional
staff. It stopped at each community down the Mackenzie River and
taught basic swimming to many hundreds of northerners. A follow-up
to this programme by the Territorial Recreation Division has been the
placement of vinyl-lined above-ground pools in a large number of
settlements. Thus the basic learn-to-swim programme continued.
Recreational swimming is also popular at these pools, as it continues
to be at lakes and, surprisingly, at places like Shallow Bay.

Spring and summer are times when many families go 'back on the
land'. While this may have essentially a subsistence function, for some
it would also seem to have a leisure component. Thus, the return to the
muskrat-trapping camp, the fish camp or whaling camp seems to be a
'labour of love' for many. Here, as their ancestors have before them,
wherever they can find a small piece of flat beach or field, northern
children play both the new games such as baseball and the old
traditional games such as the high kick or cat's cradle. For many, this
is a much-loved and culturally much-needed world where clock time no
longer exists and where children can play under the midnight sun
until, exhausted, they go to bed when they wish and rise when they
wish. At the traditional camp, time is circular like the sun that circles
unceasingly overhead. For the uninitiated, clock-bound southerner,
this can be a heady experience. Time now becomes 'when the wind is
right' or 'when the whales are in the bay'.

While many families try to get out in the bush for the summer, many
others stay in the settlement. The settlement offers a variety of
settings for play. Normally, the utilization of these is left up to the
initiative of the children themselves, although in recent years Federal
Government-funded Community Student Service workers have served
as recreation co-ordinators. All settlements have open play spaces
designated or otherwise. Schoolyards may be of varying shapes, sizes
and degrees of levelness. Most will have swings and/or teeter-totters.
Some will have very basic climbing equipment. Few will have 'creative'
playgrounds such as are being developed in the new northern towns.
This depends greatly, however, on the initiative of settlement people

and others who may touch that community. Pond Inlet is a case in point. Here a southern recreation student serving as summer recreation director facilitated the development of an innovative creative playground using such readily available materials as abandoned snowmobiles, old tyres and logs.

Again, one is struck by the generally creative nature of the play of children using these open spaces. They are also used for 'pick-up baseball', road hockey or bandy, Indian baseball, Indian football, Eskimo baseball, Eskimo football, the moose-skin ball keep-away game described above, and many others. Many of these games or sports would seem to be modified to fit the less competitive, sharing cultures of their players. It is also possible, however, that these games are aboriginal in origin and represent authentic separate games evolved from material and settings at hand. The nature of the play is in striking contrast to southern, highly structured, rule-bound competitive sport, where strictly segregated and numbered teams seem to be the rule. The mode here is rather non-competitive, with much fooling and laughter; all ages, sexes and sizes enter in and get their turn. Eskimo baseball is a good example of this. There are, of course, competitive sports teams in many communities; basketball and volleyball seeming to be the most popular.

While the practice of traditional games and dance activities has continued in a few communities such as Fort Franklin, most communities had generally stopped using these activities by the late 1960s. This was the result of several factors: active taboos by certain Christian churches, a general put-down of things native by transient southerners and apathy on the part of the people themselves. In 1970, a group of concerned northerners in the Inuvik region initiated the Northern Games. The Northern Games form a unique festival of cultural games, dance and traditional skills. Native people from throughout the many cultural groups in the Arctic gather once a year to demonstrate and share their old ways. It includes such Inuit games as the one- and two-legged high kick, the one-arm reach, the blanket toss, rope gymnastics, and such Dené games as moose-skin ball, Indian football, stick-pull and leg wrestling. A 'Good Woman' competition tests the women's skills in such traditionally vital areas as making clothes, making dry fish, skinning, starting fires, making bannock, etc. Each cultural group shares its dances and stories. The host community puts people up in tents and provides the traditional food-stuffs, such as caribou, fish and bannock. The festival lasts four days and moves annually from community to community.

The Northern Games Association and its Games are beginning to have the hoped-for impact in stimulating interest in the traditional cultural play activities. Gradually they are being rediscovered in most of the Arctic communities. Again, it is probably useful to point out the unique way that these games and activities relate to the northern cultures and environment. Most require little or no equipment; any implements used are those ready at hand; play settings are small and non-demanding; the spirit and ethos of the play is co-operative and self-testing of endurance, toughness, agility and accuracy: all necessary survival attributes in an unforgiving climate.

Seasonal Play in the New Northern Town

Towns and small cities such as Yellowknife, Fort Smith, Hay River and Inuvik have been labelled as 'New Northern Towns'. Often they are quite new in planning and development or have received major new developments in recent years. These towns are quite different in demographic structure and culture from the 'transitional settlement' described above. Ranging in size from 2,000 to 15,000, their populations are largely Euro-Canadian. Many of the people work for government or mining or petroleum concerns. Incomes will be slightly higher than for people in comparable positions in the south, but expenses are proportionately higher also.

Immediate striking contrasts in play may be seen. Basically, what can be found are literally 'southern' programmes seasonally adjusted to the northern realities. Each of these modern towns has a full-time, usually professionally trained recreation administration staff. Yellowknife, for example, has a recreation staff and programme that would make most southern cities several times its size envious. Parks and playground facilities exemplify some of the latest design and 'adventure' concepts. Fort Smith's 'Kid City' is an excellent example of the latter. Heated arenas, curling rinks, and swimming pools convert this harsh climate into the quality of indoor play environments and programmes Edmonton maintains. The programme brochure circulated by Yellowknife is very similar to Edmonton's programme. This is not to suggest that traditional cultural play activities are totally ignored; these are present, but with a much lower profile and often offered through an alternative native delivery system, such as the Tree of Peace Friendship Centre.

For instance, Inuvik exemplifies more fully the adaptation of many southern design and programme ideas to the northern situation. The most visible consideration is, of course, the need to insulate any heated structure from the perma-frost lest melting occur and cause foundation sag or buckling. All heated buildings are built on top of piles. Swimming pools must be well insulated or else level will be lost, as happened in Aklark. Autumn and early winter see cross-country skiers out on the many finely groomed trails of the Inuvik Ski Club. Formerly the home of the Canadian National Team, it still houses some excellent competitive skiers. Recreational skiing on the trails is also popular prior to arrival of the deep-freeze of winter. A very useful incorporation of the Scandinavian idea of lighting ski trails greatly extends the ski day in an area where the sun does not appear for six long weeks from late November. Maintenance of trails and lighting is of course a continual battle.

The snowmobile, although used extensively for work, is mainly a play travel vehicle. Autumn is also hunting time for the recreational as well as subsistence hunter. While the two are hard to distinguish, most transient new northerners would generally fall into the 'sport' categories. Ever-tightening regulations as to who is a 'northerner' make it more difficult or expensive for short-term northerners to hunt. In autumn and early winter children, particularly native children, spend long hours outside in creative free play, most notably sliding and rolling down wherever small slopes can be found. At school recesses and before and after class, a conventional playground is heavily used. One is immediately struck by the creativity and longevity of the native children's play. Whether this free-play feature will continue with the onset of television remains to be seen.

Most new northerners are moving indoors at this time, however, and will stay in the 'cocoon' until the warm, lengthening days of April. A once well-used outdoor rink at the Catholic school residence now lies dormant. The young who previously played hockey outdoors now welcome the shelter of the two indoor arenas. Hockey, both fun and highly competitive, forms a focal point for young men. Participation in cross-country skiing has suffered greatly as a result.

Gymnasia, at both elementary schools and secondary schools, at the Catholic student residence and at the local armed forces base, will be well used by all ages in basketball, volleyball, floor hockey, badminton and indoor soccer. Competitive leagues and clubs exist in each of these activities, often meshing with Territorial and Trans-Arctic Winter Games. A well-equipped curling rink adjacent to the hockey arena is kept busy day and night from September to May. Public skating is a popular activity particularly as 'cabin fever' sets in during the dark days, an affliction many first-winter young mothers receive.

Visiting has been replaced by television as the great indoor sport much as it has elsewhere. No community activity can hope to compete with Guy Lafleur, the Canadiens and 'Hockey Night in Canada'. Bingo is one possible exception. Bingo is almost a religion in Inuvik and every club in town raises its funds through bingo operation. Movies, hanging out at the local restaurant or the Eskimo Inn occupy many young people. The 'Zoo' — as a local bar is called — is where many social problems are 'solved', caused or perpetrated.

A new Native Friendship Centre has just been constructed which will serve as a much-needed meeting place for native peoples arriving in Inuvik. At the same time, it will form the focal point for cultural play activity development. In face of the many social problems facing native peoples in Inuvik, such a centre is long overdue, if a sense of pride is to be redeveloped.

With the lengthening sunny days of March and April, people begin to rediscover the outdoors. Cross-country ski training heats up again in preparation for the annual Top of the World Territorial Ski Championships. Day tours and picnics by ski, snowmobile or pickup truck on the ice road are highlights for some families. At the same time, the native trappers return to the muskrat or beaver line. For the old-timer and young native, this is a happy time of year in the bush — warm and insect-free. Although his activity is technically work, many aspects of the hunter-trapper's behaviour suggest a close intertwining of work and play.

With the sudden snow melt and river ice break-up in late May, summer is on. Softball is a popular competitive sport for both men and women. Everyone is outside to enjoy that brief respite before the never-ending cycle of blackflies, sandfleas, mosquitoes and deer flies begins.

The end of the school year sees a variety of activities. Many new northerners head south to visit their home areas. Others able to tolerate the insects exploit the tremendously varied opportunities for outdoor recreation — canoeing, fishing and hiking. A fortunate few are able to visit native friends at their fish and whaling camps and experience first-hand living off the earth in the land of the midnight sun. It seems a pity that so many people living in Canada's north do not get involved with and experience first-hand the unique natural and cultural opportunities before them.

Seasonal Play for the Southerner

In the last few years, the Territorial Government through Travel Arctic has encouraged a variety of tourism and outdoor recreational activities. To date, participation by southern Canadians and people from other countries has been largely in summer activities. A few exceptions are noteworthy.

Guided hunting in autumn and winter by outfitters is growing rapidly. Caribou and sheep are popular targets. Fishing for char and lake trout in summer is becoming popular with fly-ins to outpost camps. All activities are expensive and consequently provide predominantly native guides with some income supplement.

Road travel and air tourism are growing. Perhaps the most important outdoor activities growing today are canoeing and hiking-mountaineering. The new Baffin Island National Park and Kluane and Nahanni National Parks in the Yukon Territories provide hikers and mountaineers with a variety of challenges and scenery. All are a photographer's and naturalist's delight.

Canoeing in any of the major northern river systems is a great adventure and delight. The Coppermine River system beginning with a fly-in to Lac de Gras opens one's eyes to the unexpected beauty of the barrens. The beauties of the Nahanni are, of course, well known.

A Few Possibilities and Implications

Having completed this whirlwind tour of play in this land of the great national and cultural contrasts, what statements, if any, can be made of a general nature? Only a few will be attempted:

1. The indigenous play cultures of the Dené and Inuit were well adapted to their challenging environment and to their over-all world view. The values and norms of the play activities — whether games, tests of strength and endurance, or dances — celebrate their acceptance of their niche in the ecosystems of the Boreal Forest or tundra. Patience, accuracy, self-endurance, good humoured acceptance of one's lot, and sharing are all necessary parts of living together, co-operatively, in harmony with what the seasons have to offer. In human and ecological terms, materials and energies needed to prepare facilities, equipment and programmes are all economical and use what is close at hand.

2. A second related implication might stem from the recognition that really two worlds of play exist in the north — the traditional, informal, co-operative and the Euro-Canadian organized, competitive. The Territorial Government's gradual recognition of this fact and the need for alternative play delivery systems may have

implications for the provinces as well. The need for mutual exchange, modification of games and implements from one to suit the values of the other, and the possibility of mutual integration of play approaches seem to have possibilities for us all.

3. A few innovative facilities (e.g., the portable swimming pool on the river barge) were found that may trigger off possibilities for other climatic zones with similar transportation problems.

4. An obvious conclusion of such a survey is that play and recreation are vital to the individual mental health and community harmony during the long dark days, particularly in times of rapid social change.

5. Finally, while it is fair to say that the outdoors is relatively under-utilized in the north, it is well to recognize the real need for adequate community indoor facilities for the dark, cold period of winter. Proper insulation specifications and related design consideration will need to be followed if the host community is to be able to afford to operate such a facility.

Note

1. The author wishes to acknowledge audiovisual contributions from the following people: Mr Al Affleck, Mr R.G. Glassford, Mr Dennis Adams, Mr Lorne Smith, Mr Jaques Van Pelt, Mr Peter Milner, Mr Michael Van Duffelen, Ms Leslie Kroening, and Mr Gil Gilmet.

Part Two

URBAN PLANNING WITH THE CHILD IN MIND

9 RESPECT THE CHILD: URBAN PLANNING WITH THE CHILD IN MIND

Paul Davidoff[1]

> Children are capable of giving advice in the most important matters.
>
> Dostoevsky, *The Idiot*

To investigate the topic of 'Urban Planning with the Child in Mind' is a provocative, though befuddling, endeavour. First, one is challenged to deal with the idea of 'the child', of children — those awkward, questioning creatures, so often restless, noisy and, in contrast to pets, unreliably affectionate, demanding at one moment nurture and, at another, autonomy. Their nature and physique seem incongruous in an urban environment; they are easily threatened by, and often threatening to, the older inhabitants of the city. Then one is invited to think seriously about the subject of 'play': a universal, explorative, adventuresome activity — and the need of people of all ages which, being systematically denied by adult daily lives and environments, leaves the idea that 'play' is something children do. In other words, planning for play may be an unconscious concern for the needs of the spontaneous, 'insufficiently socialized' human — the child — in all of us. It may grow out of an empathy for the essential state of the child, that of an aware, perceiving powerlessness within a hostile and uncaring environment. Linking these two general concerns is the focus of this paper, the role of urban planning, of intervention by the state in the urban environment, as related to the lives and play of children.

Titled 'Respect the Child', this paper discusses issues of justice and fairness in planning for children. Respect the child: that should be the goal of planning with the child in mind. It is both a procedural and a substantive objective. Respect the child as a human being having the right to develop potential and character. Respect the child's right to receive and offer love and affection. Respect the child's right to assist in processes affecting his/her own interest. Respect the child's equality under the law with other children and adults.

It is disrespectful of the child to exclude him/her from determining his/her own interests. It is disrespectful to exclude the child from participating in processes established to plan for children's well-being.

141

The beginning of planning for the child is to plan with the child. But should the planning for the child be done by the child? It is one thing to say that the child should participate, but how much power should the child be granted to plan its future? The answer to that question is not clear; however, it is argued that the level of participation should be considerably above zero.

It is extremely difficult to get acceptance from professionals that their clients should participate; it is more difficult when the client is the child. For all the reasons that a distinction is made between the rights of adults and those of children, the difference between having reached majority age and not, children are assumed to be without capacity to 'give advice in the most important matters'. The child is assumed to be without experience, without contemplative nature, without substantial evaluative powers.

It is not known whether children would make relatively sound or unsound judgements. (But what can be said about adult judgements?) Only the smallest experiments in sharing power have been attempted. It is proposed, however, that support should be given to the undertaking of actions increasingly to involve children in the planning and administration of programmes of play. Perhaps of all the subject areas in which children are deeply concerned and engaged, play is the best one in which to develop a process that respects the child.

It is certainly the case that children are expert at play. With or without the intervention of adults, children find the means to play. Not only are children adept at play, they are well qualified to evaluate alternative play experiences. It would only be fair to note that their preferences are subject to change, sometimes to rapid change. Nevertheless, children do make intelligent judgements about play alternatives. They can give reasoned opinions supporting the values they express.

In planning, it is important to note the historic distinction between 'play' and 'recreation'. While 'play' denoted a universal, explorative, adventuresome activity by children and adults alike, the concepts of 'recreation' and 'leisure' are approximately one century old and very much tied to the history of urban-industrial society. During the middle of the nineteenth century, the inherited concept of play (or idleness) was that it was intrinsically evil and a waste of time that should be devoted to productive labour. This concept is consistent with the philosophy behind the first public school movement, the purpose of which was essentially that of 'social control': when children or youth are not occupied with productive labour, keep them in school. In a similar spirit, nineteenth-century industrialists and employers conceived of 'recreation': workers are more productive if occasionally 'recreated'.

Frederick Law Olmsted, the father of landscape architecture, was one of the most articulate and influential individuals of the nineteenth century to translate this work-oriented, or industry-oriented, philosophy into the city environment. In talking about New York City's Central Park, he wrote:

> As to the effect on public health, it has already been great. . . Physicians [have told me] : 'Where I formerly ordered patients of a certain class to give up their business altogether, and go out of town, I now often advise simply moderation, and prescribe a ride in the Park before going to their offices, and again a drive with their families before dinner. . . [Taking up this habit,] men who have been breaking down frequently recover tone rapidly, and are able to retain active and controlling influence in an important business, from which they would be otherwise forced to retire. . .
>
> . . . The lives of women and children too poor to be sent to the country, can now be saved in thousands of instances, by making them go to the Park. During a hot day in July last, I counted at one time in the Park eighteen separate groups, consisting of mothers with children, most under school age, taking picnic dinners brought from home. The practice is increasing under medical advice, especially when summer complaint is rife. (Sutton, 1971, pp. 93–4)

Public recreation was a progressive off-shoot of a primary concern with, and movement for, public health, which was a predecessor of the 'City Beautiful' and 'City Efficient' movements and thus of urban planning. At the beginning of the twentieth century, the institutionalization of the movement for recreation in the United States proceeded: between 1900 and World War I, the public recreation movement was officially organized and the National Recreation Association was founded. It was called the Playground Association of America in 1906, the Playground and Recreation Association of America in 1911, and the National Recreation Association in 1930.

Educators recognized the relationship between good schooling and recreation. The objectives enunciated by the National Education Association's Commission on the Reorganization of Secondary Education nicely sum up these complementary purposes: health, command of fundamental processes, worthy home-membership, vocation, citizenship, worthy use of leisure, and ethical character. The 1958 United Nations Declaration, Principle 7, also summed it up: 'The child shall have full opportunity for play and recreation, which should be directed to the same purposes as education.'

The development of the idea of recreation as shaping healthy young lives left little room for an idea of self-determination by children. Adults defined 'health', 'character' and 'ethics'; therefore, they would lay out the activities on the part of children which would lead toward development of these qualities.

The International Playground Association should be applauded for its leadership in taking a renewed interest in observing and respecting children's own approaches to objects and experiences, expressed in the use of 'play' as against 'recreation', the enhancement of the child's own initiatives as against a rigid establishment of adult directions and instructions. It is suggested that children's participation in planning their own play is a further step in this path.

The concern for the participation of children in public activities affecting their interests goes beyond the field of play and goes beyond concern solely with children. The realization of democratic objectives depends greatly on education of children in the practice of democracy. Exclusion of children from decision-making processes affecting their interests does not seem to be a good means to teach the substance of democracy. Democratic practices need mutual respect and affection. The practice is incompatible with exclusionary systems.

Democratic procedures are not simple; they are not quick. Time must be afforded to hear from all interested parties. Time must be afforded to hear ideas that some consider outrageous or stupid. That is why both respect and affection for co-participants are required. At a minimum, there must be tolerance for those who would extend the range of usual thinking.

In the United States, the teaching about democracy is done through reference to written documents and past practices. Children are not provided with the adventure of decision-making areas in which daily to explore the excitement and frustration of democratic choosing. Instead, reference is made to heroic figures of the American Revolution without mentioning that some were slave owners. Environments for choosing self-directions for individual or community growth, however, are not offered.

Children are not to be expected to have developed independent judgement about the proposed organization of their community, their playtime, their play equipment, their surrounding environment. Democracy is taught *at* them, not explored *with* them. From the moment they enter public school, they are ordered, not freed; they are moulded, not released. The relationship between freedom and responsibility is taught, rather than experienced.

Planning with the child in mind, with the child present, with the child planning, means empowering the child to act responsibly in accord with his/her own evaluation of goals, means and available resources.

Those who have had experience in educating graduate students know how difficult it is for many students to have to make their own choices. Adults ask teachers for directions and are often frightened of relative freedom. Having been excluded as youths from participating in decisions concerning their own education, they do not easily accept responsibility for defining their own educational needs when they mature. One of the most influential groups of students in graduate urban planning are the returning mothers. American women in their 30s, 40s, or 50s who have had much life experience are returning to many graduate programmes as they seek greater liberation. Having lived outside closed educational environments, they are more able to provide self-motivation and direction. Similar judgements were made about returning veterans after the wars of recent decades. It is contended that children without army experience and without adult experience could be enabled to make more self-directing choices were they empowered from their first day in school to participate fully in decision making about their education. In simplest terms, this means that human beings cannot evolve into affectionate, respecting decision makers in a democratic setting from experiences in which the very essence of the system — participation — has been denied.

It is suggested — though it cannot be proven — that the low level of participation in community, regional and national affairs is directly related to an educational system which is against participation, which is anti-democratic. The failure of educational systems to prepare an individual for living democratically also has negative consequences for the development of a democratic community ethic. As noted above, affection and respect are essential for the development of democratic practice. Those feelings cannot be taught only as abstract truths. They too must be experienced in a community setting where it may be learned that the sharing of rights and obligations is beneficial. Integration, oneness, unity, arise from shared experience, not from being told it is good to be that way. Racial integration does not result merely from peoples of different races occupying the same space or institutions. It is the achievement of oneness, of community. It is the desire to be a part of a community and to benefit from sharing.

The development of participatory practices in the planning of playgrounds and other planning experiences will create the possibility for a meaningful learning experience for those engaged. It is likely that much greater user responsibility and user satisfaction will result. Certainly those would represent important factors to weigh in appraising the benefits of enabling children to plan their play experiences. One could also hope that violence and destruction would be reduced; certainly, arguments could be made as to why that should be the case. The very process of evaluating the usefulness of opening the system to meaningful participation requires participation of the children. How is it that they would determine whether or not their participation had been useful?

What does participation mean, what does it require? Full participation implies the ability to engage in a decision-making process at every stage — to be heard, to be responded to, and to be counted. It means that notice of impending decisions must be given to interested parties. It means that budgets, as well as choice of equipment, should be open for the involvement of children. It means that children should have the right to participate in determining the methods by which decisions will be made and supported and implemented. In sum, their power to affect decisions should be great.

While this is of utmost importance for children, it applies as well to every other user population. With children, however, it has a special meaning — for they become us. If they have not experienced democrat practice and responsibility as children, it will be difficult to free them for it later.

The education of democratic practice and respect is serious work. The play experience, however, may lighten the mood. The planning of play may well present a wonderful initial area for challenging society's putdown of children. One of the satisfying things about exploring alternative play experiences as opposed, say, to choosing between bombs that destroy only people as opposed to those that destroy only people's property, is that most, if not all, of the alternatives represent positive outcomes. Only a few may be feared. In general, adults and children have a more playful view of play alternatives.

In terms of the right of children to participate in planning processes whether in relation to play or other functions, the argument thus far has dealt mostly with procedures for decision making. Now it is time to turn to some important substantive issues. There are what might be considered internal and external issues to be discussed. The first are those that underlie the value frame in which children are enabled more actively to share power for planning and generally participate in societal decisions, including their own education. The respect that should be shown children should include the following elements:

1. love and affection by their elders, so that their inclusion may be surrounded by warmth and support;
2. recognition of individuality;
3. recognition of commonality;
4. recognition of potential for creation and imagination;
5. recognition of difficulties they must encounter and overcome and of conditions they cannot overcome;
6. understanding of turmoil facing so many living at a time of great pain about the role of family and of mothers, women and girls, and also of fathers, men and boys.

This is an abbreviated list for cherishing as well as respecting the children who are to join with adults in guiding communities. It is important to identify some of the reasons for bringing children into the adult world of decision making. (Of course once children enter the world, it will no longer be just an adult world.)

The world surrounding children is beset with grave problems, as well as with immense joy and beauty. The external factors which must be considered in thinking about planning with the child in mind should include at least some or all of the following incomplete list:

1. Creation of a world order securing peace. No serious thought of planning for children and children's children is possible without complete devotion to creating peaceful means to resolve international conflict.
2. Creation of just distributions of the resources and opportunities of society. The worse conditions afflicting children — in terms of starvation, hunger, poverty, illness, indecent shelter, environment, play — must be eradicated as rapidly as possible.
3. Racial, ethnic and class discrimination denying children fair opportunity to play and to develop must be eliminated.
4. Elimination of sex discrimination. Elimination of burdens placed on boys and girls because of sex role models imposed on them.
5. Better understanding of the causes of anger and violence within

children. The foregoing arguments for respecting the child may, if acted upon, work to assist in this area.

6. Building of systems that are open and non-threatening.
7. Laughing uproariously at the ponderousness of formal systems that cover the absence of intelligent reasons. In other words, transmit to children knowledge of adult ineptitude. Adults, like children, are struggling to find difficult answers.
8. Transmitting a sense of pleasure that is derived from processes seeking answers to difficult questions.
9. Offering a possible option of non-participation to those who choose not to play a participatory role in public affairs. Not everyone must be actively engaged.

It suffices that the system allows for expression of interests other than those now involved in the planning and administration of communities, environments, playgrounds.

The suburbs of the United States, through many practices, deny to non-whites and to lower-income persons the right to reside within their borders. Those practices deny to the children of such families the rights that are afforded to others. They are denied the often elaborate facilities for recreation and play that are available to the affluent children of the suburbs. That process of exclusion is costly, both to those excluded and to the society, as a whole, that pays extraordinary large costs for not eliminating its under-class, which cannot fully participate productively in the work and play of society. It is argued that the exclusion of children from the right to participate productively bears similar high costs.

It is recommended that steps be taken to open responsible planning and other decision-making processes for involvement by children. Means should be established for children to engage in decisions regarding play, schooling, discipline and their other immediate concerns. Decisions having an effect on the lives and opportunities of children should be made through processes allowing children to be engaged in and to share the final decision-making power.

It is also recommended that a task force be established comprised of adults and children to examine some means for testing junior membership in certain institutions. For example, rather than excluding children from all voting rights, a half-vote might be offered to qualifying children. Qualification might be met by the passage of a test demonstrating knowledge of a system. In fact, it may be unfair to make children take tests that adults do not have to take, but it may be a useful first step in demonstrating knowledge and interest to those who act as if children, including seventeen-year-olds as well as ten-year-olds and younger, were incapacitated.

It must be demonstrated that planning with the child in mind includes planning with the child present and participating. If that step is taken, it may make an important contribution in reducing the condition Roger Hart identified as the powerlessness of the world's largest minority.

It does seem that the world – at least the United States – is on the verge of undertaking acts to enlarge the rights of children. Certainly the United Nations' identification of this as the International Year of the Child reveals the growing interest. The task is to consider and adopt steps leading to enlarged freedom for children resulting from their planning for play that is the focus of this conference and from their participation in the broader field of urban planning.

There is no obvious answer to the question of just how free should the child be to find his/her own course of action. Nor is there a specific answer to the question of just how much responsibility a child of three, five, eight or fifteen can accept or should have. It can be stated, however, that the general answer needed to questions of this order is 'more'.

The issue of the redistribution of power over the lives and opportunities of children is part of the larger ethical issue of the social distributions of rights, wealth, opportunities and justice. These are the most essential questions confronting planners as well as other public interest workers; they are also the most neglected. They represent the critical issues of the practice of urban planning. The chance to build decent communities rests on the ability to build communities that are fair and democratic.

Both fairness and democracy call for inclusionary rather than exclusionary communities. Communities in which populations, because of their poverty, race, ethnicity, sex or age, are denied equal rights to participate in public decisions and equal opportunity to sustain a decent standard and environment for living exclude such populations in ways which prohibit the creation of good communities. Precisely because the gaps between the haves and the have-nots, the whites and the blacks, the male and the female, the adult and the child, are so great in almost all urban regions, the redistributive ethic must be a paramount part of the future outlook, of value systems.

As with the question of how much freedom children should have, the question of how equal the shares of wealth and opportunities must be need not be answered directly. It is sufficient to the evil of the ubiquitous maldistribution that there be a rapid reduction of the worst conditions of inequality.

It is important to stress what is probably very obvious: the disparities in life opportunities that so disfigure urban communities afflict the area of play as much as other fields such as health, employment or housing. Wide disparities do exist in the quantity and quality of play, recreation and leisure time available to different sectors of the population. It is past time for the planning profession closely to examine the distribution of opportunities. It is time for schools of planning to teach methods for analysing resource distribution among different sectors of the population. If the reader cannot accept the redistributive ethic, then, perhaps, he/she will accept the idea that play experts and urban planners must examine the fundamental question of politics and justice — who gets what.

An examination of the urban planning literature in the United States reveals only the slightest interest in participatory planning for children and others on the part of those professionals who write for the leading professional journal of planning. It should be added that that journal is equally bereft of articles dealing with children's interests and needs. As in other areas of urban planning, spatial biases and traditions have led to the planning of facilities in accord with norms established by professionals. Professionals tend to pose planning for children in essentially technical terms; that is, as a question of supply of playgrounds and play spaces for the needs or demands of 'user groups' of various ages. So children and play are perceived as a particular design problem requiring special manipulation of the physical environment. What Herbert Gans, Thomas Reiner, Janet Scheff and other critics have demonstrated is that planners have been indifferent to the needs expressed by clients.

One of the most hopeful signs in planning in the United States is the growing tendency to devolve planning power to neighbourhoods. While it is possible that the new neighbourhood planning professionals may be as uninterested in the preferences of the users of recreation as have city and regional planners, it is suspected that the very bringing of planning power closer to the citizens will bestir a new wave of concern for the clients' substantive interests and rights to participate in decisions. Of course, Jane Jacobs deserves high praise for the growing recognition of the importance of neighbourhood-oriented planning.

A final observation concerns my only close contact with planning with children. Before undertaking my present work as an advocate for the rights of minorities to share in the growth of suburbs, and for affluent suburbs to assist poor cities, I spent over a decade in the graduate education of planners. Recently, I have had the opportunity to participate in an alternative high-school class devoted to teaching about planning. It has been a very exciting experience. For the past four years, we have had the opportunity to introduce children aged fifteen to eighteen to the concepts of rational decision making, community analysis and survey techniques, and to the taking of action within their own community. My experiences with this programme have led me to believe that the teaching of community planning directed not toward creating professional planners, but toward enabling students to know more about their community and how they can participate in shaping it, is one of the best ways to build vital, responsible citizens.

The movement to broaden the rights of children is confronted with great scepticism. Much of it masks unwillingness on the part of power holders to share power more equitably. The indifference to children shown in planning practice and literature will only stop when strong advocates for the rights of children, including their right to participate, come forward.

Note

1. I would like to thank Susan Seifert, a student in the Department of Urban and Regional Planning at the University of Toronto, for her help in the preparation of this paper.

Reference

Sutton, S. B. (ed.). 1971. *Civilizing American Cities: A Selection of Frederick Law Olmsted's Writings on City Landscapes.* Cambridge, Mass.: MIT Press.

10 PLANNING AND DESIGNING RESIDENTIAL ENVIRONMENTS WITH CHILDREN IN MIND: A DUTCH APPROACH

Domien Verwer

'Woonerf': a New Legal Concept for the Residential Environment

A process of radically reassessing the residential environment may be said to have started in the Netherlands in the 1960s, but it is only now, in the 1970s, that it has attracted the attention of the policy makers. The first body to take specific measures to give back to the street its original function was the municipality of Delft in 1971.

Creating a 'woonerf' — a street or network of streets in which pedestrians have priority over traffic — presents a multitude of problems. The use made of a street by traffic is dependent on the physical characteristics of the street, traffic laws and regulations, and the habits of road users. Everyone's thinking is based on traffic — primarily motorized traffic — circulating smoothly; legislation usually gives motorized traffic priority, which is supported by long straight roads with wide carriage-ways.

Roads are for traffic; the place for the pedestrian is the sidewalk. Thinking in any other terms is dangerous. The enormous increase in the number of cars and the parking problems they create constitute an immediate and widespread threat to the quality of the residential environment. Another consequence is the threat to the safety of children; the air is polluted with exhaust fumes and filled with ear-splitting noise. Space which is needed for walking, sitting, watching, playing and meeting friends is occupied by vehicles. People have begun to think seriously about remedying the situation.

The idea of a 'woonerf', given legal substance by the Minister of Transport and Public Works in September 1976, is an important step in the direction of preserving the quality of the residential environment. The new legal concept means that the situation can be reversed in specially designated residential areas and that the indispensable changes in thinking on the part of local residents now have legal backing even in places where there is no official 'woonerf'.

The main features of a 'woonerf' are as follows. It consists of a street or a network of streets in which:

1. there is no through traffic;
2. the buildings are primarily residential;
3. such traffic as there is (access) plays a minor role;
4. its other functions as a place where people live, stay, play, relax, meet one another, etc. play a major role;
5. there is no distinction between road and sidewalk as in traditional streets;
6. there is one area of public open space which is for everyone to walk, ride and play in and where all kinds of facilities are provided for these functions;
7. there are special provisions to restrict the speed of any traffic and to assist the other functions − in this context one thinks immediately of 'sleeping policemen' but these are not always necessary; it may be possible to narrow the space available for traffic to pass through or to introduce obstacles such as trees and fences;
8. random parking is forbidden; parking is allowed only in places indicated by a 'P' sign;
9. clear signs indicate where the 'woonerf' begins and ends.

To qualify as a 'woonerf', an area must satisfy a number of minimum requirements laid down in an Administrative Order of the Minister of Transport and Public Works; a special sign may then be erected. Once the 'woonerf' sign has been placed in position, a number of specific rules apply to the area:

1. pedestrians may have access to the entire area;
2. traffic may not move faster than walking pace;
3. drivers must pay particular attention to pedestrians, children and obstacles;
4. bicycles and mopeds coming from the right have priority;
5. drivers may not impede the path of pedestrians;
6. pedestrians may not unnecessarily hinder drivers of vehicles;
7. parking is permitted only in those places specially indicated.

Many of the suggestions which will be made below about the residential environment may be put into practice in the form of a 'woonerf'; in any event, the new legislative provisions allow for experiments. It will also be clear that considerable research work will have to be undertaken to develop varied and different types of 'woonerf'.

The 'woonerf' is by no means the only way of 'humanizing' a street;

a less radical approach may be desirable, especially if the street plays no important role for through traffic. In any event, care must be taken against adopting a stereotyped approach to streets and squares simply because legislation lays down certain minimum demands and conditions which a 'woonerf' must fulfil. It is vital that the aim of all these efforts and, therefore, the reason for specific measures should remain crystal-clear. Every new street and neighbourhood must have its own special characteristics providing a basis for working out new ways of making it more safe and congenial. At the same time, there will be greater variation and each individual area will acquire its own separate identity.

An examination of planning practice and background research on this topic will now be presented.

Outline of the Administrative System in the Netherlands

Town and country planning and housing in the Netherlands have been governed by the Physical Planning Act and the Housing Act since 1965. Their principal instruments of implementation are local plans and municipal building permits respectively. Local plans establish, where necessary, the specific use of land, containing provisions for its further development and for the buildings on it. The principal instruments for the implementation of local plans are building permits and expropriation.

Great importance is attached in the Netherlands to the administrative autonomy of the municipalities. At the same time, however, the high population density and the small size of the country mean that certain responsibilities must be retained by the provincial and central government authorities. The term 'complementary government' used in this connection thus refers to these three interacting levels of government. In the area of building and planning, the municipalities are free to initiate activities and to direct the implementation of building plans. Though the term 'complementary government' is a useful means of indicating the interaction between the different levels of administration, it in fact refers to the entire system of centralized and decentralized government. Dutch law would seem to place particular emphasis on taking decisions at the appropriate level, and no higher. Nevertheless a strong tendency towards centralization is generated by the fact that plans drawn up at the lower levels of government require the approval of the higher levels providing the requisite funds. The demands of legal equality are best met when the criteria governing approval are set out in the form of regulations.

Though this carries within itself the seeds of social uniformity, it also ensures equal treatment for everyone in the matter of living standards. Regulations of this kind, which usually contain guidelines, norms, criteria and basic assumptions, constitute a semi-legal basis, as it were, for recreational amenities in residential districts. They have the merit of facilitating an objective approach on the part of the higher administrative levels assessing them, for which reason they are generally more quantitative than qualitative. Over the past five years, qualitative concepts have been taken more into account; the quantitative norms applied have become more flexible in that they are more oriented to specific local situations.

Standards and Guidelines for Land Use in Housing Plans

Housing construction in the Netherlands, as in other countries, is subject to national regulations, especially as regards subsidized housing. These regulations relate chiefly to such points as layout, size of rooms, etc. and to structural, material and other technical requirements. Standards for the residential environment are given in 'Basic Housing Costs', a booklet published by the Association of Netherlands Municipalities in association with the Ministry of Physical Planning and Housing in 1968. It is the sole official publication listing the main land-use categories in housing plans, such as the net area allotted for dwellings, public parks and gardens, roads and pavements, and sewage systems (see Table 10.1). This is the only indication of official standards obtainable in print. Nevertheless, as the booklet itself states, they do not guarantee either the quality or the 'economy' of a particular plan. Indeed, these standards cannot be used to measure quality as such.

Residential areas built according to these standards have no lack of space in terms of square metres. They do suffer, however, from lack of quality. Most residents have failed to feel sheltered or to experience any feelings of intimacy or safety in their new surroundings. In fact, all that they have is housing built according to what were then the latest standards, an otherwise important fact in a country long afflicted by a housing shortage. Once the quantitative shortage had been alleviated somewhat, there was a demand for better-quality housing, as regards both the dwellings themselves and their surroundings. The quality gradually improved, with higher standards of comfort, better sound insulation and more space. Most residential environments, however, still lacked the qualities essential to satisfactory living. This situation was subject to a growing amount of criticism in the 1960s from young

Table 10.1: Official Dutch Standards

Land Use	Ground Area Per Dwelling		
	Terraced houses (m²)	Flats (m²)	High-rise flats (m²)
Net ground allocation	160	100	70
public parks, etc.	60	60	60
combined	(220)	(160)	(130)
Roads and pavements	80	60	50
total	300	220	180
Length of sewage	7 m	4½ m	3½ m

architects, social scientists and others.

The rising tide of criticism brought forth the 'Stichting Ruimte voor de Jeugd', established with the aid of the government and a large number of private organizations. At first, it focused its activities on the need for safe playgrounds and indoor amenities for children and young people, without losing sight of its principal objective of integrating the planning and provision of such facilities with those for people of all ages. The underlying idea was that children should not be isolated from the adults in whose world they must learn to live, while at the same time adults should be able to enjoy having children around them. Children need adults as models for their games and teenagers need to come into contact with them from time to time, even if for no other reason than to rebel against them. Contact is the essential term here, and thus the major task is to ensure that there are places in which all members of the community can meet — outdoors, in the streets and parks and in specially designated play areas; and indoors, in youth clubs and in local centres and clubs.

Though there is as yet no solid legal basis for recreational amenities, the community recognizes their importance, the definite need for them. They are often referred to as social and cultural facilities — a term which covers the entire range from a simple bench at the street corner and a sandpit to an extensive community centre.

Planning for Play and Outdoor Recreation in the Immediate Environment of the Home

To offset the extreme functionalism of much town planning, a more integrated approach to the housing and recreational aspects is now being developed in the Netherlands. The entire gamut of recreational facilities is being integrated into plans for new residential districts, one element of which is regulation of the flow of traffic in such a way that pedestrian areas and traffic areas exist side by side. This greatly improves the general quality of those residential districts, as the residents can again take possession of the streets they had lost to traffic. The original functions of the street as an extension of the home, as a place in which to meet others, to relax, are in this way restored. The official introduction of the 'woonerf' as a legal and town-planning concept has contributed much to these improvements. This will be discussed in greater detail below.

Qualitative Norms

In the summer of 1974, the Stichting Ruimte (1974)[1] published a report entitled *Youth and the Residential Environment: criteria for 'humanized' residential areas,* which lists the demands made on the residential environment by the various age categories up to 25 years. The major points are as follows:

1. play and recreational facilities must constitute an integral part of the surroundings of the home — children must be able to play in all parts of their residential environment, though of course some places will be more suitable than others and this distinction will remain;
2. it is important to give thought to all parts of the residential environment with a view to their use by young people and their elders, and to their principal and subsidiary functions in all seasons, day and night, now and in the future;
3. a residential environment (neighbourhood, district) should be regarded as a complete unit that is constantly changing.

The report also stresses seven requirements to be met in planning or assessing residential areas:

1. For a safe residential area, traffic must be subject to special provisions making it subservient to pedestrians and cyclists. A network of paths and tracks for pedestrians and cyclists constitutes the main means of communication between houses and between the latter and schools, recreational facilities, etc.
2. There must be tolerance in town planning and architectural design making full allowance for the activities of children and adults. A residential environment must encourage children's games;

prohibitions must be kept to an absolute minimum.

3. Shelter from the weather increases the choice of activities: if it rains, blows or is too cold children must be able to play indoors. This is of particular importance in areas with high-rise residences.

4. Intimacy is essential for small children because of their limited capacity to adjust to situations and to tolerate them. They need orientation points close to home. Children under 6 years of age need to be able to play within 100 metres of their homes, i.e., within calling distance, and they require small-scale design such as small sandpits, shallow ponds, low walls, and little variation in height.

5. A direct relation between indoors and outdoors is important in that it facilitates children's use of their homes as a base, indicating that high-rise flats are not to be recommended for small children unless they are equipped with easily worked lifts, bells and entry phones. Buildings no higher than three storeys provide the best possibilities for the spontaneous play which is important for children's harmonious development.

6. Variation in design and materials is necessary for diverse purposes: large and small play areas, sand and water, brick and wood, high and low, open and closed, crowded and quiet.

7. Different heights, natural and artificial, slight (for the small children) and great (for the bigger children), as an element of design add quality to the living environment. Children enjoy experimenting with different heights; heavy rainfall leaves streams and puddles to play in; sledges can be used in winter, etc.

The report contains only two quantitative norms for the planning and designing of facilities for children under the neighbourhood level:

1. Children under six years of age usually play close to their homes, i.e., within a radius of 100 metres. As they grow older their action radius gradually increases.

2. The distance for children up to approximately 12 years of age is 300 to 400 metres from their homes.

An Evaluative Study of Residential Environments: The Roermond Research Project

This research (conducted in Roermond in 1976) was concerned with one of the most important ways in which the residential environment can be used, i.e., for playing and recreation. In accordance with the changes which have already been outlined, three important new ways of thinking about this aspect of the use of the residential environment can be distinguished (Verwer and Bakers, 1977):

1. recognition must be given to the fact that children and other residents are entitled to use their entire residential environment for such purposes and not just specially provided facilities within that environment;
2. quality is preferred to quantity (this does not mean, however, that the statistical approach will have no role to play in the future);
3. the designing and location of playing facilities should be integrated into town planning as a whole.

An increasing number of municipalities are adopting these new ways of thinking, often simply on the basis of intuition: however, when it comes to turning them into specific measures, there are problems.

The municipality of Roermond consulted the Stichting Ruimte for advice in the spring of 1976 when it was faced with the necessity of developing solidly based policy to deal with the extremely large number of neighbourhoods and streets in need of renewal within the municipality. Decisions were needed on the kinds of improvements to be made and where they should be made. It was proposed that the new policy should be relatively forward-looking in accordance with the three criteria referred to above. The municipality asked the Stichting Ruimte to attempt to translate the ideas about the residential environment set out in its report entitled *Jeugd en Wonen* (1974) into practical terms. This invitation was accepted by the Stichting, which then proposed a programme of work consisting of the three following aspects:

1. analysis of existing neighbourhoods in relation to the guidelines for a humane residential environment developed in the report;
2. examination of the possibility of converting them into traffic-limited residential areas;
3. the need to provide formal play facilities.

In co-operation with a group of local government officials, and through discussions with the various groups concerned within the municipality, a research project was carried out. Initially, attention was primarily devoted to the first of these three points.

Structure of the Research

The evaluation of the different residential environments was primarily based on systematic observation on the basis of the guidelines contained in *Jeugd en Wonen.* The observations focused on the environment as it affected the research worker and included everything that occurred or did not occur during one, two or three visits to the area. This method lays particular emphasis on the physical and spatial qualities of the environment, and is based on the assumption that there are certain definite links between the particular physical characteristics of an environment and the qualities which make it an attractive area in which people may live (guidelines).

The physical characteristics were arranged in a systematically graded order for the purpose of this project (though not always exhaustively) and labelled 'criteria'. The systematic observation of the residential environment then consisted of an analysis of its physical characteristics in the light of these criteria, which at the same time provides a description. This enabled certain key problems to be singled out and suggestions to be made for possible improvements. Most of this work was undertaken in verbal terms, occasionally with explanatory drawings, As far as possible, all the evaluations were written out in full in the interests of objectivity and accuracy; this approach provided the people most involved (i.e., the residents themselves) with a means of checking how the evaluations were compiled.

An important consideration in this kind of research project is that it must be possible to discuss all the different elements with all the parties concerned. The evaluations are by no means final; they are rather initial assessments, or part of a whole series of comparable evaluations which can set a number of processes in motion, both in the neighbourhoods and in the town halls, and thus lead in due course to definitive evaluations.

At all stages of the project a need was felt for information supplementary to that which could be verified first-hand. Discussions were held with a number of experts and local government representatives. Moreover, chance contacts, sometimes spontaneously and sometimes on request, threw light on various areas, routes, relationships or the location of particular facilities.

The prime emphasis of the project, however, was on X-raying the environment, using the eight guidelines and devoting particular attention to physical and material aspects. This was based on the assumption that certain physical characteristics of a living environment play a vital role in determining its quality. The research was based on the eight criteria set out below; some are qualities or other points which deserve special attention. That they could have been grouped together or labelled otherwise is immaterial; what matters is the total number of features of the environment to which they refer. The following is a simplified description of the criteria:

1. Safety — in relation to road traffic, other users, waterways, construction work, situations;
2. Congeniality — feeling of being protected, intimacy;
3. Tolerance — plan providing for varied kinds of use; attitudes of residents/authorities to use;
4. Indoor-outdoor relation — accessibility of environment from dwellings;
5. Variation — space: design and use of materials; time: multiple use, susceptibility to change, seasons;
6. Paths and tracks — pedestrian paths and bicycle tracks; location of play areas in relation to pedestrian and other routes;
7. Play facilities — location, layout and arrangement; open space for . . . . ;
8. Involvement — care, maintenance, and supervision of use by users, municipal authorities and other responsible bodies.

Utility of the Method

The method used was based on quality and had little if anything to do with statistical standards. It consisted of scrutinizing the living environment against the background of the eight criteria listed above. This meant that the scrutiny had to be thorough, i.e., based on experience and capable of providing reliable results. In research of this kind, the client and the research workers must share a number of basic premises if the results are to be at all significant. (Compare this with an approach based on quantity, i.e., so many square metres of amenities according to statistical norms.)

In Roermond, the municipality and the Stichting Ruimte shared the views on which the qualitative method used was based, and the subsequent report was completely accepted by the municipal authorities. It contains a detailed account of each of the various residential environments by the young people who live there. This provides a general picture of the situation and, in particular, of the

shortcomings and the changes required. Moreover, after the residents of
the areas concerned have been given the opportunity to express their
views, it is suitable for use as the basis for a programme of priorities for
action. A number of vital questions were raised:

1. Having decided on the close scrutiny method of investigation, which
   requires experience and must be reliable, can it be entrusted to a
   number of observers without the sheer size of the target area (such
   as a whole municipality) presenting them with insurmountable
   problems?
2. Is every type of residential environment suitable for evaluation by
   this means? Experience has shown, for instance, that problems arise
   when it is utilized for a certain type of residential area consisting of
   large detached houses in which the public area consists largely of
   roads. Presumably no useful results can be expected from the
   application of this method, as the principles underlying this
   particular kind of land use are diametrically opposed to those
   contained in our evaluation.
3. To what extent is it wise to base the evaluation primarily on physical
   factors? Would it be advisable to add to the criteria a number of
   aspects connected with use and experience?
4. Would it be desirable for the research worker from outside to work
   in co-operation with somebody local, both for practical reasons and
   in principle? This would enable the investigation to be conducted
   with inside knowledge of the local situation.
5. Are we in a position to make our criteria more objective? One of the
   biggest questions is whether the research field is such that its
   qualities can be fully expressed in words.

The development of this qualitative approach and the increasing
demand for it may be regarded as a positive change in thinking about
the residential environment. In time, it may be possible to learn and
understand so much more as a matter of course that many of our
present difficulties will simply evaporate.

Arguments for and against Statistics

*The Significance of Quantitative and Qualitative Data (Norms) for
Planning and the Provision of Facilities in the Immediate Residential
Environment*

The local authority draws up a land-use plan which contains provision for a residential environment as part of a residential area. The land-use plan, as its name suggests, specifies the different uses to which land in a given municipality is to be put; it defines the areas precisely and states their use in specific or general terms. Thus, it also indicates the total amount of space available for specific purposes. It is at this stage that the problems dealt with in this paper occur.

At an early planning stage it is necessary to determine the extent of certain types of land use, but on what basis does this take place? Theoretically the following norms could be used:

1. a particular facility has fixed dimensions by which its nature is partly determined;
2. the interested parties (residents, organizations) claim the facilities they require at this early planning stage;
3. experience gained in similar situations forms the basis of land-use planning.

The first possibility relates to amenities for activities which are governed by fixed rules, such as all official types of sporting competition. Even so, the total amount of space required, including that for the sport itself and for a variety of supplementary related activities, may vary considerably from case to case.

The second possibility forms an important basis for physical planning. The active participation of the interested parties as an essential part of the planning process is known as social planning. Their participation in the process of preparing local land-use plans has become generally accepted in the seventies, after a stormy beginning in the late sixties. When every conceivable type of organization and group within society began to demand direct involvement in the decision-making processes, a desire for co-determination awoke among all levels of the population. The authorities tended to regard this as a passing fad which, though bothersome and time-consuming, had nevertheless to be incorporated within the policy-framing process. Subsequent experience with participation has gradually revealed its true significance: it should not be regarded as replacing the work of experts and those who are politically responsible for planning, but rather as an aid to planning, which it can stimulate and modify by helping it to keep both feet firmly on the ground. The real importance of participation in planning by the people most directly affected is that it causes them to become involved with the object of the planning and consequently means that the facilities which are being planned are likely to have a higher chance of success.

The third criterion on which planning is based, that of information gleaned from past experience, is the most important in this context. In principle, in certain circumstances it could be enough in itself; but even in circumstances where the first two criteria apply, information based on past experience has an extremely important role to play either explicitly or implicitly.

If a particular municipality plans a specific project, behind the designation there lies a conception of the project based on someone's practical or theoretical experience. The substance of the conception consists of a number of elements:

1. a definition or description containing a reference to the principal functions and objectives and to the target groups;
2. the dimensions in broad outline;
3. composite functions/elements of the project.

Throughout the entire process of planning, there is a need for information based on past experience (van den Berg and Werf-Zijlstra, 1975). The generally accepted data in the form of official standards, guidelines or norms are particularly important; they invest the planning process with a certain measure of authority. The norms for this type of planning are primarily quantitative, with the emphasis on designating the amount of space which will be taken up by amenities in the residential environment. This is expressed in terms of the number of square metres required for each category of amenity per dwelling or inhabitant, which enables the planners to determine the number of people who can be housed on a particular site or, conversely, the amount of land required to house a certain number of people (van den Berg and Werf-Zijlstra, p. 30). What the amenities actually consist of is not taken into account.

Hard and Soft Sectors as a Planning Context

The planning of welfare provisions, whether as part of land-use and structure plans or otherwise, does not take place in a vacuum: it is part of the harsh reality of policy making. The various policy sectors concerned are to some extent involved in a struggle with one another to ensure that their claims are met in the plan which eventually takes shape. In view of the scarcity of land, the various provisions must be evaluated one against the other and a choice made: more for one means less for another and so on. The various sectors competing with one another for space do so on the basis of statistical norms which count for more to the extent that they become more official and institutionalized (van den Berg and Werf-Zijlstra). The personal welfare services are inclined to undersell themselves by ignoring the hard statistical approach and instead constantly referring to the quality of the provisions (Stichting Ruimte, 1974). Of course, this sector is relatively young still, and not very institutionalized (Kuypers, 1978). It is precisely this sector which wishes to base its approach on the contributions of the people affected because it has democratic objectives. This means that it takes a long time before the amenities which are ultimately to be provided assume a definite shape, and the relevant programmes and the forms they are to take often vary considerably. The members of the general public who are involved must be able to identify with both the decision-making process and the facilities finally provided. They are after all the consumers; and if their requirements are not met, then the amenities in question are nothing more than the pointless claims of one policy sector.

In essence this amounts to the fact that the welfare sector must become familiar with social planning. In other words, the planning aspect of the total policy process must be linked to the special demands of democratization, decentralization, and participation of all of the parties concerned. There is, however, an extra complication here: welfare provisions often have links with other sectors, which means that demands must be made of these other sectors at an early stage if their essential qualities are to be retained. A good example of what is meant here is to be found in recreational facilities in the immediate vicinity of the residential environment. Such facilities are so closely interwoven with their immediate physical setting and therefore with the entire town planning structure that their quality and their potential have already been largely determined. It is becoming increasingly clear that the 'soft' sectors cannot bypass planning, even though planning in itself does not guarantee quality; planning is one thing, but actual results are another (Kuypers, p. 48). For example, if in the past a municipal parks department was granted the space to lay out a park and an area in which children could play, this was regarded as an achievement in itself. People put faith in norms based exclusively on size, but even if the struggle with other sectors was successful it had to be admitted that the provision of the best possible play and recreational facilities did not always proceed very smoothly. The problems here can be analysed in essence as follows:

1. The division of local and central government into policy sectors to a large extent determines the problems and possibilities of preparing and implementing good recreational facilities in the immediate vicinity of the residential environment.
2. This division into policy sectors was consistent with the organization of town planning after 1945, and especially with the element of rationalization in both. It seemed then as if everything could be planned . . . except quality (Kuypers, p. 148). Planning encourages a quantitative approach.
3. In view of the planning process in municipal policy, the following questions need to be answered: what must, what can, and what may be determined according to quantitative guidelines and why are qualitative guidelines necessary?

Further elaboration on these three problems follows.

Sectors Which Conflict with One Another. It is a common feature of bureaucratic organizations that separate elements of the administrative machinery conflict with one another. Of primary concern here are conflicts between, for instance, the municipal Town Planning Department (or the Public Works Department) and the various welfare and parks departments (which often come under the Public Works Department). Both sectors draw up plans in the same field but from different standpoints and with different frames of reference. Which sector or department is best equipped to win the financial round? When this is no longer a difficulty the least problematical provisions — those from neighbourhood level upwards — are those which are clearly defined and circumscribed (outdoor recreation).

Amenities such as parks in urban areas of all sizes require planning, but play and recreational facilities in the immediate vicinity do not. The latter are so closely interwoven with the town planning structure — if it is sound — that they are largely determined by it. Play and recreational facilities are closely connected with the way in which the land has been divided up, population density, traffic structure, and the arrangement and use of materials in the public sections of the living environment. De Zeeuw includes, for example, squares, street corners, wide footpaths, pedestrian walkways, terraces, market squares, etc. This means that separate quantitative norms for such features are neither necessary nor possible. An important quality of a living environment is that it can be used for a variety of purposes both simultaneously and successively.

The various claims which could be made by the different functions cannot simply be added together; in many cases they relate to one and the same area and must be directly provided for by the town planners. Moreover, other guidelines and standards (Ministry of Housing and Physical Planning, 1976) apply to the planning of housing because other demands such as light, distance between dwellings, view, car space, road surfacing and greenery have to be met. Here, too, there are many points in need of review.

Planning Versus Quality. Planning by no means guarantees quality. Earlier in this account it was shown how in many instances planning has become a necessary prerequisite for quality: provisions requiring a large amount of space need to be planned well in advance if they are ever to come into being. Provisions in the immediate residential environment – the lowest town planning level – are, however, precisely the ones in which effectiveness is determined largely by their actual substance, which in turn is often so closely bound up with other sectors of town planning that it seems to derive from them. Whether a street makes a good play street is determined by its architecture, traffic, parking facilities, layout, landscaping, the materials used in constructing the surfaces, and the people who live in it. The quality of the facility and its recreational value for all residents and users is determined by the sum total of all these factors.

A good example of planning, in this case municipal planning, which relates to the recreational use of streets by their residents is to be found in the structure plan currently in preparation for parks, gardens and recreational facilities in the second-largest city in the Netherlands, The Hague. Traditionally, structure plans usually began with large-scale provisions at city level and worked down to neighbourhood or street level; in this process, objectives were defined in terms of numerical targets by a certain date in a particular area. The Hague has reversed this process in the present planning and is working upwards, starting with the people who live in the streets for which the plans are being drawn up. Such a method begins by ascertaining what facilities they need for recreation in their immediate environment, moving on from there to the question of the facilities required at neighbourhood, area and city levels. Communicative planning, as this is called, which proceeds from the users rather than the facilities, is a marked improvement on old-style planning as it takes greater account of such aspects as user satisfaction, accessibility and the actual desires of residents than does planning from above.

Guidelines and Criteria. These two terms convey the difference between thinking based largely on quantity and that based largely on quality. In the foregoing, it has been seen that urban planning requires quantification by all the sectors concerned. In principle, this presents no major problems for recreational facilities at neighbourhood level and higher. Naturally, there may be different opinions regarding the necessary or desirable extent of particular facilities, but there is at least some point in discussing the size of parks or playgrounds and the number of them required. If these facilities are actually to be provided, however, criteria must be applied to decide what kind of facilities they should be and what they should contain. Here the relationship between the two categories of norms is somewhat clearer than it is at the lower level of the immediate residential environment, i.e., the street.

Current thinking about what constitutes a good residential environment is that it should not be split up into facilities with separate functions which have been planned by different sectors. The immediate residential environment should be viewed and planned as a whole. Any guidelines for the planning of this environment must therefore relate to the whole. The different sectors can make a contribution here, but they must not insist on norms which are weighted heavily in favour of the type of facilities they themselves provide.

The question now requiring an answer is how can such guidelines be given a solid basis to ensure their soundness, particularly as far as play and recreational facilities are concerned.

Conclusions

The main problem concerns establishing and applying norms for the lowest level, that of the immediate residential environment. Perhaps a distinction should be made between:

1. residential areas in which the problems are of such dimensions that they cannot all be tackled at once, in any case not in the short term, and in which special facilities for play and recreation will be required; guidelines on the basis of field-work statistics could be useful here; and
2. situations which can be tackled as a whole and made more suitable for play and recreation for children and adults. As the space required for recreation cannot be regarded as a separate factor in such circumstances, the statistical norms cannot be applied here.

Perhaps the best approach would be to plan urban centres so that areas suitable for play and recreation for children and adults should not be regarded as separate factors. This may be the breakthrough required to stop the ever-increasing demands (as laid down in quantitative guidelines and standards) for more recreational facilities. This problem is especially acute in The Netherlands where the extremely high density of the population requires that a great deal of attention be paid to the quality of the total residential environment; the problem is particularly evident in many of the new lower-density residential areas where the large open spaces are relatively empty, probably because of low quality of design. It must also be considered that use itself can improve the quality of the area by increasing liveliness, social contacts, etc.; because the probability of use is much greater in higher-density areas, the often lower design quality of those areas may be somewhat overcome by the greater use itself.

It is suggested that the 'woonerf' development is one means of overcoming many of the problems noted above by providing an integrated approach to urban planning. This is not to say that such an approach is, in reality, simple to achieve, but that it would appear to be a useful innovation from which planners can learn and adapt. In closing, the question – which must remain unanswered for now – arises as to the degree to which this Dutch approach can work in other countries.

Note

1. The Stichting Ruimte is a centre for the development of social and cultural facilities for the young and old in residential areas. Further information can be obtained from Stichting Ruimte, Weena 732, Post Office Box 20732, Rotterdam, The Netherlands.

References

Allen of Hurtwood, Lady Marjory. 1968. *Planning for Play.* London: Thames and Hudson.
Bengtsson, Arvid. 1972. *Adventure Playgrounds.* London: Crosby and Lockwood.
Gans, H. J. 1972. 'The potential environment and the effective environment', in *People and Plans.* New York: Pelican Books.
Jacobs, J. 1965. *The Death and Life of Great American Cities.* London: Penguin.
Kuypers, P. 1978. 'Decentralisatie is versterking van de Staatsmacht', *Vorming,* 3, pp. 143–51.
Ministry of Housing and Physical Planning. 1976. *Housing in the Netherlands.* The Hague: Information Department.
Moore, R. C. 1973. 'The diary of a volunteer playground', *Landscape Architecture,* April, pp. 216–21.
Proshansky, H., W. H. Ittelson and L. G. Rivkin (eds). 1976. *Environmental Psychology: Man and his Physical Setting.* New York: Holt, Rinehart and Winston.

———1970. 'Freedom of choice and behavior in a physical setting', in H. M. Proshansky (ed.), *Individual Needs in the Organization of the Environment*. New York: Holt, Rinehart and Winston.

Rapoport, A. and R. E. Kantor. 1967. 'Complexity and ambiguity in environmental design', *Journal of the American Institute of Planners*, July.

Sandels, S. 1970. 'Young children in traffic', *British Journal of Educational Psychology*, 40, 2, pp. 111–16.

Stichting Ruimte voor de Jeugd. *Spelen in de woonomgeving*. Rotterdam: Stichting Ruimte voor de Jeugd.

———1974. *Jeugd en Wonen*. Den Haag: Provinciale Jeugdraad Zuid-Holland.

van den Berg, M. and D. Werf-Zijlstra. 1975. *Het Ruimtegebruik in stedelijke milieu-eenheden*. Den Haag: RPD.

Vermeer, E. A. A. 1972. *Spel en pedagogische problemen (Proefschrift)*. Utrecht: Bijlevelk.

Verwer, D. and B. Bakers. 1977. *Onderzoek Spelen in de Woonomgeving Roermond*. Rotterdam: Stichting Ruimte.

Ward, C. 1977. *The Child in the City*. London: Architectural Press.

Welten, V. 1973. 'De betekenis van de adolescentieperiode', *Jeugd en Samenleving*, 3, 10, pp. 596–610. Utrecht: Stichting Jeugd en Samenleving.

White, L. E. 1953. 'The outdoor play of children living in flats', in H. Proshansky *et al.* (eds), *Environmental Psychology*, New York: Holt, Rinehart and Winston.

OUTDOOR PLAY IN HOUSING AREAS
Elizabeth Chace and George Ishmael

Introduction

Within Western industrialized society, with its emphasis upon the
nuclear family, the most important influence on children is
undoubtedly the home environment, as determined by the life-style
of the parents. A useful indicator of conditions for children is the
social grouping to which their parents belong. Children of the lower
social group may be in overcrowded conditions, with both parents
working all day in order to pay the rent. Such children are obviously
at a disadvantage in relation to other children whose parents have
better economic conditions and can afford to have one parent at home
or to pay for day care, etc. Education obviously plays a part here
also – the parents may not realize the importance of play to the child
so, even with one parent at home, conditions may not necessarily
improve. During the evening, when the family may be together for a
period, the time may be filled by a non-social activity such as
television watching. Other factors may also have an influence upon
the children's conditions; e.g., religion and the respect for the Sabbath
amongst the crofting communities of Highland Scotland may be so
strong as to prohibit the outdoor play of children on Sundays.

It can be seen that within this complex society there are many
influences affecting the conditions for children. In providing for the
children's needs, who actually makes the decisions, and who influences
these decisions? The main influence is the home, and the modern
play movement is clearly a result of parental reaction to the poor
conditions for children. This movement is a product of the twentieth
century and differs essentially from pre-industrial conditions in that it
has become a highly organized institution. Public concern and pressure
have over a long period resulted eventually in government intervention
on behalf of children, in terms of compulsory education and physical
provision for play. In this way, the school has become the second most
important influence on the child's life; and teachers, who may have
more time to realize the importance of play, can become a stabilizing
influence on the child's life.

The insights of the professionals have had only a small and slow influence on social planners and activists. For most of the twentieth century, the industrial society has concentrated resources on the development of an educational system which teaches academic and physical skills essential to the industrial and commercial world. The social system has also concentrated primarily on providing resources to meet the basic and obvious material social needs of society. It is only just recently that a number of factors have caused more attention to be directed towards the promotion of individual development by means of more widespread provision of opportunities for children's play.

Criticism of the formal education system itself — and the observed failure of the system to promote the development of many children — has led educationists to re-emphasize the importance of play. The comments made by many professionals today point to the importance of play and the need to provide for creative and adventure play.

The greatest restrictions on play occur in urban — particularly inner urban — areas; however, it is easy to accept the false belief that it is only in urban environments that play restrictions occur. Land is a valuable yet scarce commodity in most modern living areas, since nearly every type of community activity requires land. Even in the countryside, modern agriculture is a highly efficient, capital-intensive industry and the environment it produces is often not conducive to children's play.

It is obvious that the industrial society has resulted in poor conditions for children, particularly for the children of the working class. Not only are children often deprived of the contact with parents which is so essential, but they are also cut off from the economic activity of the community, and their play activities are structured by adult society, which dictates when and where play should occur. This has stifled the basic spontaneity of play and reduced many of the possibilities for play by offering rather sterile environments.

It is due to the recognition and promotion of the importance of play by social activists and others that play has finally become an expanding feature of the community and educational activities. Recognition of the basic needs has been forced to some extent by the huge increase in juvenile crime, truancy and vandalism in Western industrialized societies. The improvements necessarily made by the ruling classes, however, are generally carried out in a very half-hearted way, in order that the efficient running of the existing system is least interfered with. Thus, even when legislation exists it is often so inflexible as to be almost useless. For example, in Britain there are government standards for play space that apply to all new local authority housing schemes. These, however, specify only standard sizes of play area with standard equipment to be chosen from a standard list. There is a tacit assumption that play facilities can be provided at capital cost alone, and no mention is made of supervised play space, including contact with adults. Such statutory play space provision may be well intentioned, but shows a total lack of understanding for both the problems involved and the very nature of children's play. The space thus provided is often unsuitably sited and may indeed be comprised of whatever space is left over when the developer — public or private — has satisfied his own demands. Provision of play space is always a major source of trouble in the design of housing layouts and in the subsequent use of the area; the losers are always the children, even when the law seems to support them. In order to qualify for grant aid, the play areas must usually be constructed before completion of the scheme, and thus it is difficult to know to which age groups the play area should cater and it is practically impossible to involve the residents in its design and construction.

In the United States, a major stumbling block is the strict insurance regulations for children's safety. Lady Allen of Hurtwood (1965) once commented that it appeared as though American playgrounds are designed more for insurance companies than for children.

It can be seen, therefore, that the children — the real users of the play areas — have no say in how these should be provided, and that those who do make the decisions — the politicians and officials who supply and maintain the sources and amenities of urban life — are those least affected by the results. The parents — falling somewhere between the two extremes — could have an important influence on behalf of the children, but in many cases do not appreciate the real need, or are never consulted. Their role is therefore limited. This might not be so important if it were not for the fact that these designated areas are often the only available play spaces for the children.

In attempting to evaluate the significance of the physical environment in the development of children, it is well to recognize that this physical environment is to a large extent a product of the culture in which they live, varying according to the particular life-style of the parents. The socio-economic conditions of the parents will be of crucial importance to the children, and if such conditions are poor then no amount of physical provision of play facilities will compensate. This is not to say, however, that the physical environment is not important; as the framework within which the play pattern must be structured, it obviously is influential – for good or ill.

The allocation of space under present planning policies rarely caters to the real needs of children except when public opinion forces it. One has only to think of the implications for children of most urban planning, and of traffic planning in particular, to realize to whose demands the plans really cater. There is no systematic relationship between the provision of play facilities and the actual needs of children. The major determining factors are instead the availability of space, administrative convenience and financial consideration. Natural play space is taken over for buildings, streets, motorways and car parks, and the child is increasingly confined to specified areas which too often become 'child ghettos'.

The effect of the built environment upon the satisfaction of the basic needs of children has centred on three major issues:

1. the conflict with traffic;
2. the particular problems of high-rise living; and
3. the provision of adequate play space.

Traffic

The rapid increase in car ownership, and road traffic in general, especially since 1945, has created severe problems for children. They had previously been able to play in the street in relative safety and to participate in the community life which went on there. The increase in traffic meant that children were increasingly pushed into 'play areas' off the street, but also away from contact with other age groups and community life in general, although this too was disrupted by the increased traffic.

Inadequate traffic segregation leads to:

1. An increased accident risk: since children have an inherently limited traffic sense up to the age of 12, children cannot judge the speed at which cars are travelling towards them, and their hearing ability has not yet reached adult standards. When playing, they will run out into the street without thinking of danger. The risk to these age groups is reflected in official statistics.
2. A restriction upon the movements of children: i.e., the child's geographical range away from the home base will be limited by the presence of busy traffic thoroughfares. Often parents will not allow their children to cross such roads, even though the only available

playground lies on the other side.

High-rise Living

Several studies have shown that children living above the third floor of
a high-rise building play outdoors less than children living near the
ground. For example, a British survey of families with young children
living in high-rise flats found that over 58 per cent of the families
restricted their children's play. This, coupled with other factors such
as the space available for play in the flats and noise problems, has led
researchers to conclude that high-rise life for children is damaging,
since their environment is so restricting.

Although in cities such as London and Copenhagen there seems to
be a move away from the construction of more high-rise residential
developments or perhaps a move to house families with children on or
near the ground, many children continue to live in high-rise apartments,
and building of these developments continues in many countries. The
problem will therefore remain with us for the foreseeable future.

The Provision of Adequate Play Space

Many residential areas, particularly the older ones, are lacking in play
space. Even in those developments which have a sufficient amount of
space, this may be of an unsuitable nature that does not cater to the
real needs of the children for which it is supposedly intended. Bits of
left-over space are often designated as play spaces after the housing
layout has been planned. These play spaces inevitably prove to be
inadequate as part of a total housing environment and often conflict
with traffic or the privacy of other residents.

Tingbjerg: a Case Study

In today's world, one usually finds uninteresting play areas that
conform for the most part to the requirements of administrators, and
least of all to the needs of children. They are characterized by low-
maintenance, non-moving equipment in a low-maintenance sea of
asphalt or concrete – an unchangeable, non-manipulable environment
that quickly becomes redundant in terms of meeting children's needs,
producing boredom and perhaps vandalism. Such environments are in
extreme contrast to those of the pre-industrial economy, where the
child was exposed to a wealth of experiences.

Faced with a choice between the places designed for them by adults
and the far more stimulating and dangerous street environment,
children will obviously choose the latter. Left alone to play, they will

choose the dirt and gravel — the environmental elements they can experience by touch, smell, sight, taste, and over which they have some individual control. Given the opportunity and the raw materials, children will design a playground far better than most facilities designed for them by adults.

It would be interesting to take as a case study a modern planned housing development, to illustrate not only the problems for children, but also some attempted solutions. In this respect, Tingbjerg, lying about 8 km northwest of Copenhagen, Denmark, is a good example, as it was planned by Steen Eiler Rasmussen with the specific intention of catering to the needs of all age groups, and to children in particular.

Tingbjerg was constructed during the years 1956–70 and contains about 2,500 dwellings built by traditional methods (brick and tile). Approximately 6,500 people live here, in blocks of flats of varying heights, the majority being three-storey:

Tingbjerg was planned with several clear intentions in mind:

1. to provide a self-contained housing environment which would combine the advantages of urban living with good opportunities for social contact: 'a housing milieu where all age groups can feel comfortable and at home';
2. to obtain an economic and efficient use not only of the buildings, but also of the open spaces between them, to ensure maximum utilization of the site and to conform to the floor/space ratio as regulated in the Housing Act;
3. to design a rational and economic project that fully exploits the advantages of uniformity; such uniformity in terms of equal-sized rooms and buildings is determined both by function and the economics of building technique, and is characteristic of all large post-war housing developments.

In planning to create a 'neighbourhood' with a real feel of community, it was realized that certain pitfalls must be avoided. For the sake of the children in particular, it was declared necessary to try to create a neighbourhood with people from all social (class) standings, occupations and age groups. This would be the determining factor in the 'spirit' found in the area:

> . . . it is hoped that there will come a broad segment of Danish society with people from both the trade and liberal professions. If it is possible for one to create a milieu with an attractive appearance,

it should be possible to populate it with people who can take an active part in the growth and development of the neighborhood. (Rasmussen, 1963, p. 2)

Rasmussen also realized, however, that this was optimistic and that as long as the housing shortage existed there would be a one-sided representation of age groups among the residents, with mostly young families, many children, and young people moving in. Consequently, his provisions were aimed very much at the children and youth who were to live the the area, while aiming also to satisfy the needs of a more representative society, which he hoped would eventually materialize. In addition, an attempt was made to balance the age structure by providing homes and facilities for the disabled and old-age pensioners. At least 10 per cent of all the housing was built specifically for these groups.

By offering a varied environment with equal opportunity for the young of all classes Rasmussen hoped to give a greater number of possibilities to each individual and to create a sense of solidarity and belonging. In this way, by combating sterility and lack of communication, it would be possible to overcome many of the inherent problems facing residents of extensive new housing areas.

The landscape design was carried out in conjunction with C. Th. Sorensen, who believed that, in order better to satisfy the needs of children, there had to be more than just ordinary playgrounds with the usual equipment included in the design. His belief was that children needed access to the various landscape forms that could be found in the Danish countryside. Under the existing urban conditions, he attempted to distill the essential elements of those landscapes into a form which could exist within the narrow framework of the town, and be maintained without too much trouble. Instead of the beach appeared the sandpit; instead of the meadow, the lawn; and instead of the woodland, trees would be planted.

Profile of Social Conditions

In an attempt to gain insight into some of the behaviour patterns and the general state of well-being of the residents of Tingbjerg, and to find out whether factors connected with the physical layout do in fact influence their welfare, an interview was conducted with Erik Poulsen who, with his wife, Mette Kint, lives in Tingbjerg, where they are employed as the 'paedagogue familie', or family counsellors. The existence of such a team is not as yet found elsewhere in Denmark.

Administered by Kobenhavn Kommune, the thinking behind the pedagogue family is the provision of human rather than bureaucratic help through person-to-person contact within the living environment. Erik and Mette work as co-ordinators between the institutional or bureaucratic structures and the residents themselves, in an attempt to catch problems in the early stages, and work to solve them.

There are approximately 2,500 family groups among the population of just over 6,500 in Tingbjerg. Pensioners number approximately 300, and there is a substantial number of handicapped residents. Monthly rent at Tingbjerg is approximately 1,700 kroner per month for a three-room, 90 m² flat. One out of ten dwellings houses more than three people per two rooms.

In terms of social status, the occupants are chiefly from the lower-middle class and the skilled-worker group. Although one of the chief objectives in the formulation of Tingbjerg was to have all sectors of society represented in the population, this idea was an illusion, as Rasmussen readily admits. It is not possible to plan the social make-up of the projected residential population, and in turn to determine their respective life-styles on paper. It seems that the residents of Tingbjerg have only to some extent developed the intended feel of the self-contained neighbourhood community with many qualities of the old town. There are an estimated 400 single mothers living in Tingbjerg, and between 300 and 400 residents are presently unemployed. This high rate of unemployment is not due solely to the situation in Denmark today, but also to the fact that many of these people are unemployable due to lack of training or education. Those with jobs are employed mostly as labourers or trade workers, some with training.

The differences in social standing are reflected in the life-styles characteristic of the residents. There are three fairly distinct groups that may be identified:

1. Those that are educated, holding semi-skilled or skilled positions. They are basically a responsible and conforming group which forms a stable core within the community.
2. A more unsettled faction, with hopes of living only temporarily in the area, moving when they can afford to.
3. Those that are unemployed and uneducated, dissatisfied with their life situation, but unable to view their situation realistically. Most of the social problems at Tingbjerg lie within this group. Alcoholism, drug problems, loneliness and boredom, frustration and apathy, are characteristics of this group.

Sixty per cent of the residents have lived in Tingbjerg for over six years, and 10–11 per cent move each year, with an equal replacement rate. Survey results found that nearly 50 per cent of the residents would like to move away if it were possible, a fairly average figure for a large housing area.

The Children's Situation

Although the physical layout of Tingbjerg was designed specifically to serve the needs of the young, the actual effects of this 'special' environment are not easily discernible. It has been found that nearly one-quarter of the children tend to play in busy traffic and pedestrian areas rather than in the spaces intended for play purposes. Contrary to expectations, the adventure playgrounds at Tingbjerg are used to a rather limited extent, the children preferring the smaller playgrounds and courtyards. In a study of six similar housing areas in Denmark, it was found that children in Tingbjerg tend to spend fewer hours playing outside.

A large proportion of the families living in Tingbjerg have more than two children – close to 2,500 children under the age of 18 live there. Nearly 50 per cent of them are under the care of the many existing institutions run either by the municipality or by the organization called SBBU.[1] The differences in the social standing of the parents is reflected in many instances in their children. Thievery and delinquency occur much more frequently among the lower-class families. Though the institutional facilities are numerous and extensive in Tingbjerg, there is a danger stemming from this strong system: that of institutional replacement of family responsibility. Parents can in effect choose to let the strong institutional network at Tingbjerg care for their children almost around the clock, freeing them of any responsibility or parental interaction with their children. SBBU is a strong organization providing a great number of facilities that are well used, yet this provision becomes in many ways compensation for the generally poor conditions for children in our society. Administrative responsibilities must not end at the organizational and structural level; the actual processes, not the product (e.g., impressive facilities, activities and participation statistics), must be dealt with. It is the personal rapport and guidance skills that must be fully emphasized.

It can be seen from official statistical evidence, the results of a number of independent surveys, and conversations with people concerned with children's welfare (both in official and parental capacity), that socio-economic factors are crucial in determining the over-all conditions for the children. In terms of physical design there is little, if anything, that can be done to influence these factors. It is equally clear, however, that the physical environment provides the framework for living and play activities. It may either inhibit these activities or stimulate activity and allow a range of possibilities to materialize.

How successful is Tingbjerg in providing this physical framework?

It has been said that the three major problems of post-war housing layouts are:

1. their sheer size and inhuman scale;
2. their mass-produced, 'designed for the average man' style; and
3. their impersonality, due to the lack of residents' influence upon the design.

Since Tingbjerg was designed with the specific intention of creating a friendly neighbourhood with a feel of community, some interesting solutions to these problems might be expected.

Tingbjerg does have a more human scale, being broken down into small units of three-storey apartment blocks surrounding open green 'yards'. This layout, however, has also tended to isolate each housing group to the extent that there seems to be little feel of 'neighbourhood', but rather a sense of belonging to a particular unit or yard. This feeling is reinforced by the fact that the traffic system around each unit tends to act as a barrier to movement, particularly that of children. They tend to stay in their own yard until quite a late age (11 or 12 years), when they start to explore around a little more and may visit schoolfriends living in other units. Since this layout results in the children spending much of their outdoor time in a restricted area, both physically and visually, it is unfortunate that the individual yards are rather monotonous, surrounded as they are by continuous housing blocks of equal height with no view and nothing to break up the bulk of the buildings. This latter problem may be solved when the trees get bigger, but a much more varied and dense planting will be required really to improve the situation. It is also unfortunate that little adult activity occurs in the individual yards. It might have been better to have dispersed the shops and services more evenly throughout the neighbourhood, thereby utilizing the activity generated to bring a little more life to the yards. There may be economic arguments against such a move, but dispersal of this kind has occurred naturally, for example, in Avedore, also on the outskirts of

Copenhagen and with a similar physical layout. Many Swedish housing areas have this more dispersed arrangement and seem more active as a result.

Although the needs of all resident groups have been considered at the neighbourhood level, there has been little consideration at the level of the physical layout, so that in reality there is little social benefit to be gained from mixing the different groups. There is an unfortunate tendency for different age groups to become geographically segregated, so that even though the age structure within the neighbourhood is reasonably balanced, it is meaningless in terms of each housing unit. Thus, due to the physical layout of the housing, the pensioners live clustered together in a group of small flats. They are somewhat isolated and possibilities for interaction with other age groups are fewer as a result. Similarly, single people tend to live in the older section of Tingbjerg because the flats there are cheaper. Presumably the economic considerations of construction outweighed the social considerations. This is further evidenced by the many problems arising from the use of cheap materials.

The needs of preschool-age children could certainly be better met. The main problem lies in the conflict between traffic and the possibilities for doorstep play. Ideally, of course, ground-floor dwellings should be available for all families with children, and should have a small garden or semi-private area fronting onto public open space, with no danger from traffic. Present conditions could be improved if some of the short streets immediately outside dwellings could be designated 'play streets' or completely devoted to pedestrians.

Although the physical layout has not encouraged a natural neighbourliness, the organization SBBU has acted as the catalyst to co-ordinate the fight for better facilities (e.g., bus service, playgrounds) and in so doing has helped build up a certain sense of community among the residents, who now see themselves as able to have some direct influence over their environment.

In the organization of children's facilities, it has been said that there is a tendency to take away responsibility from the parents. This aspect should not be over-emphasized, since, under the present conditions of Western society, where parents are often unable to cope with the needs of their children, a service such as SBBU offers is clearly essential. An organization such as SBBU can direct the pressure for improvements to the children's conditions and force action on the part of the authorities. Undoubtedly, and unavoidably, there is a political side to the organization, but it is equally certain that, in the struggle to improve children's conditions, SBBU offers something of a model for provision in other housing environments. Needless to say, if such an organization exists from the start, before people move into an area, it can grow along with the community, in response to its ever-changing needs.

In conclusion, it can be said that play opportunities at Tingbjerg are far better than those in other housing developments of similar age and residential mix. This fact is undoubtedly due to the excellent facilities provided by SBBU.

As well as 'traditional' playgrounds — which too often fail to satisfy real needs — other facilities offer diversity, challenge and the chance directly to affect the environment. The 'active' playgrounds are very successful, as are the small allotment gardens provided for children, in allowing decisions and experimentation to be made. These activities lack real meaning, of course, but as necessary substitutes they perform extremely well.

Where SBBU is really successful, however, is in the provision of adult help, supervision and stimulation to the children during their play hours, thus compensating to some extent for their unsatisfactory home conditions.

In terms of satisfying the real needs of children, it is better, once sufficient open space has been provided, to spend available money on organization (e.g., provision of play leaders, day-care centres) rather than facilities such as playgrounds, which could better be produced by children and parents under guidance. It is important, however, that this organization be directly responsible to the residents of the area, rather than to any local government authority. Money spent by a local authority could be used to grant aid to such an organization, either directly or by provision of accommodation, open space, or specific items of equipment. Payment of staff could be, at least in part, by levy of a rate on residents in the neighbourhood. This would also have the advantage of making the organization directly answerable to the residents, and thereby much more responsive to their needs.

The Child's Physical Environment

The pre-industrial age provided an ideal physical framework within which play could occur. Furthermore, society was in better balance with nature; people were more 'sociable' in general; and work was not the 'be-all and end-all' of existence. Children, although having no rights as such, were an integral part of the community and took part in the work process. They came into contact with a variety of people and age groups: life was a rich experience.

Western society — with its individualistic approach to life, its compartmentalization of work, dwelling and recreation, its tendency towards standardization, and its confused attitude towards nature — results in an environment that is sterile and lacking in diversity and richness of experience. This is not something that can be remedied merely by taking the physical structures of the past and reconstructing them now, under entirely different conditions.

The over-all conditions for children are determined by diverse factors which act and interact in complex ways. Individual factors may be emphasized from time to time in an attempt to improve conditions. Hence, since the mid-nineteenth century, there has been a gradual improvement in factors such as health, education and children's legal rights to an extent that they now exceed the standard that existed before the Industrial Revolution. On the other hand, these improvements have been paralleled by a gradual deterioration in the physical environment and a gradual segregation of age groups. The child has also been separated from the work process. Factors such as these now limit any further improvement in over-all conditions. Although attention is now turning in this direction, it is important to remember that, even if, for example, the ideal physical environment is provided, over-all conditions may not improve because of limitations from some other factor such as the economic conditions of the family or the parents' understanding of the child's needs. Hence, the rate of progress is determined by the rate of improvement in the lowest, or limiting, factor. The operation of such a 'law of limiting factors' means that all factors must be constantly improved if progress in improving over-all conditions is to be sustained.

With these points in mind, the question of the child's physical environment, and some attempts that have been made to reverse the trend of its gradual deterioration, will be examined. The problem will be considered on several levels, including planning, layout and design — major determinants of play conditions.

It must be emphasized that the research described here gives a highly unbalanced picture of children's conditions. It deals only with the more obvious physical manifestations of the environment. Thus the question of safety is considered only in terms of the traffic problem, an entirely modern phenomenon, but one which has had a tremendous impact upon the landscape and thereby upon the child's everyday behaviour, much more than, for instance, a particular disease. Thus, although neglected in this study, the question of health is important and directly related to the state of the physical environment. Disease was a real and ever-present threat in earlier days, as was the possibility of physical violence.

To complete the picture, a socio-economic study is necessary. What was the daily routine of children in these various environments? Could they, for example, take advantage of the play opportunities offered by the physical environment of the pre-industrial village?

The aim of this particular study is to examine the physical framework within which the child lives and plays. How can the physical environment, and specifically that of modern housing areas, be so designed as to meet the child's need for play, or at least to provide the possibility for this need to be met?

In designing for play, layout has a highly significant contribution to make, since it determines the distribution of suitable play space and its degree of accessibility. Furthermore, it can do much to avoid or reduce conflict between the needs of the child and the needs of other groups.

The neighbourhood planning process determines the presence or absence of the major preconditions to be satisfied. Once provided, they must then be arranged in a physical pattern, or layout, conducive to the use of the area as an outdoor play space. Thus, although the amount of open space *per se* is determined largely at the planning level when densities are decided, the chosen housing type and its layout greatly influence the actual amount of usable public open space.

Many countries have introduced standards whereby a certain area is set aside for use as both public open space, in general, and children's play space, in particular. This guarantees the provision of space, but does not attempt to locate it in the actual physical layout. Thus, although enough space may exist, because of poor location it is often not used — or is even misused. Standards, as they presently exist, appear to be too rigid in nature and hence unable to adapt to the unique needs of residents in any one area at any particular time.

Ideally, the needs of the residents should be known in advance before play areas are located and designed in detail. Since each age group has different requirements, it is essential to know for whom one is designing at any particular point in time. Of course, it is a feature of modern housing areas that as time passes the age structure changes and therefore the needs of the residents change also.

In this connection, it is of interest to note which groups make most use of the external environments of modern housing developments. Obviously it is those groups confined to the area for most of the day, either because they lack mobility — the preschool age, the handicapped, the aged — or because their work ties them to their home — the 'mother/housewife'.

As has been pointed out above, the external environment tends to be designed not for these groups, but for the wage earner/car owner, exactly the group that spends the least time on the housing estate, and even this time predominantly when light/weather conditions are often not conducive to outdoor activity. Furthermore, layouts tend to be inflexible and unable to respond to the varied and ever-changing needs of residents.

Accessibility

Since play occurs informally and is essentially a spontaneous activity, the entire housing layout must be regarded as potential play space. Although 'playgrounds' have an important function, they too often become child 'ghettos' in an otherwise barren environment. The entire housing area must be regarded as potential play space, just as children themselves regard it.

Any layout should take into account the facts that children play near the home and that as age increases, so does their radius of activity from the home base. Failure to recognize these facts is common in poor residential environments, i.e., poor in terms of fulfilling the needs of children and poor in terms of appearance (since children will play, and wear and tear will occur, in areas not designated to take it).

There are three types of accessibility, which are now mentioned.

Physical Accessibility. Play spaces must be available well within the housing area and linked with safe (i.e., traffic-free) circulation routes to allow maximum freedom of movement.

It is vital for children under five years of age to be in close physical proximity to the home; in fact, most children play within a few metres of home. Every family house, children's establishment and school must be in direct contact with suitable play space. Such space should extend throughout the housing area as a series of linked public open spaces, with private or semi-private open space immediately off them.

The provisions for each age group should be looked at separately, although always with the possibility in mind of interaction with the other groups. It is, therefore, not a good idea totally to segregate children by age groups, as adjacent facilities will provide interaction. The linked spaces concept, therefore, not only aids safety, but also facilitates the process of transition between one age group and the next which can otherwise be a problem, e.g., the transition from individual to group play in the toddler at two to three years old, and the transition from the pre-adolescent to the adolescent group. Some degree of physical segregation is often necessary, however, in order to satisfy safety requirements.

Visual Accessibility. Play space, and playgrounds in particular, should be 'where the action is', i.e., on main pedestrian routes, preferably at a junction, and not hidden away in some isolated area. Children at play should ideally be in view of the home.

Acoustic Accessibility. This is of particular importance to children under five years of age, who need readily to hear, and be heard by, the parents.

The Avoidance of Conflict

Although play spaces should be sited to give the maximum contact with people and 'things', certain potential areas of conflict should be avoided at the early planning stage.

Conflict with Other Resident Groups. Spaces designed for play should be located away from dwellings intended for elderly people or adults without children. It is usually the noise that gives rise to problems, but also the physical proximity can create difficulties, e.g., the kicking and throwing of balls into gardens or against gable-end walls. This is not to say that isolation should be encouraged, but that people should be given a choice: elderly people may like to watch children playing and this should be made possible, as for example at Tingbjerg.

Much can be done further to resolve this conflict when detailed design comes to be considered.

Conflict with Management. This is an all too common occurrence. For example, poorly designed circulation may lead to short-cutting across planted areas, causing excessive wear or even total destruction. If play areas are situated too far from the house and decorative planting schemes provided immediately outside the home, then of course the plant bed becomes the 'sandpit' and a conflict occurs with management and other resident groups who dislike the mess.

The layout of open space must attempt to resolve such conflict before it arises.

Detailed Design of the Housing Area

The maximum amount of space around family dwellings should be usable as play space, and in this respect the detailed design of the area is of great significance. Of particular importance is the design of the interface between the private zone (within the house) and the public zone (in the street). The dwelling and its immediate environs should be physically, visually and acoustically well integrated.

Ideally, all family dwellings should have a garden or yard in intimate contact with the inner living area (preferably the kitchen or living-room), but also in contact with the public comings and goings of the area. In this way, the young child can make contact with other children playing nearby and eventually move out to join them. Adequate fencing may be necessary in the child's early years, but this does not preclude the possibility of visual contact.

A sense of enclosure — but not of isolation — adds greatly to the attractiveness of the environment near the home. Enclosure can also help to reduce noise and screen untidy play areas (e.g., adventure playgrounds). It can be achieved in various ways: structures such as walls and fences, vegetation to form hedges and screens, or earth contouring.

This sense of enclosure should be combined with shelter from extreme weather conditions, e.g., wind, rain, strong sunlight. Creation of a satisfactory micro-climate positively encourages outdoor play and should be a primary aim in the design of all housing areas. For example, in northern Europe, play space for children under five years of age should take advantage of sunlight in the late morning and early afternoon, when outdoor play occurs.

The various components of the built environment (e.g., steps, railings, paved areas) should be designed to provide play possibilities, but must be robust enough to withstand such play. A variety of hard-wearing surfaces should be provided. Children prefer hard surfaces for street games and a variety of pattern and texture not only offers visual stimulation but can also suggest different uses to children. Circulation areas around family dwellings can be designed positively to encourage children's play, e.g., the use of ramps rather than steps not only allows the use of wheeled toys but also enables physically handicapped children to join in.

Since active manipulation of the physical environment is a necessity, there should be areas for 'natural play', particularly digging and building. In the case of older children, such needs can be satisfied in nearby wild areas or in the adventure playground, but young children need such provision close to home in the form of a sandpit and paddling pool. This may be provided in the private garden, but could also be provided communally for each group of dwellings, as at Saettedammen, Denmark. Several recent housing developments in Denmark have 'play woods' adjoining equipped play spaces. These are small patches of rapidly growing trees or shrubs (e.g., willow or dogwood) that are resistant to harsh treatment.

If not intended for play, planting must either be protected by careful siting, or be robust enough to withstand wear and tear, i.e., fast-growing or prickly material such as Pyracantha. In either case, fencing is advisable, at least while the plants establish. Alternatively, plants can be placed in raised beds out of harm's way. Planting can function as a buffer between spaces, to control the movement of children and also to give shelter and a sense of enclosure.

Grass areas intended for play should be large enough to avoid over-intensity of use, and have a number of access points in order to reduce excessive wear and tear. If not intended for play, lawns should be raised above path level or carefully mounded at least to discourage ball games.

Careful choice of plants will give not only year-round aesthetic pleasure, to stimulate the senses of sight, sound and smell, but can also attract wildlife to the area — obviously an added benefit to children.

It is evident from this brief survey that, in planning the physical environment from the point of view of satisfying children's play requirements, much more should be provided than just 'swings and slides' on a piece of fenced-off ground.

It is noticeable that the most successful schemes offer a great diversity of opportunities within the total environment, and it seems well to follow this principle of diversity when designing new residential environments. Needs vary with age and with the individual and it is obvious that the more diverse the environment, then the more needs it is likely to fulfil. The goal should be a rich environment in which children can develop their various skills — physical, social and psychological.

Flexibility is another great asset to a housing environment, at all levels, from the planning of the neighbourhood to the layout of the various functions, and even to the way in which, for example, a fence can be designed to fulfil a number of purposes.

Progress to Date

Some achievements to date and some practical proposals (at the neighbourhood level) within the industrialized countries will now be considered.

In terms of housing, social facilities and traffic links, progress has been made, at least in so far as children and the improvement of their physical environment are concerned. These improvements have been the result of conscious effort at the planning level to reverse the trend of deterioration, and have often involved a considerable measure of state intervention. Such efforts are by no means universal and even where they do exist the problem may not be solved.

Housing

The general trend is still towards large areas of uniformity in terms of house type, size and cost. This in turn produces uniformity in social terms, all of which is unsuitable for the balanced development of children. There are, however, a number of schemes which provide diversity and some degree of social mixture (e.g., the British New Towns), so it is possible to create such neighbourhoods in present Western society. It is arguable whether these attempts have been successful in creating more social interaction, but at least from the point of view of children they ensure some diversity within their social environment, particularly at school. Surely, just from this point of view, the effort is justified.

Social Facilities

There is now a growing trend towards the provision of communal facilities in housing areas, and it is to be hoped that this continues. As has been demonstrated (e.g., Vaerebro Park, Denmark), however, the provision even of extensive facilities need not of itself result in improved conditions. There are many other factors to be considered, e.g., physical layout and, not least, socio-economic factors.

It is essential, under present conditions, where both parents often go out to work, that supervised facilities be provided for the children. This type of facility is often in short supply or totally non-existent, but schemes like that at Tingbjerg (SBBU) point the way.

Traffic Links

Much progress has been made in this field, with consequent benefit to children. Sweden is particularly rich in examples of traffic-segregated housing environments, and sets an example to the world. Often, however, little attention seems to be paid to this problem: the traffic planner frequently seems more concerned with achieving a smooth flow of traffic than with child safety.

Work

As regards the child's relationship to the work process and his relationship to nature, little progress has been made. The separation of the child from the work process (and hence the real world) has been one of the less fortunate aspects of industrialization from the child's point of view. Any attempt to solve the problem is fraught with difficulties, as children doing meaningful (i.e., economically valuable) work are often seen as being exploited. Over-protection has led to legal requirements which further complicate the situation. Obviously, there was a need for this in the early days of industrialization when child exploitation occurred on a large scale, but it is time now that the situation was reassessed.

Children need to experience diversity, challenge and the chance to manipulate and directly affect their environment. Failure to meet these needs constructively will result in them being met elsewhere, perhaps destructively. Vandalism can be seen as the expression of a basic need to influence the environment: to make one's mark. It also has to do with pushing the limits within which society confines one, a need which could be met constructively. The energy and drive of youth needs some aim; otherwise it dissipates itself in wasteful acts either destructive or, at best, meaningless. The teenager in particular must be allowed to make decisions and influence his environment.

Not all countries see the need for cutting the child off from the work process. Indeed, some see it as an essential part of a child's education. In Albania, for example, food production is very labour-intensive and during the summer children and pensioners (who often suffer from this same problem) help with market garden and greenhouse cultivation. The children of all industrialized countries used to participate in harvest work, but farm mechanization has gradually reduced the need for their labour. It may well be that this is an inevitable process, but some methods of food production are, by their nature, labour-intensive. The provision of allotment gardens in housing areas means that children and pensioners have the possibility to participate in meaningful work. This aspect of provision should not be under-estimated: it should not be a purely economic argument for the provision of allotment space. It is of course important that such gardens be well integrated in the layout and not beyond easy walking distance at the most.

Child work is often seen as child exploitation, but the child's world has its own values and there is no rigid distinction between work and play. In the learning process, that which adults call 'work' has a vital contribution to make to the balanced development of the child.

It is an unfortunate over-reaction to the appalling conditions created at the outset of industrialization that planning authorities are now over-cautious in allowing some mixing of industry and housing. It shows a certain lack of self-confidence on their part that they often refuse even to allow small craft workshops of a non-polluting kind to be integrated once more with housing and thereby bring some activity back to these lifeless areas.

Conclusion

In this effort to examine and evaluate the physical environment from an interdisciplinary approach, on the basis of the authors' training and experience as architect and sociologist, it becomes readily apparent that problems relating to children's play in today's living environments cannot be solved by either the architect or the sociologist alone; the two fields are inextricably bound, whether this is acknowledged openly or not.

The function and relative success of a particular physical environment are undoubtedly influenced by the character and social make-up of the population itself; and the attitudes and general life-style of its members are, in turn, unavoidably affected by the physical design of their environment, even if this is not consciously recognized. Organizational and bureaucratic bodies have determining power over both of these aspects, often ignoring the actual social, physical and psychological needs, concentrating instead on political or financial matters. In the attempt to obtain good value for money, these real needs cannot afford to be ignored.

Both the architect and the human scientist admit the great importance of the physical environment, yet from different approaches. The sociologist tends to be a bit more realistic, perhaps, yet cannot begin to grasp the problems with which an architect or planner must contend. The architect, however, is too often absorbed with aesthetics and concentrates on the product — the end-result. Although this product is indeed important, it is the process of living, working, building in an integrated society that should be of primary concern to those involved in the planning and functioning of the built environment.

Note

1. The SBBU or 'Foreningen Socialt Boligbyggeri's Ungdomsklubbers' (The Organization for Social Housing's Youth Clubs) is an organization which receives state and local funding for the purpose of improving leisure-time conditions for youth in the suburbs of Copenhagen.

References

Abernathy, W. D. 1961. *Playgrounds.* London: National Playing Fields Association.

Allen of Hurtwood, Lady. 1965. *Design for Play.* London: E. T. Heron.

Andersen, Finn. 1971. *Leg I Byplan Aktiv Leg.* Arosopgave: Dansk Fritidshjemsseminarium.

Arkitektens Forlag. 1952. *Legepladser.* Kobenhavn: Arkitektens Forlag.

Arnold, Paul, Roger Hart, Clare Cooper Marcus, Robin C. Moore and Audrey Penn Rogers. 1974. 'The Children's Landscape.' Series of articles in *Landscape Architecture*, October, pp. 354–416.

Bengtsson, Arvid. 1972. *Adventure Playgrounds.* London: Crosby Lockwood.

——1974. *The Child's Right to Play.* London: International Playground Association.

Dattner, Richard. 1969. *Design for Play.* New York: Van Nostrand.

Department of the Environment. 1973. *The Estate Outside the Dwelling.* London: Her Majesty's Stationery Office.

Department of Landscape Architecture, University of Edinburgh. 1974. *Applecross Study 2.* Edinburgh.

El'Konin, D. B. 1960. 'Some results of the study of the mental development of children of pre-school age', in *Psikhologicheskaia nauka, USSR*, Volume 2. Moscow: Academy of Physical Sciences. English translation: *Psychological Science in the USSR*, Volume 2. Washington: Office of Technical Services.

European Leisure and Recreation Association. 1970. 'ELRA Recommendations 1–7', June. ELRA: Zurich.

——1975. 'Play and Recreation Facilities in Switzerland'. ELRA: Zurich.

Eversley, D. E. C. 1968. 'The child, the family and the built environment', *Town and Country Planning* (special issue: 'Children and Planning'), Oct.–Nov. London.

Friedberg, M. Paul. 1970. *Play and Interplay.* New York: Macmillan.

Frobelseminariet. 1975. 'Borns opvoekstvilkar i et forholdvis nyt boligomrade.' Kobenhavn: Frobelseminariet.

Guttinger, V. A. 1977. 'Small children and residential traffic', *Ekistics*, 43, p. 255.

Holme, A. and P. Massie. 1970. *Children's Play.* London: Michael Joseph.

Jacobsen, C., E. Petersen and B. Vibholm. 1978. 'Legepladser: i gammelt og nyt boligbyggen med Focus pa christianshaun og Tingbjerg.' Det Socialpaedagogiske Seminarium Personalehojskolen.

Kluckhorn, Clyde and Dorothea Leighton. 1974. *Children of the People.* Cambridge, Mass.: Harvard University Press.

Ledermann, A. and A. Traschel. 1968. *Creative Playgrounds and Recreational Places.* New York: Praeger.

Lozar, Charles, 1970. 'Playground Aesthetics', *Educational Products Reports*, May.

Martini, Sten. 1974. *Nyere forstadmiljoer.* Kobenhavn: Socialforskningsinstitutet, publication G1.

Piaget, Jean. 1951. *Play, Dreams and Imitation in Childhood.* New York: Heinemann.

Pollowy, Anne-Marie. 1977. *The Urban Nest.* New York: Dowden, Hutchinson and Ross, Inc., Community Development Series.

Rasmussen, Steen Eiler. 1963. *The Tingbjerg Project.* (English translation by Evy Pedersen and Pia Jensen.) Copenhagen: Royal Danish Academy.

Sigsgaard, Jens. 1965. 'The Playground in Modern Danish Housing', *Danish Foreign Office Journal*, 54, October.

Socialpaedagogiske Seminarium Personalehojskolen. 1978. *Legepladser.* Specialopgave. February.

Statens Offentliga Utredningar. 1970. 'Barns Utemiljo.' Stockholm.

Wharton, K. 1970. 'Sad storeys for children', *The Architect and Building News*, October.

Whiting, B. B. 1963. *Six Cultures: Studies of Child Rearing.* New York: Wiley.

12 CAN CHILDREN PLAY AT HOME?

Louise Gaunt

Introduction

During recent years, children's play environments have been the focus of much debate. The discussion has almost solely concerned the outdoor environment, or the neighbourhood's form and content with respect to children's play and activities. It is the contention of this paper that children's indoor environments must be included, in order to give a picture of the total environment for children today. What restrictions and what possibilities does the indoor environment offer for children's activities? First, a short summary will be presented of the results of a newly completed empirical investigation about children's dwelling habits which has been undertaken at the National Swedish Institute for Building Research within the project 'Dwelling Habits and Housing Design'. These results will then be discussed in reference to development theory. Finally, there will be an examination of some of the consequences of this research for housing design and parental attitudes towards children's activities.

Method

In late 1975 and early 1976, an interview investigation was carried out with 300 households in 30 different housing types in Sweden. Of these households, 120 included children between two and seven years of age: altogether, there were 158 children in 19 housing types. The aim of the investigation was to show how the dwelling is used and the importance of housing design for dwelling habits. The results will be used in a discussion about the form and content of Swedish design standards (Statens Institut for Byggnadsforskning, Årsbok, 1977). Each interview took about two hours and included the drawing of a floor plan in which the furniture was marked and photographs of the dwelling. A special part of the interview was dedicated to the children's activities in the dwelling. From a check-list of play types and activities, the parents were asked what their children had been doing during the last week. The parents were also asked what rooms the children used and where they were not supposed to be. Visits by playmates and the children's participation in adult activities were also recorded.

To this quantitative part of the investigation was added a qualitative section. The parents of twelve of the children were asked to make a diary during two days with notes on all child activities taking place in the home: what, where and with whom. The diaries were followed up by a long tape-recorded interview with parents and children about play during the diary days and about the conflicts and difficulties that had arisen.

The investigation concentrated on the indoor environment, but some notes were also recorded on outdoor play. These notes and a survey of the neighbourhoods give the same picture of passive play patterns and unstimulating environment that so many earlier studies of outdoor play have presented (Björklid-Chu, 1974; Dahlén, 1977).

Results

What Rooms Did the Children Use?

The parents were asked to estimate the children's time in each room in the home. The children spent half of the time in their own rooms, about a third in the kitchen, and the rest in the living-room. They were hardly at all in the parents' bedroom. The children's play mainly took place in their bedrooms and to a certain degree in the kitchen. In the living-room they were mainly occupied with quiet activities, such as watching television, listening to music and talking to parents. Parents preferred the play to take place in children's bedrooms and kitchen; only a quarter of the children were allowed to play everywhere in the home. Small children and children in large families were more restricted than older children in small families. This means that children in small families not only often have a bedroom of their own, but can also play in the rest of the dwelling, while children in large families often share a bedroom and have restrictions about the use of the rest of the dwelling.

Some English studies report that children in many families have the living-room as their main playroom, the mothers wanting to keep bedrooms free from play. This is especially true for houses with kitchen and living-room on the ground floor and the bedrooms upstairs (Gittus, 1976; Newson and Newson, 1976). German dwelling habits, on the other hand, seem to be more like the Swedish, as far as the children's use of the living-room is concerned (Oesterle-Schwerin, 1976; Zinn, 1973).

Although the parents usually did not want the children to play in the living-room, they had some understanding that play could require a lot of space. In one-child families living in two-bedroom flats, the child usually got the smallest bedroom, whereas in half of the households with two-bedroom flats and two or more children the children were given the largest bedroom. Figure 12.1 shows two of the dwelling types in the investigation, marked with the children's main areas.

What Did the Children Play at Home?

The children's activities were recorded from a check-list which included activities representative of all-round play. The term 'all-round play' is a description of the various contents of play according to developmental theory. This description can be made in many different ways according to the aim of the study. (See Figure 12.2.)

Figure 12.3 shows the types of play in which the children had taken part at least once during the week previous to the interview. Almost all children had watched television, drawn with a pencil, looked at books, and listened to stories and music some time during the last week. Somewhat fewer children played with building blocks, Lego, cars or trains, built a tent or hut, played mother and child, or painted. The least frequent activities during the last week were cards, chequers, playing music, carpentry, playing with a pet and riding a tricycle.

The parents were also asked to name the three activities that the children had been doing most often ('Often last week', Figure 12.3). Playing with building blocks, Lego, cars or trains had been one of the most common activities for about half of the children, as was drawing for almost as many of them. A quarter of the children often played with dolls and looked at books. Hardly any children at all, however, had played often with balls, danced or done gymnastics, climbed or played on a swing, baked or cooked, played cards, chequers, etc., or made music.

It is clear that passive, receptive activities were very common among the children in the investigation, while active play was more uncommon. The least common were the really noisy and messy activities. This issue will be raised again in the discussion of the results in view of developmental theory.

The diaries were mainly used to study how often the children changed activities during the day. The twelve diary children changed occupation on average every ten minutes. This does not mean that they changed at that pace all the time: sometimes they changed every minute, sometimes they could be occupied by the same activity for up to twenty minutes or half an hour. They often broke off an activity

Figure 12.1: Two of the Dwellings in the Investigation

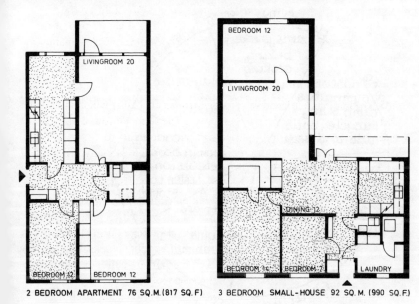

2 BEDROOM APARTMENT 76 SQ.M.(817 SQ.F)   3 BEDROOM SMALL-HOUSE 92 SQ.M. (990 SQ.F.)

for a short while, to eat or to play with something else, but they would usually return to the same activity many times during the day. Quite often they had more than one activity going on at the same time in different parts of the room or the dwelling. This occurred more often for children with more available space, than for children with less available space. As a result it is impossible to clean up between each game; the toys must remain where they are. Most parents did not bother to clean up during the day, but before bedtime they wanted the toys to be put away. Making room for many games at the same time puts great demands on children, parents, and the shape and size of the room. These demands become even greater if two or more children share the same bedroom. Conflicts occurred many times between the children when they wanted to do different things or when the younger destroyed what the older had built up.

What Did the Children Do Together with Adults?

In earlier societies, it was natural for children to participate in adult work. As soon as possible, they had to be useful in household work.

Figure 12.2: All-round Play Activities in the Investigation

Carrying fuel, looking after smaller children and watching the cattle were common chores for children. Today the economic necessity of such chores is of little importance. Lately, however, the pedagogical importance of children's participation in adult activities has been pointed out (even if, of course, nobody wants child labour back). Children need not merely play with toys, but should also take part in useful activities together with adults, for instance household work or gardening. Within the Swedish preschool training programme, this is called 'everyday pedagogics'.

The children in the investigation participated sporadically in adult activities, more often the mother's than the father's. Half of the children at some time during the week had participated in baking or cooking; a third had helped with laundry, laying the table or washing up; and a third with cleaning and putting away toys. Of the father's activities, a quarter of the children had worked with him at the family's weekend cottage, in the garden or on the car, and a tenth with carpentry or repair. Only 7 per cent had participated in the father's

Figure 12.3: Proportion of Children Who Engaged in Activity

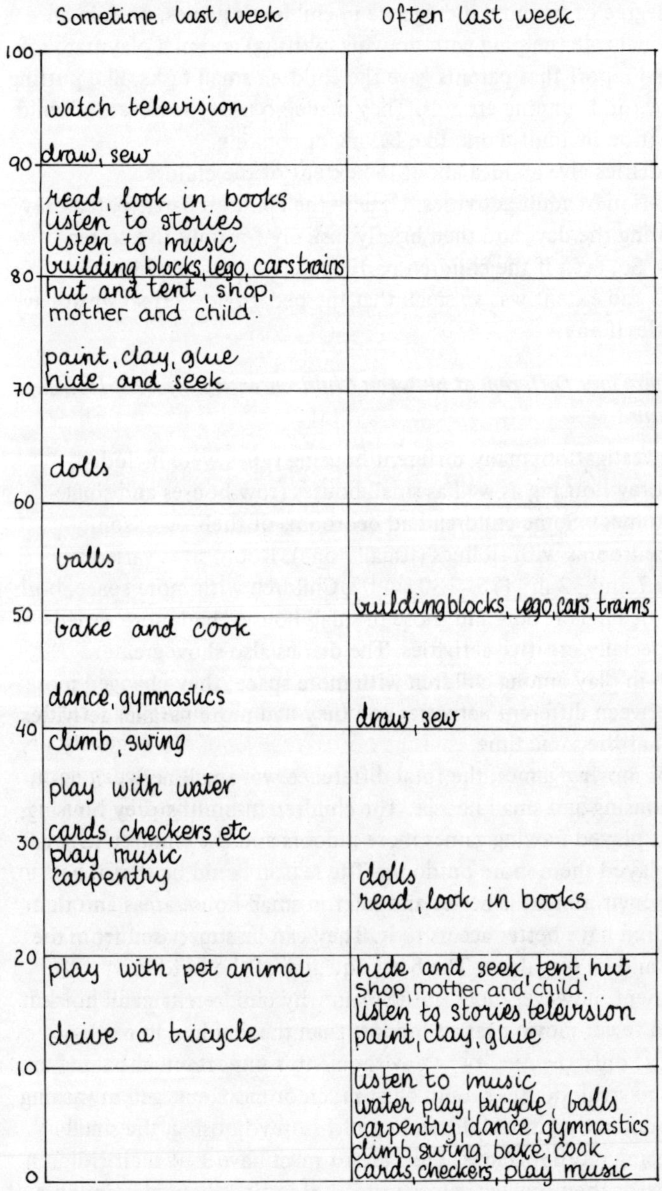

Sometime last week	Often last week
100	
watch television	
90 draw, sew	
read, look in books	
listen to stories	
listen to music	
80 building blocks, lego, cars trains	
hut and tent, shop,	
mother and child.	
paint, clay, glue	
70 hide and seek	
dolls	
60	
balls	
50	building blocks, lego, cars, trains
bake and cook	
dance, gymnastics	
40 climb, swing	draw, sew
play with water	
cards, checkers, etc	
30 play music	
carpentry	dolls
	read, look in books
20 play with pet animal	hide and seek, tent, hut
	shop, mother and child.
drive a tricycle	listen to stories, television
	paint, clay, glue
10	listen to music
	water play, tricycle, balls
	carpentry, dance, gymnastics
0	climb, swing, bake, cook
	cards, checkers, play music

household work. A fifth of the children had not done anything with their parents during the last week. Newson and Newson (1976) report a high degree of parental indulgence in children's games, both in an educational role (helping with drawing, writing) and in a playmate role. They also report that parents gave the children small tasks, like putting away toys and running errands. They made no note, however, of child participation in adult work, like baking or cooking.

The diaries give an idea about the extent of the children's participation in adult activities. Usually the children participated only once during the day, and then briefly, usually for only five to ten minutes. So, even if the children participated once in a while, the duration and extent was so small that the pedagogical effect must have been little, if any.

Were There any Differences between Children with Different Housing Conditions?

In the investigation, many different housing types were included, multi-storey housing as well as small houses (row-houses and single-family homes). Some children had bedrooms of their own; some shared bedrooms with siblings (usually one). Room sizes varied between 7 and 12 m^2 (75–130 sq. ft). Children with more space, both those with single rooms and those in small houses, had more varied play, especially creative activities. The diaries also show greater variation in play among children with more space; they changed more often between different activities and they had more parallel activities going on at the same time.

As for moving games, the total difference was small between multi-storey housing and small houses. The children in multi-storey housing, however, played moving games more indoors and the children in small houses played them more outdoors. The reason could be that the outdoor environment is better and safer in small-house areas and that the children have better access to it. They can be supervised from the window and be out alone. The better quality of the outdoor environment, however, does not explain why children in small houses engage in fewer moving games indoors than the children in multi-storey housing. If only the quality of environment is important, the children in small houses should be as much or more engaged in moving games indoors than the children in multi-storey housing, the small houses being more spacious. The parents must have sent their children outdoors for their moving games instead of letting them play indoors as well.

The explanation of the differences between children living in different housing types must be twofold: more space invites more varied and creative play, but parental attitudes are equally important in deciding the suitable form and extent of play.

Evaluation of the Results

The activities examined in the investigation can be grouped according to their requirements on the surroundings, the physical environment and the adults' patience. The results fit into the following pattern. The activities that put the least demands on space and the adults were the most common (e.g., watching television, drawing, reading and looking at books, listening to stories, playing with building blocks, Lego, cars or trains, and playing with dolls). Less common were the activities that put somewhat greater demands on the dwelling and the adults (e.g., listening to music, building a hut or a tent, painting, playing hide and seek, baking and cooking). The activities that put the greatest demands on the dwelling and the adults were also the least common (e.g,, playing with balls, dancing and gymnastics, climbing and swinging, playing with water except when bathing, playing music, carpentry, riding a tricycle).

From developmental psychology and particularly cognitive theory, it is known that all activities are equally important, that it is important for children to engage in many different types of activities. For concept training, children need both to draw or paint and to do carpentry, both to listen to music and to play music, to do both quiet things and more lively things, to be both neat and messy. The active manipulation and exploration of concrete objects in early childhood create the foundation from which children can progress towards theoretical thinking in adolescence. For Piaget, active exploration of the physical environment is the basic requirement for the child's developmental process. This process is piecemeal: children assimilate from their environment that which they can adapt to their earlier experience. At the same time, the pattern of their earlier knowledge is accommodated to a better coherence with their new experience.

If the child's free investigation of the environment is stopped or held back, however, the whole developmental process will be disturbed.[1] On the other hand, the richer and more complex children's collected experiences are, the better they can deal with abstract problems when they get older.

During the children's exploration and manipulation of their environment, they come into conflict with adult rules and goals for upbringing. If, for example, the living environment is unsuitably formed, dangerous, too small or restricted, the parents have to put many limits on children's activity. If conflict and aggression are solved through discipline and obedience, that may become the rule for the child's own actions when an adult (Zinn, 1973). Even if the parents' goals for upbringing, social group, work situation and childhood are more important factors for socialization, it is beyond doubt that the physical environment also has importance in forming the child's personality.

The children in the investigation had been occupied mainly with quiet and passive activities. This means that they had been restricted in their manipulation and exploration of the environment and that they did not get all the concrete experiences which they needed. Developmental psychologists would say that these restrictions do not come from within the children themselves; children have a natural curiosity to try everything with which they come into contact. The restrictions lie outside the child both in a uniform and limited environment and in the adults' rule systems. Psychologists also state that the consequences are twofold: cognitive and social (Zinn, 1973).

For example, children's participation in baking and cooking can be studied. Half of the children had done this at some time, but very few had participated in such household work continuously. On the other hand, this activity is available all the time in the home. It is also extremely well suited from a pedagogical standpoint. In household work, children can do meaningful things together with adults, learn co-operation and take responsibility. In addition, they will see the results of their work, which is not so common in other child activities. Kitchen work also includes many things that offer useful early training for children, e.g., motor activities (stir, sweep, pour), explorative activities (different kinds of food and their preparation, hot-cold, moist-dry, hard-soft) and creative activities (kneading and forming of dough).

One reason the children are not as active in the kitchen as would be desirable is that the kitchen is not designed to meet their requirements. Another is the adult lack of knowledge about how important it is to let children participate in cooking. If small children are to prepare food, an adult must stand beside them as they cannot manage on their own. They must share the working surface, which in Swedish kitchens is located between stove and sink. This working surface is designed for one person's effective work (size 80 cm x 60 cm or 32 inches x 24 inches). Very small children work best if they sit on the working surface, but this is not very safe. Somewhat older children have to stand on a chair to reach, but this is also bothersome, for example when something in one of the drawers under the working surface is needed. (Down from the chair, away with the chair, get the needed things from the drawer, back with the chair and up again.) Mess and flour on the floor are unavoidable.

Other working surfaces in the kitchen also involve problems. The kitchen table may be occupied by other things or must be cleared for laying. The adult may not feel inclined or have time to move his work from his regular working place as soon as the children want to participate. Under circumstances like these, both patience and conviction are needed if the children are to be continuously allowed to participate in daily food preparation. For a busy parent, it is easier to send the children to their rooms or to ask them to take care of simple chores like laying the table or running errands.

Even if the housing standard today in industrialized countries is high, compared to the housing standard in the past, present housing and housing areas lack much of the variation that earlier — especially rural — environments had. Before, children had access to many types of buildings, areas and activities in barns, workshops, etc. Many adults were occupied with varied types of work close to the home. Children also took on responsibility for certain chores at an early age. Today housing is separated from working; in that way, housing areas have become uniform and stereotyped, both outdoors and indoors. As the environment is so free from variations, the possibilities for a varied and active play are limited. The active exploration of the environment becomes restricted. The lack of adult work close to home also contributes to passive play, as the children lack adult models to imitate. Even in the adult work that still remains in the home, the children are not allowed to participate as much as would be desirable.

Conclusion

The consequences following from the results of this investigation are of two kinds. One is that children's access to space must be improved. The other is that parents require more knowledge about children's needs in the home as well as in the neighbourhood. In countries with a cold or wet climate, the improvement of children's indoor conditions is, of course, more important than in countries where children spend most of their time outdoors.

Children need free space for their play indoors. What is left over between beds, table and wardrobe in a small bedroom is not enough.

Even the simplest games require a floor area of about 2 m x 2 m (6 ft x 6 ft). If two or more children should play different games at the same time, they need a larger floor area than that, for instance 2 m x 3 m (6 ft x 10 ft). Swedish housing standards do not include any floor area at all for play. German housing standards require 1.2 m x 1.8 m (4 ft x 6 ft) in the children's bedroom or in the dining area (DIN 18011). Norwegian guidelines, which are not official standards, suggest a free floor area for play in the bedroom of 1.4 m x 2.5 m (5 ft x 8 ft). These guidelines also state that an adult playing around on the floor with the child needs 2.4 m x 3.0 m (6 ft x 10 ft) so that 'the play should not end with crying and a bump on the forehead' (Svennar, 1975).

The kitchen too needs greater floor area for children's play. Small children especially prefer to play close to a parent wherever he/she is working. The kitchen working surface must be designed not only for effective adult work, but also for children's participation. The main working surface must be large enough and located in such a way that drawers and cupboards are not hidden by the chair that children stand on.

Better indoor play conditions could be created in different ways. One way is simply to enlarge dwellings to include floor area for play in bedrooms and kitchen. Another is to redistribute the available floor area and diminish the adult part of the dwelling in favour of the children's part. Single-family homes and row-houses especially have lately become much larger, but this growth has mainly taken place in living-rooms and parents' bedrooms. This tendency has to be re-examined in view of children's needs. A third way is to add a neighbourhood centre to the housing area. During the day it can be used by children and parents for common activities — playing in large rooms, working with paint, clay and carpentry — and serve as a meeting place for children and parents, etc. In the evenings it can be open for adolescent and grown-up activities. A fourth way is to give all children access to preschool activities in day-care centres. The way to improve children's indoor space conditions depends of course on many factors, for instance energy forecasting, female employment and local traditions.

The results of the investigation showed that most parents did not want their children to play in the living-room or the parents' bedroom. This was true even for dwellings with quite large living-rooms and small bedrooms. The conclusion is that no general improvement will benefit the children unless adult attitudes towards children's play are changed. In parental education it is, therefore, important that information on children's need for play space and their need to explore the environment are included. Information should also be spread about how the home can be furnished to suit the wishes and needs of all family members, adults as well as children.

Note

1. 'Wenn das Handeln fehlt, versagt auch die Anshauung.' (Piaget and Inhelder, 1971).

References

Björklid-Chu, Pia. 1974. *Kartläggning av barns aktiviteter inom två moderna förortsområden. (Mapping of child activities in two modern neighbourhoods.)* Stockholm: National Swedish Institute for Building Research.

Dahlén, Uno. 1977. *Småhusbarnen. (The small-house children.)* Stockholm.

Gaunt, Louise. 1977. *158 småbarns bostadsanvändning. (The dwelling habits of 158 small children.)* Stockholm: National Swedish Institute for Building Research, Bulletin M1977: 1.

Gittus, Elizabeth. 1976. *Flats, families and the under-fives.* London: Routledge and Kegan Paul.

Newson, John and Elizabeth Newson. 1976. *Four years old in an Urban Community.* London: Pelican.

Oesterle-Schwerin. 1976. *Mit Kindern wohnen.* Wiesbaden und Berlin: Bauverlag GMBH.

Piaget, J. and B. Inhelder. 1971. *Die Entwicklung des räumlichen Denkens beim Kinde.* Stuttgart.

Statens Institut for Byggnadsforskning. 1977. Arsbok.

Svennar, Elsa. 1975. *Boligens planløsning.* Oslo: Håndbok 25, Norges Byggforsknings-institutt.

Zinn, Hermann. 1973. *Familie-Wohnbereich-Städteplanung.* Monatschrift für Kinderheilkunde, Jg 121.

13 HOW HIGH SHALL WE RISE? THE GREAT UNANSWERED QUESTION

Otto Weininger

Introduction

For a variety of reasons, there has recently been a drastic slowdown in the building of high-rise apartments in North America. Whether or not much more housing of this type will be built is not clear. What is clear is that a large number of families with children are going to have to continue to live in high-rise apartments.

This slowdown — this opportunity even temporarily to avoid committing ourselves to a controversial form of housing — can provide a chance at least to pause briefly and look objectively at what has been created in the past decade-and-a-half before plunging ahead with more of the same.

The question that needs to be asked is: what does high-rise living do to people, especially children?

It is essential to stop assuming that negative proof is the only proof acceptable. By this I mean that it is foolhardy at best to wait around for one of every three high-rise children to become psychotic, or two of every five fathers to testify to feeling emasculated, or three of every four mothers of preschool children to leave footprints on the walls before being carted away. One should be asking for positive proof of an improvement in the human condition resulting directly from high-rise living before one gives up the fight and lets the developers take over all the towns. The rationale always given for having a nice single-family house in the suburbs is that it gives children room to play, fathers room to putter, mothers room to breathe, families room to learn to enjoy each other without intense pressures in terms of space.

Given that it is no longer economically feasible in terms of land and construction costs — not to mention space and travel time — for every family in a city the size of Toronto to have its own home, alternatives need to be found. That does not mean that the first experiment, the high-rise, should be accepted as the only alternative, the finished, no-questions-to-ask, absolute winner suggestion. Alternatives must certainly be feasible on economic grounds, but if people are to live in them, or if other people are forced to live in them (which should be the same thing, but is not, somehow; the average developer surely does not subject *his* family to a raw, twelfth-floor, windswept, high-rise development), then it must be ensured that the alternatives fit people's needs, rather than building first and then squeezing the edges off people to fit into them.

Review of the Literature

So what do people want in terms of fit? It is not true now (if it ever was) that every family dreams of a house in the suburbs. Many people like living downtown; others prefer the country; some do not like lawns and gardens and cannot stand the large numbers of children that suburban living entails; others want or need to be close to their job, or to a particular hospital, relative or even hobby. What people want is what fits them — not 'the typical Canadian middle-income family of four' — but *them*: some place they can change to fit all the curves and oddities of their particular requirements. This important point will be returned to later.

The study done for the Board of Education in North York[1] in September 1971 by Crawford and Virgin (1971) began with this question: do pupils who live in high-rise apartments demonstrate lower performance on measures of academic and social skills than pupils who live in single-family homes? They carefully chose their criteria as follows:

1. one-half from grade five, one-half from grade one;
2. one-half male, one-half female at each grade level;
3. one-half lived with both parents in apartment at each grade level; one-half lived with both parents in single-family dwelling at each grade level;
4. apartment dwellers lived above fourth floor;
5. the area was comprised mainly of middle-income families.

Each pupil completed the vocabulary, reading and mathematics sections of the Metropolitan Achievement Test (MAT), a self-appraisal inventory and four motor ability tests. In addition, each student was rated by the teacher in terms of eight dimensions of his/her social behaviour within the classroom, and the grade-five students completed a questionnaire on the amount of time they spent in various out-of-school activities.

By and large, the results of this exceedingly well-planned study showed no real differences except in the area of motor development (grade-one boys from single-family homes scored higher in agility, running and balance items). No difference in sports participation was shown, however. Boys in apartments, as might be expected, helped with fewer chores, and children, especially boys, in apartments watched a little more television, and seemed to play outside more and inside less. Perhaps they simply played less, period. Boys listed swimming, the playgrounds, and playing in the halls as advantages of apartment living, the elevators and noise restrictions and unpleasant superintendents as disadvantages; the girls listed swimming, being close to friends, the balcony as advantages, but complained of lack of space and rules forbidding pets and seemed more sure than boys that they would like houses better. The authors of the study comment that, although there are obviously no gross pathologies associated with living in a middle-class high-rise, there could be problems more subtle than a measuring device could detect. They also note that there are often far greater differences between children in two different apartments than between children in high-rise and single-family dwellings. This point will be returned to later, as well.

Dr Ph. H. Fieldelij Dop[2] described a study done in Amsterdam which also brings forth some interesting points. It was found that 30 per cent of apartment children showed difficulties in arithmetic in the primary grades, especially in the area of space perception: understanding distances, size and three-dimensional relationships. This was related to problems in co-ordination, body image and identity. Another finding was that less construction play goes on with apartment children; two-year-olds seemed to play at putting materials into cupboards rather than building things – they seemed to be taught to be 'tidy'. When asked what they do when they play, children in the four-to-seven-year range said they were 'supposed to play on the street', as there was not much space for playing except in the organized playgrounds, which they did not like, and that they were bored. This may partly be because architects often do not understand the needs of young children for play space; they assume the needs, build to them, and as a result the space is not used by children as it was intended. Moreover, parents seem to fear more for their children when they cannot see them at ground level – the result is less freedom to play, use of a more circumscribed area, such as a playground, and less time for play. The effects are that children have more trouble concentrating and lack the experiences necessary for optimum learning and growth.

The Amsterdam study also found that adolescent rebellion was

ghtened and that school was used as a scapegoat for hostility toward
hority due to lack of privacy both in terms of space and personal
ssures. Normal adolescent fantasies are heightened to the point
ere the child tries to act out his/her fantasy in generally
-destructive ways.

An earlier study, by Kumove (1966), indicated that there was
reasing emasculation of the male due to the absence of work space
 the traditional role of fixing appliances and other home-oriented
res. Small children, imprisoned because they could not reach the
vator button, were tied to their mother's apron-strings for too long,
ich could, by extending the weaning syndrome, cause greater
enile delinquency and gang participation in later life. Loneliness and
nation were the chief hallmarks of those he studied.

An article in the *Montreal Star* in 1969, discussing Vancouver and
'cube children', quotes a group worker in a high-rise area:

Children here are totally oriented to being indoors. I recently took
a group of small boys down to the woods to play commander; and
though they said, 'Is it alright to go where you can't see us?' I knew
they meant, 'I don't want to go where I can't see you.'

lescription of a Christmas party for these same children is bleak:

Undisciplined, extremely hyperactive, they darted about like
mindless molecules. Confronting one another for, at most, a minute
or two, they would stand and stare, then begin running again. The
wonderful world of child communication has passed them by. They
do not know how to play.

Other information on the effects of high-rise living comes from
ious workers in the fields of sociology and urban development.
ppon (1971), one of the foremost critics of high-rise life, sees many
blems as arising from apartment-life deprivations: a stifling factor
 noisy play, a lack of outlets for aggression, a lack of chances for
etic development, passivity because of time and effort required to
 to the ground, a struggle for identity in the 'massive sameness',
rly socialized children due to their proximity to tense and irritable
lts, fewer neighbourhood peers and activities, nothing for
lescents to do — with a resulting tendency to escapism and a high
dalism rate — great feelings of replaceability and an insecure dwarf
ge leading to poorly developed egos due to the inhuman scale of the

high-rise. His conclusion appears to be that high-rise living may lead to anti-social children, males deprived of normal masculine outlets and adults who become passive watchers of television.

All these factors common to high-rises are greatly intensified by the pressures of low-income living. Fabian Jennings, who works with children in St James Town,[3] was quoted in April 1971:

> It is really getting to the children. They have such hostility and tension to overcome before you can even get through to them. They live in a keyed up environment. They live in concrete. There is no grass. What do you expect? They respond to their environment. (*Toronto Telegram*, 1971)

He sees children as unable to get along with him, with their parents and teachers, unable to play team sports without great hostility and fighting, constantly testing adult limits, lying shamelessly, defensive and unhappy.

Vera Denty (*Toronto Star*, 1971), a psychologist at Scarborough Mental Health Clinic, reported that space limitations, as well as affecting the children who have no backyards to play in, affect the mothers who 'feel that the walls are coming in on them'. She sees this as extremely draining and says such mothers feel isolated and alone.

The Nature of the Problem

So back to the problem — how does society go about making houses for people? Beneath all this information, much of it easily and immediately available in more informal ways — like going and talking to any three or four families in any high-rise building about their complaints, dissatisfactions and hopes — is discernible one slightly less obvious but, I feel, crucial issue. The North York school board study noted that differences between children in two different families or two different apartment buildings were often far greater than those between house children and apartment children. It is suggested that this gnaws at the edges of the problem underneath the questions about high-rise living, the problem of making houses fit people.

The hypothesis presented here is that high-rise living accentuates, intensifies and magnifies existing problems within families and within the community at large; thus one family may be quite comfortable in a high-rise, and not feel their children are hard done by, providing other outlets are available for their play — long vacations, day camp, YMCA membership, family outings and so forth. This family may have strong friendships to sustain them, an adequate income, perhaps extended family living nearby, a car with which to get away from it all, a father satisfied in his job and secure in his relationships with his wife and children, a wife who either enjoys staying at home or is occupied, part-time or full-time, in something she finds fulfilling and with no worries about the care her children are receiving. In short, this family is functioning truly as a family and would probably be just as happy wherever they were living — within reason, of course.

At the other end of the spectrum is, perhaps, the single parent, raising children on his/her own, always short of time and money, harassed by the tension of working full-time, worrying about where the children are, guilty about shortchanging the children, lonely and missing someone to share the burdens of housekeeping and child-rearing, without a family close at hand, with few friends outside the family because he/she feels different and spends what little time when not working with the children. The parent is starved, emotionally and materially, and often so are the children. Life would not be easy for this family under any circumstances and the isolation and sameness and lack of friendly neighbours and play space of an apartment just make it that much worse.

Between these two poles are the thousands of families living in high-rise apartments in Toronto. As their circumstances differ, so do their reactions to the inconveniences and/or deprivations of apartment life. The mother of two preschool children who does not know any of her neighbours, either from shyness or from newness, may view the winter and the apartment as her enemies, out to destroy her sanity; she may be right. The mother of two preschool children who has a friend with children down the hall to talk to, complain to, share with, laugh with and swap children with for shopping and emergencies, may feel the winter is gone almost before it starts.

Some Possible Solutions

People's needs must determine how they are going to live, where and with whom — not money, or lack of it, not high-rise developers destroying any other possibility in their drive for profits. The supports must be made available to strengthen family life in whatever setting people want and need. Instead of stuffing people, choiceless, into slabs of concrete in identical little cubes on long, impersonal hallways full of closed doors and antiseptic smells and superintendents who go 'shhh!!', cat-less and dog-less and children's noise-less, it is necessary to apply pressure to developers and governments, and approach them armed with long lists of things to make apartment living — if it is indeed economically necessary — more responsive to the needs of the people living in it. A few essentials suggest themselves immediately; some might be expensive, some impractical, many doubtless inconvenient for property managers; but that is not the author's concern, nor should it be theirs.

1. Buildings built around open space (instead of surrounded by it) forming a safe courtyard large enough for children to play in.

2. Fewer formal gardens; more wild grass, tall grass, rocks, trees and sand for children — no concrete playgrounds with high, wire fences.

3. Staggered layout apartments, perhaps two-storey apartments, for greater internal space more easily adjusted to individual family needs.

4. Fewer long corridors and central elevator banks; more four to six-storey buildings where one can walk up and down to different entrances, with only five or six apartments on a hallway. Maybe even different coloured doors!

5. Big playrooms on each floor; a huge room (or rooms) with perhaps a small kitchen, like college dorms have, so that groups of mothers could gather with their children, enjoying lots of space for running and things to climb on without worrying about the noise; space for teenagers to congregate and listen to records, for men to have space to paint or refinish furniture. At least the amount of space equal to one apartment on each floor, bright and comfy, the joint responsibility of all the neighbours together — not a professionally run recreation centre a block away with a room for everything and over-organized activites for everyone.

6. Laundry rooms, small, on every floor, and a co-op nursery and day-care centre at nominal or subsidized cost in every building, including lunch-time and after-school care and hot lunches for school-age children.

7. Much less emphasis on rules for the sake of rules, especially about pets, decorating apartments, hanging things on walls, bringing tricycles and prams into buildings, children making noise in corridors, and not walking on the grass.

8. Much more emphasis on communal responsibility for common areas, on helping new tenants to get to know others.

9. Rents strictly controlled so that they do not exceed the one quarter of people's incomes recommended by most economists. In Toronto today, rents are much closer to one-half of many people's incomes without fulfilling basic space and personal needs.

10. More flexibility in renting practices: why cannot two women, both separated with children, share one apartment or house and make their own arrangements about working and child care without landlord interference or petty zoning regulations? Or two men? Or four working women? Or two older retired ladies? Or six college students of both sexes? Why not apartment buildings that reflect the cross-section of life in a big city instead of being virtually ghettos of young families with children, abandoned, as are most suburbs, by all males over 16 during daylight hours?

Conclusion

These are just a few of the many suggestions that the thousands of people now living in apartments could present if anyone cared enough to ask them. No changes, of course, would make apartment living amenable to everyone, but at least if some attempt is made to change current building and living patterns a greater variety of style can be offered to everyone than at present. Perhaps one more step could be taken to stop the endless haggling, the 'Yes it does hurt people – no it doesn't hurt people' war. The question has been answered for anyone who really wants to look at it honestly; high-rise living rubs on many people like an ill-fitting and unwanted shoe. Now the real question must be posed and answers found fast, before it is too late. How can houses and apartments be built to fit people better?

Notes

1. Suburb of Metropolitan Toronto.
2. Personal communication, 1971.
3. A large high-rise apartment complex in Toronto which contains some subsidized buildings for low-income families.

References

Cappon, Daniel. 1971. 'Mental health in the high-rise', *Canadian Journal of Public Health*, 62, 5, pp. 426–31.

Crawford, Patricia and A. E. Virgin. 1971. *The Effects of High-Rise Living on School Behaviour.* Totonto: North York Board of Education Research Department.

Kumove, Leon. 1966. 'Nobody starves', *Canadian Welfare*, September/October, 42, pp. 198–201 and 203–6.

Montreal Star. 31 May 1969. Article on Vancouver and its 'cube' children.

Toronto Star. 26 June 1971. Article on joyful but difficult time experienced by mother of preschoolers, described by Vera Denty, a psychologist at Scarborough Mental Health Clinic.

Toronto Telegram. 13 April 1971. Article about interview with Fabian Jennings, who worked with children who live in St James Town, in which he asserts there is just no real place for kids to play.

14 CHILDREN'S PLAY IN INDOOR SPACES: FOCUS ON HIGH-RISE

Anne-Marie Pollowy

Problematique and Objectives

The problem examined in this paper concerns the lack of recognition of and provision for young children's activities within the body of multi-family dwelling units, particularly as it applies to high-rise apartment buildings above three storeys in height.[1] This condition most seriously affects families and children who live in restricted and restrictive high-rise dwellings where children's activities are restrained and developmentally limited by:

1. the lack of space within the dwelling;
2. the lack of adequate acoustic separation between dwellings;
3. the lack of planned activity spaces within the proximity of the dwelling;
4. the lack of adequate integration of functional, acoustic and visual relations among the various semi-public spaces, in terms of children's activity requirements;
5. the unsafe use of semi-public areas such as corridors, elevator waiting areas, laundry and public storage facilities.

Why is there a need to focus on this problem when there are already other overwhelming social issues — such as a shortage of decent housing, crime and inflation — which are apparently more important? There are two major reasons:

1. Consciousness of the problem and of its possible resolutions can lead to a child-oriented consideration of spaces within any specific dwelling and within semi-public areas among the dwellings. It may be possible to satisfy children's developmental requirements — to increase and improve effective space allocation for children's activities — without incurring considerable additional expenditures.
2. There appears to be a possible overlap between child-oriented design and crime-preventive design. This dual response to two critical conditions has been suggested by Newman's (1972) studies of

criminal activities in high-rise public housing projects. He indicates an increase in the crime rate with increased building height, and a preponderance of crimes within the body of the buildings. According to Newman (p. 32), 'a criminal probably perceives that the interior public areas of the building are where his victims are most vulnerable, and where the possibility of his being seen or apprehended is minimal.' As an alternative, he suggests reducing the size of interior public spaces or electronically monitoring them. He also mentions, all too briefly, the possibility of altering interior semi-public spaces within the framework of a comprehensive design for children.

Within the context of this problematique, the objectives of this paper are:

1. to identify some of the historical and cultural conditions that have led society to ignore child-oriented high-rise design;
2. to identify some mechanisms for the implementation of child-oriented design;
3. to identify available design knowledge and information that can assist in resolving the problems in existing developments and prevent them in future ones.

Historical and Cultural Conditions of the High-rise

In the early nineteenth century, the major cities of the northwestern United States were still bright and airy, particularly in comparison with most Western European cities of the period. This condition did not last. By 1830, areas of New York were noted for their misery, filth and overcrowding. Outbreaks of typhoid, dysentery, typhus and cholera were common, and malaria and consumption killed many city dwellers. The victims were most frequently immigrants, whose influx created a drastic housing shortage in the cities. Immigrants clustered in the areas of the burgeoning factories where houses were converted to tenements and the intense housing shortage caused the rental of basements, attics and lofts. As immigration expanded, the cellar-dwelling population increased. The increasing number of urban residents necessitated the development of additional housing. Two major trends took place: the affluent escaped from the city; and the immigrants and poor workers were housed in tenements.

The development of mass public transportation led to the rise of the first suburbs. Promoters emphasized the advantages of suburban life in areas 'unsurpassed for healthfulness, removed from the smoke and dust of the city, enjoying pure air and wholesome water'. The swell of the affluent population's move out of the city can best be demonstrated by looking at two examples: (1) by the 1870s Chicago had about 100 suburbs with an aggregate population of 50,000; and (2) between 1870 and 1900 the suburban Boston population increased from 60,000 to 227,000 (Glaab and Brown, 1967). In a study of Boston, Warner (1962) comments on this pattern of suburbanization:

> To be sure, the costs of new construction were such as to exclude at least half the families of Boston; but the suburban half, the middle class, was the dominant class in the society. To middle class families, the suburbs gave a safe, sanitary environment, new houses in styles somewhat in keeping with their conception of family life, and temporary neighborhoods of people with similar outlook.

While the hope of relief from urban congestion was realized for the upper and middle classes, conditions were not alleviated for the immigrant or the poor worker as the poorer districts of many cities continued to show an increase in density of population even after the general introduction of street cars (Glaab and Brown). Contemporary social conditions and economic conditions, where annual returns from 10 per cent to 20 per cent were common on rental property and annual returns as high as 40 per cent were possible, encouraged new methods of housing and innovations in building. The demand and the lack of supply encouraged urban property owners to make maximum use of valuable urban land sites (Glaab and Brown). These conditions led to the infamous tenements, the precursors of the contemporary constricting high-rises. An extreme case, New York, had 43,700 tenements housing 1,585,000 people by 1900.

This optimization of economic gains at the expense of the poorer segment of the population could easily be explained away on social and moralistic grounds. Historically, most members of the upper classes found poverty and the social structure of the cities 'natural and proper' and, despite their regret about prevailing conditions, it was obvious to them that the poorer segments of the population were of lower moral character. Thus, for them, tenements and high-rises were linked with a morally inferior population and with a sanitarily inferior way of life. This ideology reinforced the desirability of the single-family suburban house (the house owned by the opinion makers who establish the ideological norms) which thus became a material symbol of moral (and economic) superiority and a desired goal for inner-city residents. Thus, high-rise housing developed in an historical association with housing for the disenfranchized; it became — and, for many, remained — a minimum shelter solution, ideologically and materially inferior to the suburban house.

Cultural Norms and Patterns

To understand the historical implications of high-rise housing for children, it is necessary to relate the historical context to the development and meaning of cultural norms. These norms are society- and time-specific standards that define that society's range of normative ideas, actions and material culture. They identify the set of interdependent beliefs, actions/interactions and technological state-of-the-art held by a community; they identify what is considered true or false, right or wrong, good or bad, etc. This set of interdependent beliefs also defines that society's range of conformity (i.e., what is considered 'normal') as well as its deviations (i.e., what is considered abnormal, 'unnatural', or 'unheard of'). These norms thus act as referents for everything people do, think or have — establishing patterns that constrain and limit that society's ideas, actions and technological alternatives at a given period in time. Thus, historical developments may in fact become normalized patterns, standards for ways of thinking, for the actions taken, and for the things people have or want. In these early periods of the high-rises in the United States, the patterns that were established and the norms or standards that were created became referents for today's actions, leading to the beliefs that high-rise dwelling was inferior to single-family housing and that children could not — or could not adequately — be raised in high-rise units. Both standards must be re-examined because of the reality of:

1. the increasing scarcity of land;
2. the increasing cost of single-family units;
3. continued high-rise development;
4. the number of children raised in high-rises.

It is the position of this paper that high-rises can potentially be extremely viable despite the fact that the current, traditional forms of the high-rise, within the contemporary socio-cultural context, may not be acceptable to a large percentage of the population within the contemporary set of ideological norms and standards.

Cultural Norms and Social Priorities

A society's or a community's priorities are related to its cultural norms, i.e., to its value structure. Of primary concern for the resolution of the identified problem is the priority of allocation of scarce resources, and, related to it, control over the selection of priorities and over the resource allocation process, i.e., what is provided for whom and with what conditions.

High-rise residents form an ideologically disenfranchised social sector of a society whose ideology is oriented toward the 'rightness' of the single-family dwelling. They also form a materially disenfranchised social sector in which the simple need for adequate housing is already a major issue; a social sector in which 'normative' play spaces such as parks or playgrounds are generally lacking, and in which the implementation of suitable alternatives such as vest-pocket parks gets entangled in the bureaucratic red tape. The problem of interior play spaces thus becomes but another issue to be added to the long list of shortages.

Given the long list of social priorities and the general anti-high-rise ideology, the problem of children's play in interior places may go unperceived by the authorities in a context in which adequate facilities and provisions are not part of the 'normative', standard amenities or requirements of housing designs. Even if perceived, it may not be a priority consideration unless its relative importance can be justified and documented. Since importance has been amply demonstrated from a purely developmental point of view as well as from a general user point of view,[2] what remains is the validation of this need in terms of the economic system and its priorities. Thus, the linkage between child-oriented design and crime-preventive design becomes critical, while children may not be given preference in resource allocation in terms of child spaces, a high-priority treatment is surely accorded to crime-reducing and crime-preventive designs for crimes against both people and property, designs that may assist in preventing continued ghetto approaches to the high-rise.

If the objective is implementation of adequate child spaces, it must also be realized that priorities and related policy are set at different levels of the political hierarchy and that policies at one level can — and frequently do — countermand policies or requirements set at a lower level. In this case, the traditional conflict of institutions versus the community — namely the bureaucracy versus the users — is often encountered. Obviously, the political hierarchy affects — or, more accurately, controls – some of the priorities that are established and also the allocation of public resources. Thus, one must deal with a potential trade-off of priorities that may lead to a trade-off of resources. How can this be achieved? From the institutional side, it must be assumed, again based on past performance, that while some priorities may attempt to deal with the provision of minimal 'decent' housing for all, this is not likely to include adequate considerations for children's needs. It must also be assumed that institutional priorities, in accordance with economic priorities, do deal with crime, particularly with crime against property. In terms of the concerned community, it must be assumed that its priorities deal much more specifically with the daily experience of decent housing, with crime prevention against people and property, and with child-rearing considerations. Thus, it may be assumed that a mutually satisfactory trade-off can be arrived at by encompassing child-need satisfaction in the larger but directly relevant and crucial issues of (1) decent housing, and (2) crime-preventive design. Strategies for implementation must be planned accordingly.

The Design of Alternatives – Focus on Process

In terms of the process, there are five components that have to be considered:

1. the provision of space and facilities for interior play spaces in high-rise housing;
2. the maintenance of these facilities;
3. the security of these facilities in terms of the children and in terms of protection from undesirable outsiders;
4. the supervision of these facilities;
5. the red tape involved in all of the above.

No attempt will be made here to detail what is involved in these five components of the process; they have been fully detailed by others in terms of playgrounds, adventure playgrounds, vest-pocket parks, etc. The principles are the same in most conditions. The focus here, however, will be on three types of processes that can be used for the resolution of any of the above five components and also for their integration; variations can be found within each of these processes, different organizational procedures can also be used and overlaps too may exist. For example, while one may be selected for the maintenance function, another may be selected for the supervisory function. These three processes consist of:

1. a process *for* the community — a traditional and often a directive
   approach in which a given group or organization possessing decision-
   making and financial control (e.g., the state or the city) attempts to
   provide for the users what it believes the users require;
2. a process *with* the community — in which the above-mentioned
   groups/organizations are actively involved with the user community
   in identifying requirements and in satisfying these requirements; and
3. a process *by* the community — in which the decision-making and
   management control over the process lies with the members of the
   community. Generally a process with and by the community can
   be closely related, and the decision-making and resource allocation
   control functions may shift depending on the phase of the general
   process. Many of the co-operative rehabilitation projects fall into
   these latter two categories and their success was frequently ensured
   only by the co-operative involvement of the community.

For a resolution of the problem identified, emphasis will be placed
on *with* and *by* approaches. The citizens' active involvement is
essential in all stages of the process, including the initial problem-
identification stage. They have to be involved because they alone can
adequately indicate their preferences, priorities and patterns of
behaviour — the critical elements of successful design and
implementation. Also, since they will be using — or not using — the
facilities, they must ensure through their daily behaviours that the
design does not become another white elephant. For this sort of
complete involvement and support one must turn to the successful
precedents of housing rehabilitation projects and vest-pocket parks.
Success can be said to depend on community involvement and on the
citizens' ability and willingness to deal with the alternatives required for
satisfactory results.

The Design of Alternatives — Focus on Product

The product is a facility or facilities for children within the housing
environment. There is no need to belabour the relationships between
behaviour and the physical environment, or the fact that spatial
conditions can encourage and facilitate, or constrain and limit, human
behaviour. Children's play activities are necessary to their development.
Play occurs in all places, whether these have been 'designed' for
children's play or not. Environmental design enters into the situation

only as a facilitator or inhibitor of children's activities, thus intervening in the satisfaction or frustration of both children and adults.

In the residential milieu, two factors affect the child/physical environment situation the most: the age of the child or his/her stage of development; and the dwelling type. Regarding child development, the design implications of physical growth patterns, of environmental cognition, of attachment behaviour, of exploratory behaviour, and of socializing behaviour have already been explored and researched. A summary of these findings and related design recommendations is also available (e.g., Pollowy, 1977a, 1977b). A review of the data indicates that exploration and spontaneous socialization opportunities are closely linked to each other and are particularly lacking in the high-rise setting. Environmentally, the sphere of action of children radiates from the dwelling, to its immediate vicinity, to the neighbourhood, and eventually to the entire community. Obviously, dwelling proximity and accessibility will be key factors in when and with whom children will play. In this period of early socialization, up to about school age, social and cognitive development through play with peers can be encouraged only if a child can have contact with other children and adults close to the home.

There have been a number of traditional responses to the problem of children's activities in high-rise settings. The most prevalent one simply ignores any attempt towards a resolution by supporting the ideology that children should not live in high-rises. Yet the high-rise population includes children. Thus, environmentally the problem exists and will continue to exist; wishing it away by ignoring it would only create a self-fulfilling prophecy. Other responses have included the provision of some public parks, playgrounds and, more recently, vest-pocket parks. Most newer high-rise developments also provide some outdoor recreational facilities for small children. In this vein, various agencies and publications, such as the Central Mortgage and Housing Corporation's (1978) *Play Spaces for Preschoolers*, provide guidelines for the design of ground-level outdoor facilities. Yet, one of the problems adults and children have is directly caused by these provisions being outdoors and at ground level: because of climatic considerations, because children's access to these places requires adult escort, and because children's activities require constant adult supervision away from the dwelling. Despite these factors, outdoor ground-level playgrounds are generally all there is, and this well-intentioned but limited solution is continually being perpetuated by various organizations and individuals as a holistic answer to the housing/play problem.

Child-specific environments provide a more adequate design response to children's activities, when these take place away from the residential setting. Child-specific spaces such as day-care centres, nurseries and kindergartens have been studied and design guidelines are numerous (e.g., Osmon, 1971). In more commercial situations, interior playgrounds have been established by profit-oriented enterprises such as shopping centres. Consequently precedents do exist for both interior play spaces and for play spaces in the residential high-rise setting. The objective is to combine the two in an attempt to provide a more adequate environment for children's activities.

The provision of facilities will not, however, automatically guarantee specific human behaviours. It is known that behaviour is culture-specific and, although one may know the general cultural context, given communities have their own sub-cultures that differ radically one from the other. As such, one cannot generalize too rapidly on environment—behaviour relations, particularly when these also involve cultural child-rearing patterns. For example, while some communities have a lively and rich street culture, in others people would not sit in front of their homes under any circumstances; some have an informal kitchen culture, while others would never consider entertaining anyone in the kitchen. These cultural variations of space usage also effect the children's use of space both within the dwelling and outside it (Pollowy, 1977a, 1977b). Each spatial use will now be examined.

Dwelling use is cultural and it varies with the age of the child and the number of children within the household. Consequently, the current rigidity of the dwelling space distribution seems to be antithetical to the requirements of a dynamically changing family situation. In terms of product, a community may, therefore, wish to explore some of the flexible housing alternatives that have been offered and that are technologically feasible, but the use of which are generally discouraged by vested interests. To reach these alternatives, however, the community needs adequate information – the provision of such information being the primary realm of the professional's responsibility. In addition to information regarding flexibility, the community must also have information regarding alternatives in the use of the space currently available to them. Here the professional's responsibility is the development of alternatives *with* the community and its members, to take advantage of the full potential that the physical environment may have to offer.

Literature also exists outlining some of the issues and problems that affect children in the semi-public realm of the housing development (e.g., Cooper-Marcus and Hogue, 1977; Newman, 1972; Pollowy, 1977a, 1977b). This literature may be used for the initial approach to the resolution of these problems since some design guidelines are suggested. Another rich body of literature, also extremely useful, deals with the design of spaces that have been traditionally child-specific. Some of the excellent publications pertaining to child-care centres (e.g., Osmon, 1971) may be particularly suitable, since they deal with the functional distribution of child and adult spaces, and with the interrelationships among these spaces. Much of this type of information is also within the domain of the playground designer. The critical issue then is the synthesis of these bodies of information and their dissemination to the community for use in the provision of play spaces in housing.

Implications

An attempt has been made to outline the problem of children's play in the indoor realm of the high-rise from both an historical/ideological stance and from the developmental, experiential stance. An attempt has also been made to indicate approaches for the resolution of this problem in terms of (1) available information; (2) possible resource trade-offs where crime-preventive design is a priority; and (3) implementation processes. These approaches lead to some specific tasks or objectives in terms of total implementation.

First, there is a need for the synthesis of available information with the focus on existing interior child spaces in high-rise housing.

Second, there is a need for an intensive survey of relevant crime-preventive designs in terms of their implications for the implementation of child spaces.

Third, there is a need for an equally intensive survey of community-based housing rehabilitation projects in terms of their consideration for and resolution of both the crime-prevention problem and the child-play problem. This undertaking seems particularly critical since the provision of facilities that will actually be used appears feasible only through the active involvement of the concerned community in the whole process of implementation. The community must be involved since play-space design has traditionally been design for communality, for social interaction — it is the design of culturally specific socializing space for both children and adults. It is also design that is able to identify and relate functional territories while encouraging the users' sense of affective territoriality. It is also design that encourages the mutual surveillance of the play environment by both the children and the adults. As such, it is design that could prove vitally important for the development of all types of communal spaces — it may be a vital initial step in the development of popular spatially communal alternative spaces.

Notes

1. Starting with low-rise dwellings, observations tend to indicate that a higher proportion of children under 11 years of age play outdoors in a low-rise setting than in either the mixed or the medium-rise setting. Generally, small children are more frequently allowed to play outside if they are within view of the dwelling (Cooper and Hackett, 1968). The most important contributing factor for playing outside for this age group seems to be ready and easy access.

2. For some reviews of the research literature see Cooper-Marcus and Hogue (1977) and Pollowy (1977a and 1977b).

References

Central Mortgage and Housing Corporation. 1978. *Play Spaces for Preschoolers.* Ottawa: Central Mortgage and Housing Corporation.

Cooper, C. and P. Hackett. 1968. *Analysis of the Design of Two Moderate Income Housing Developments.* Berkeley: Institute of Urban and Regional Development, University of California.

Cooper-Marcus, C. and L. Hogue. 1977. 'Design guidelines for high-rise family housing', in D. J. Conway (ed.), *Human Response in Tall Buildings.* Stroudsburg, Pennsylvania: Dowden, Hutchinson and Ross.

Glaab, C. N. and T. A. Brown. 1967. *A History of Urban America.* New York: Macmillan.

Newman, O. 1972. *Defensible Space.* New York: Macmillan.

Osmon, F. L. 1971. *Patterns for Designing Children's Centers.* New York: Educational Facilities Laboratories.

Pollowy, A. M. 1977a. *The Urban Nest.* Stroudsburg, Pennsylvania: Dowden, Hutchinson and Ross.

———— 1977b. 'Children in high-rise buildings', in D. J. Conway (ed.), *Human Response in Tall Buildings.* Stroudsburg, Pennsylvania: Dowden, Hutchinson and Ross.

Warner, S. B., Jr. 1962. *Streetcar Suburbs: The Process of Growth in Boston.* Cambridge: MIT and Harvard University Press.

15 CITY STREETS: THE CHILD'S IMAGE AS A BASIS FOR DESIGN

Galia Weiser

Introduction

The street is a world of experience and participation. But in our society it is no longer the milieu where vital contacts with other human beings and with the environment are laid. Only for the child, perhaps this is not so.

Tjeerd Deelstra

The urban street, due to current design approaches, is rapidly becoming a dull, sterile and sometimes even hostile environment. Although children do their best to prevent this process, it seems they cannot do so by themselves. The huge mechanism which determines the shape of the city is stronger. The result is, as Van Eyck (1968, p. 53) describes: 'A city which overlooks the child's presence is a poor place. Its movement will be incomplete and oppressive. The child cannot rediscover the city unless the city rediscovers the child.' The 'rediscovery' of the street, by the design of a more satisfactory environment, is especially important for children, because they 'live' in the street more than any other age group and their activities are limited to a relatively small area. This work is an attempt to help make the city street once again 'a world of experience and participation' for children, as well as for adults.

Children's Image of Their Street

The experience of 'being in the world' is a process through which man's relations with the physical environment are gradually developed. As a result, the nature of one's interaction with one's surroundings changes at the different stages of life. In order to be able to build an urban environment which is also satisfactory for children, it is necessary to understand their typical relations with it.

The design studies in this paper are based on the child's image of his/her street, as described in a previous research project (Weiser, 1977), which attempted to identify some significant design aspects of the relations between children and their immediate surroundings, in

225

Figure 15.1: Children 'Modify' Their Street

particular the street on which they live. The analysis of the data, collected from children in the fourth and sixth grades, living on three different streets in Haifa, Israel, led to the conclusion that children perceive and define the street on which they live in two different ways simultaneously. On the one hand, they are aware of the continuity of the 'objective' street and try to define it according to its planner's intentions. On the other hand, the meaningful area for them is a sub-unit of the street, perceived as a whole within a whole, as 'my street' within the 'objective street'. This area is connected with the concept of 'home' and serves as an extension of their private domain, conveying a sense of belonging to the immediate surroundings of the house. The range of this area varies from about 50 metres to about 150 metres from home. Under certain physical conditions, such as the separation of pedestrian and vehicular traffic and the locations of foci of attraction, the range of 'my street' grows to 300 metres. These results are in agreement with Bengtsson (1970) who mentions a similar-sized area.

The relationship to home determines the nature of children's existence in the street. In spite of the fact that the streets examined were designed as paths only, the children structured the street similarly to the way a house is primarily structured, as a place to be in, to dwell. Norberg-Schulz (1971, p. 20) has written: 'A place is basically round . . . the notions of proximity, centralization and closure therefore work together to form a more concrete existential concept, the concept of *place*.' Figure 15.2, a drawing of the street by a twelve-year-old girl, is an interesting example which sums up childrens' perception of the street as place. In this drawing, the circle which expresses the concept of place is turned into an ellipse due to the longitudinal characteristics of the street.

Children's activities take place everywhere in the street, in places 'suitable' or 'unsuitable' for them, as was also noted by Churchman (1976). Since the street is seen as a place to be, among the various street's activities mentioned by the children were some typical dwelling activities, such as reading a book, knitting and talking with friends. The children are mainly attracted to, and their activities are centred around, the general functions of the street: the natural elements, the entrances to the houses, the public functions, the parking lots, and the objects spread in the street. The places designed especially for children − the playgrounds which are located farther than 300 metres from most of the houses − play a minor role in the image.

The spatial definition of the street, as seen by the children, is similar to the spatial definition of the 'house'. It is defined by its walls, surfaces and the objects located in it. The street space is structured by these elements in two scales. On the one hand, space is defined by the large elements, the houses and the large trees. These are perceived from a distance and are, in general, described schematically, two-dimensionally, and with few details. On the other hand, the meaningful definition of space is by the small-scale elements with which children have direct concrete relations. These are the elements which are accurately described by them in a detailed three-dimensional way: the fences, the edge of the sidewalk, the garden, the grass, the sign posts, the garbage cans and the flowers. As in Read's (1958, p. 68) conception, 'Children, like savages, like animals, experience life directly, not at a mental distance.'

From the above, it appears that the child's image of the street is a product of an interaction between the child and the environment. Through the process described by Piaget and Inhelder (1974) as assimilation and accommodation in which children act upon the

Figure 15.2: The Street as Place — a Drawing by a 12-year-old Girl, Haifa, Israel

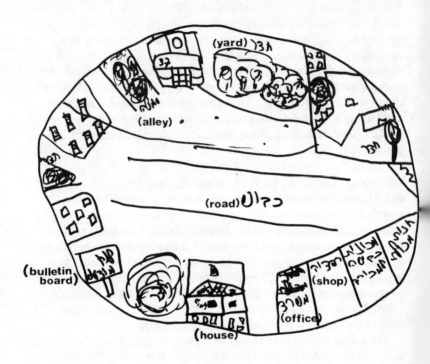

environment as well as the opposite state, children 'modify' the street to meet their wishes and dreams. As a result, they experience and act in an 'objective' street which is 'improved' by them to the one in the image. When the gap between the concrete reality and their image is too wide, their activities are disturbed and in turn their activities present a disturbance to the environment.

Design Concepts Based on the Image

The main object of this work is to try by means of design approaches to 'concretize' aspects of the child's image, and thus help create a more satisfactory urban residential environment for children.[1] The basic design unit dealt with in this work is that meaningful part of the street which is conceived by the child as 'my street'. It is that outdoor area near home in which the child can satisfy his/her interests and curiosity, play, learn and do things conveniently when and where he/she wants to without having 'to go somewhere to do them by plan, officially' (Jacobs, 1961, p. 96). The design unit is structured to fulfil the criteria of such a street. Its range from home varies from about 50 metres (the immediate surroundings of the house) up to about 150 metres, or even 300 metres under certain conditions, as described previously.

The various ranges of the basic street unit stem from and express the hierarchical nature of the foci of attraction on which they are centred. These foci are based on the elements that attract the children as reflected in the image. The lowest level in the hierarchy is the entrance to the house itself. This focus appears in the residential environment in the highest frequency and depends on the site layout and the types of buildings. In general, and in the scheme presented, a few foci of this type are located within the 150-metre range. The importance of this focus is in the immediate direct relationship it has with the house itself. In this part of the street, actually being inside the house and being in the street near the house are complementary parts of one continuous experience. The entrance itself, which belongs at the same time to both the house and the street, connects the two parts.

The second level in the hierarchy is characterized by the potential relations with 'the public'. This focus integrates some small public functions which serve a relatively small number of people and which generally reappear several times in relatively short distances in the residential environment, such as kindergartens, nursery schools and different shops. The location of these functions in the distance module of 150 metres enables them to become an integral part of the children's everyday city life, and thus to make it more vivid and interesting.

The highest level in the hierarchy is mainly public. It is comprised of functions which usually appear once in a relatively large area of the residential environment, such as a school, a clinic, a post office, a day-care centre, a club, a cafe, a bus stop and different shops.[2] The variety of functions and the open spaces of some within the range of 'my street' add extra dimensions to the child's daily activity. As was shown above, under certain conditions it is possible to locate those functions within 300 metres' distance from the house with the same results.

The 'residential street' (in the broad sense of the term) is created by the combination of the three foci in an hierarchical succession. The continuity of the street is structured by two parallel processes, those of connecting and dividing, which take place at the same time, so that each unit exists independently and as a part of a larger whole. This particular structure enables each child to define within the continuity his suitable territory. This territory can adapt itself to the child's needs as he grows. Figure 15.3 summarizes these relationships.

Each of the interrelated units of the street has the qualities to become a potential extension of the home. The street is designed as a place to be in, to play, to learn and to meet people and children, all of which give a feeling of belonging to the immediate physical and social environment.

Contrary to current design approaches and the layout of many residential areas today which tend to separate children's activities into mono-functional buildings, it is important to integrate the children in the spectrum of the daily street activities. These activities are the 'city' with which the children have direct daily intensive contact and which may contribute to their education and to a more interesting life for the urban child. The rigid frames which these days usually isolate activities and age groups are avoided. The functions are integrated into one whole system in which the children can move freely from one part to another and create mutual relations between themselves and other groups, and between their activities and the general street activities, thus stimulating one another.

The 'Children's Street'

This interaction is developed hierarchically in three stages, as shown in Figure 15.4. In the focus of the lowest level in the hierarchy, the child is in contact with children's activities relating on the one hand to the activities of the private domain, and on the other hand to a relatively large variety of street activities: the pedestrian movement in the street, the movement to the apartments, the vehicular traffic in the parking lots, green areas, senior citizens' activities, mothers with babies, and other children's activities. At the focus of the second level in the hierarchy, the contact with the private domain is weakened and the contact with other activities, such as street movement and meeting of people, becomes more colourful and intricate. At the third level, the interaction with the public activities is enriched to an ever fuller extent.

The integration of children's activities with the general street activities calls for special attention to the subject of vehicular traffic. Different kinds of relationships can be created. One way is entirely to exclude the vehicular traffic from the designated area for the children's activities. In this case, these areas will be safe, but will lose an element of interest. In addition, there is no guarantee that children will not play

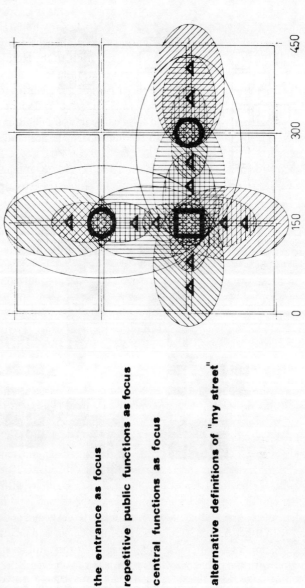

Figure 15.3: The Inner Structure of the Street

the entrance as focus

repetitive public functions as focus

central functions as focus

alternative definitions of "my street"

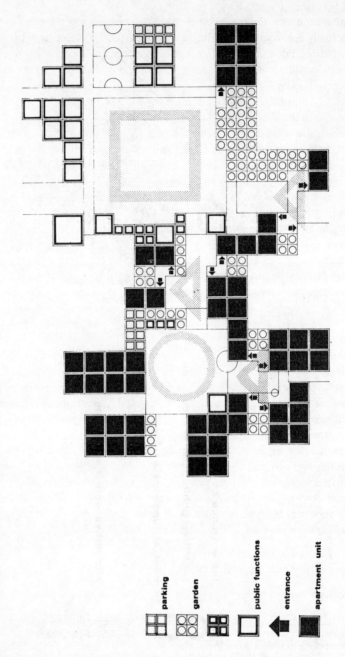

Figure 15.4: Integration of Functions in Three Levels

parking

garden

public functions

entrance

apartment unit

where the cars, the buses, the horses, the carriages and the bicycles actually are. Another possibility is only partially to separate these activities. For example, one can prevent the vehicular traffic from passing either in the lowest hierarchy or in both the first and the second hierarchies and let it pass through the focus of the central functions only. A third alternative is to integrate the vehicular traffic in all three levels. In this case, a new type of relationship has to be created in which the vehicular traffic adapts itself to the rules of an environment of children, as was done in Delft (The Netherlands), for example.

A variety of interwoven spaces which develop in three hierarchies, from the small, intimate, semi-private enclosure to the large green areas and public piazzas, creates the conditions for many street activities different in group size, age and nature. The spatial definition of the street is enriched and emphasized by additional nuances which stem from a child's attitude to the physical environment, that is, the definition of the small scale. These are the elements to which children can directly relate (i.e., see closely, touch, sit on, jump from, climb, etc.). A possible combination of the different scales is shown in Figure 15.5.

The variety of multi-purpose walls, surfaces and objects in the street, shown in Figures 15.6 and 15.7, enriches and stimulates children's activities. For example, the stairs to the apartments can be designed also to serve as seats or rest areas, or as stairs to slides. A hoop on a wall located in a widening of the street can make the street a basketball court. The numbers of the houses can serve as a basis for different ball games.

When all of the above concepts are combined, a 'children's street' results. (See Figure 15.8.) Designing streets with consideration of their image ought to lead to the creation of more suitable urban environments for children by turning large parts of the urban environment into places for play and enjoyment. Thus, the child's point of view may bring back to our cities something of the fun and drama which were inseparable from them in the past, as in Fongin's verses:

Les rues seront des théâtres
on jouera sur les trottoires.

Notes

1. Although the conclusions concerning the child's image of his street presented in the previous section are still somewhat tentative, they are sufficiently compelling to motivate this preliminary design.
2. These data are based on contemporary Israeli standards.

Figure 15.5: Hierarchy of Spaces Defined by Two Scales

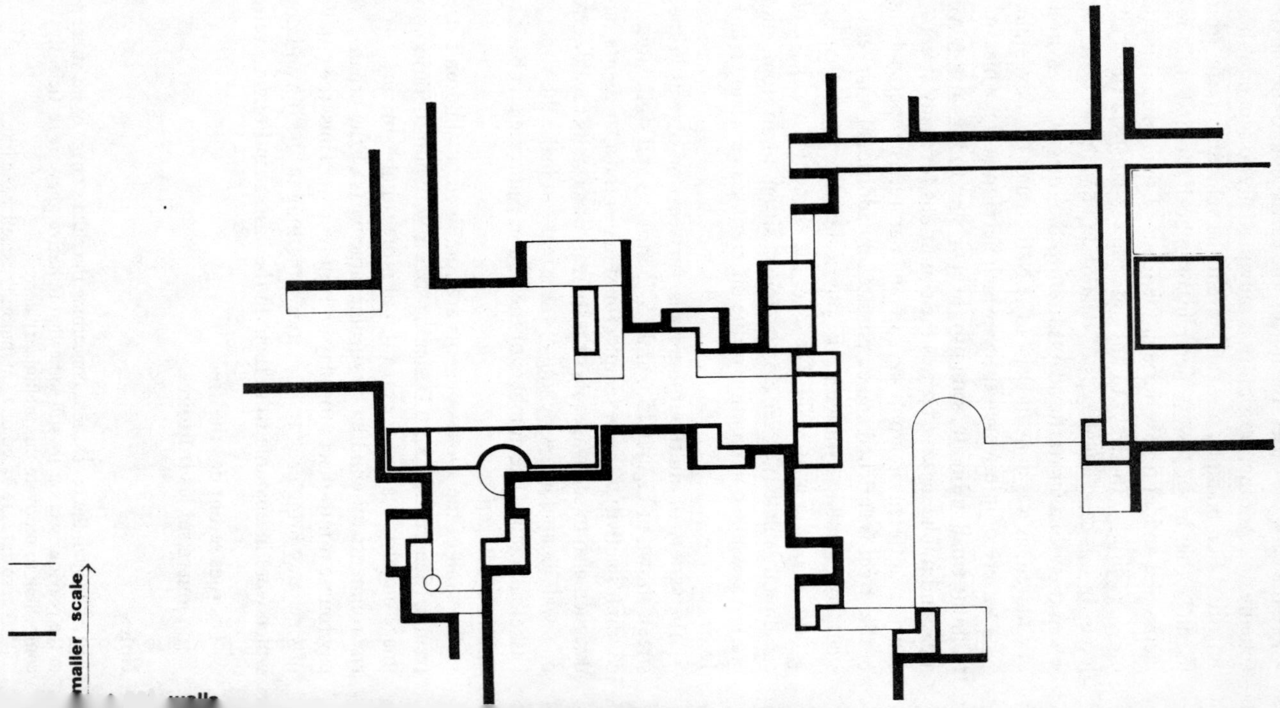

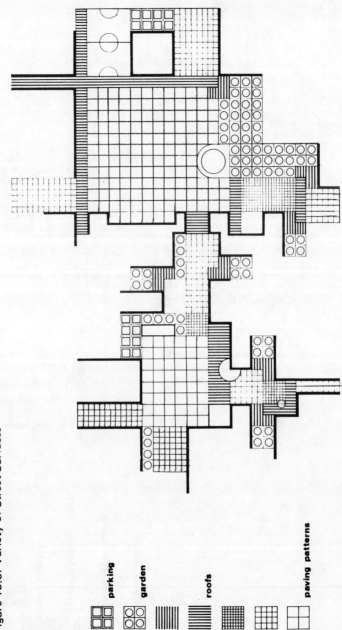

Figure 15.6: Variety of Street Surfaces

parking

garden

roofs

paving patterns

Figure 15.7: Continuity of Multi-functional Objects in the Street

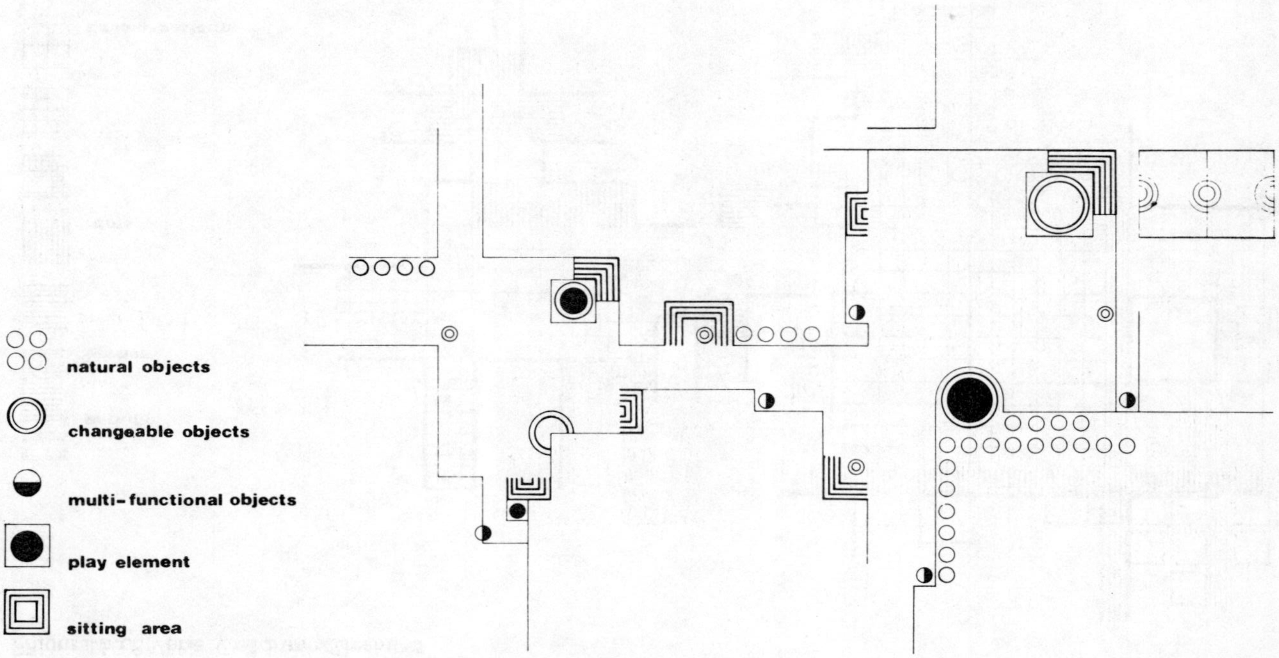

natural objects

changeable objects

multi-functional objects

play element

sitting area

Figure 15.8: The 'Children's Street'

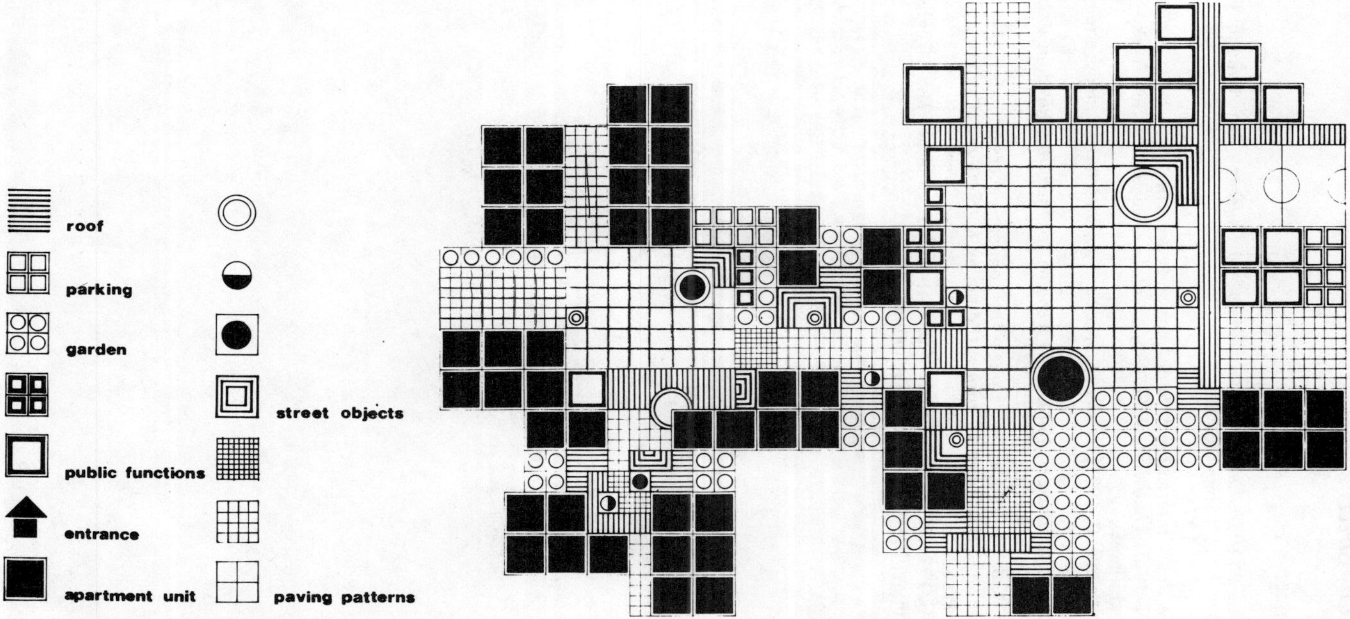

street objects

roof

parking

garden

public functions

entrance

apartment unit

paving patterns

References

Bengtsson, A. 1970. *Environmental Planning for Children's Play*. London: Crosby Lockwood and Sons Ltd.

Churchman, A. 1976. 'Children's street play: can it be accommodated?' *Proceedings*, International Conference on Pedestrian Safety. Haifa, Israel.

Jacobs, J. 1961. *The Death and Life of Great American Cities*. New York: Penguin Books.

Norberg-Schulz, C. 1971. *Existence, Space and Architecture*. London: Studio Vista.

Piaget, J. and B. Inhelder. 1974. *The Psychology of the Child*. London: Routledge and Kegan Paul Ltd.

Read, H. E. 1958. *Education Through Art*. London: Faber and Faber.

Van Eyck, A. 1968. *Team 10 Primer*. (Edited by A. Smithson.) Cambridge, Mass.: MIT Press.

Weiser, G. 1977. 'Children's image of their street.' Unpublished M.Sc. Thesis, Technion, Israel Institute of Technology, Haifa, Israel.

16 STREET PLAY: RE-CREATING NETWORKS FOR THE URBAN CHILD

Ellen Jacobs and Peter Jacobs

Introduction

The history of play and recreation in North American cities is a relatively short one. Play was commonly believed to be a child's activity and childhood itself only gained status in the early twentieth century when child labour was eliminated through legislative acts in North America as well as in Western Europe.

Parks were designated as play areas and were located away from the mainstream of community activity so that this exuberant and uncontrolled form of behaviour would not interfere with adult life. Jacobs and Derevensky (1977) found that urban children were dissatisfied with this form of segregated recreational planning and as a result abandoned the parks in favour of the streets. Gold (1977) suggests that the traditional approach to providing urban space and leisure services, which is currently being challenged by theoreticians and practitioners, will result in a new generation of recreation plans and programmes. Adults of the 1970s find themselves with more leisure time than ever before and are pressing for a change in the leisure services of the cities. Further, the economic situation of this decade calls for a realistic consideration of the financial feasibility of all leisure plans and programmes lest they be undertaken and abandoned due to a lack of funds. Jacobs and Charney (1975) have proposed that the repatriation of the street and street-related activities might be a solution to the recreational problem in the cities. The street as a public resource is presently the unofficial recreational space used for athletic practices as well as community gathering points, by young and old respectively. This paper attempts to present the children's perceptions of official and unofficial urban play areas, their preferred play spaces and the reasons for their choices. Emphasis is placed on a process-oriented approach to urban play developed through the full participation of those most directly involved, the children and parents of the community.

Both the history of play and the history of the use of urban space in the last two centuries have tended towards increasingly complex and segregative approaches to their respective subject matter. On the one hand, the taxonomy of recreation types, standards and age/income groups has led to sophisticated statistical analyses of the patterns and values of play, while the approach to zoning and segregated land uses in the city has all but eliminated messy and non-conforming uses of the urban milieu.

The urban park is but one of many specialized uses of urban space. Tot lots and playgrounds are equally specialized concepts of age-related play activities. While neither of these specialized sets of concepts is inherently bad, they do tend to prestate solutions to perceived problems of urban resources, green spaces, or existing social values. The urban park evolved as a solution to a set of nineteenth-century social values and concerns. Observations outlined in this paper suggest that many of these values and the proposed solution — the urban park — are no longer relevant to young urban children nor to their guardians.

In order to clarify the relationship of urban place to urban play, the first part of this paper traces the evolution of urban recreation in Montreal as a means of establishing some context for observations of the child's use of the city as a place to play. The paper concludes that neither urban space nor urban play can be profitably segregated from the integrative process through which the city is used and enjoyed by urban dwellers of all ages.

The Public Parks and Beyond

Urban space in the initial settlement of Montreal was constrained by the perimeter fortifications of a city set in the wilderness adjacent to the St Lawrence River. Within these walls the city was parcelled into large land holdings dominated by a large number of religious institutions all of which contained formal courtyards which were in turn walled and therefore restricted. Enclosed in these secondary sets of walls lay farmland which was cultivated for medicinal herbs, vegetables fruit trees and flowers. Major urban spaces within the walled city were essentially private and the view of the city in the early nineteenth century was of a tightly knit community pierced by the church steeples of the major religious institutions.

At the end of the eighteenth century, emerging nationalism provided a legitimation of play (Stone, 1971). Play was conceived of as a way of preparing young people for military service, and Le Champ de Mars, which was one of the first public squares in Montreal, was used almost exclusively as a military parade ground. It was in the mid-nineteenth century that public parks were created from private gardens to serve as meeting places and for civic functions. In Montreal, Place Viger was designed with fountains, gardens and a bandshell, and was one of the first conscious efforts made to accommodate public urban recreation, providing a pleasant gathering spot for evening promenades and outdoor concerts adjacent to the city centre.

The necessity for public parks was created by the growing density and congestion of the city core. As the city expanded toward the mountain and away from the older more commercial segment of the city, two lush cemeteries were established on the mountain's northern flank. Apart from their obvious function, they served as the first urban parks, as the term is now used, and provided the first experience of a public natural setting for the urban population.

By 1870 the residential suburbs had been established at the base of the mountain by those who could afford the move, leaving the densely industrialized city centre to the workers. People who recognized the need for a public park near the harbour pressured the government until 1873 when the Government of Canada ceded an unused artillery range, Lafontaine Park, and the island defence installations, St Helen's Island, to the city of Montreal. Concurrently, Frederick Law Olmsted Sr. was invited to propose a plan for a public park on Mount Royal Mountain. Thus, in a period of less than ten years the majority of Montreal's major public park system was established.

In commissioning Olmsted in 1875, the City Council recognized full well that the conditions of urban life were quite simply oppressive within the city core. Air pollution, traffic congestion, crowded urban housing and long working hours afforded little or no opportunity for (popular) recreation in the urban core. Olmsted believed that urban America required a physical setting that would provide the urban population with a sense of beauty, calm and recreation opportunity.

If the first cycle of urban recreation towards the end of the nineteenth century focused on large urban parks, the second cycle was committed to the community sportsfield, athletic centres and other active indoor centres of urban recreation. To a large extent the rapid growth of public services, including public and private transportation modes, created a vastly expanded and predominantly gridded city fabric. As a by-product of expansion, the centroids of urban population shifted farther and farther away from the first urban squares, frequently bisected by the very transportation paths that supported urban growth in the early twentieth century. Major urban parks, once at the periphery of the city, were now surrounded by dense residential communities.

By the middle of the twentieth century, the vast majority of the older surviving urban squares and institutional grounds, the major urban parks, the sportsfields and playing grounds were established, and for all intents and purposes the greening of the city stopped. The enormous increase of land values all but prohibited the purchase of additional urban space, a resource that was considered to be both non-renewable and rare. Competition by various groups for the resources of urban parks and an increased incidence of crime were countered by public investments in the maintenance, patrolling and services provided for public family use. In addition, popular cultural festivals and artistic exhibitions were located within these parks to increase their appeal to an urban population increasingly aware of the changing role and balance between the vastly expanded urban commercial core and the mountain park which once dominated the walled city and seemed so inaccessible in 1876, when it was first established.

Commercial expansion and the pressure on land values not only arrested the acquisition of parkland but, coupled with the diminishing public role of the religious institutions throughout Montreal, began to threaten many of the historic green spaces of the city. Many of these spaces, such as the Sulpician property, served as unofficial passive recreation centres at the edge of the expanded city core. Similarly, in areas with extremely low ratios of open space to population, mature religious properties developed during the nineteenth century (such as the Villa Maria property) to serve as informal parks for neighbouring residents. Downtown, small parcels of land attached to Protestant churches, established in the first English suburbs outside the walled city, now serve as isolated spots of green in an otherwise hard-edged scene.

In the late 1960s and mid-1970s, a clear dichotomy in recreation priorities was apparent. On the one hand, the informal family use of the parks movement is enjoying an important renaissance. Montrealers discovered the historic, cultural and natural richness of their urban heritage virtually at the same time as official gestures, of an immense magnitude, were devoted to universal exhibitions and to Olympic sports.

Between the mountain and island parks, between the official gests of grandeur and the community playing field, live the people of the city. What of their milieu? Do the initial arguments that stimulated the parks movement as an antidote to the industrial city during the middle and late nineteenth century still hold true?

The initial impetus that generated the parks movement in the 1850s developed from a perceived social necessity to counteract the congested city devoted to economic production and to profit. Gradually the nineteenth-century grid pattern of streets became animated with large central parks and with smaller neighbourhood parks and, by the early twentieth century, recreation standards were established to aid municipalities in the provision of open space. Simultaneously, the conservation ethic and demand for outdoor recreation during the first three-quarters of the twentieth century stimulated the purchase of vast areas of the country, acquired for national, provincial and regional parks, well beyond the urban fringe. In fact, almost 92 per cent of the province of Quebec is owned by the public. Many sectors of the urban population began to colonize the countryside with summer cottages, then winterized residences and, more recently, permanent residences from which they commute to the periphery of the city where more and more jobs are located. These communities, seen as recreation resources in and of themselves, are increasingly subject to official planning intervention, such as their expropriation for provincial parks (Jacobs, 1975). Thus, by the middle of the twentieth century, while the city grew enormously, the recreational use of the city changed substantially. In fact, the polarity of the city as a place to work and the country as a place to recreate was, and continues to be, reinforced by officially sanctioned recreation and tourism facilities located farther and farther away from the city by provincial and federal agencies.

This trend is being reversed in areas such as Ottawa, Edmonton and Halifax; but, by and large, the urban record of support for managed open space in Canada is less than encouraging. Particularly in municipalities experiencing rapid growth, the concern for a viable tax base, other competing public services and limited perception of recreation needs tend to militate against all but the most minimal provisions of new managed open space. Frequently 'the park' is used as a promotional device to attract new residents to an emerging urban concentration with little or no provision for improving, maintaining or operating what is essentially a large vacant lot.

The apparent conflict between projections of future needs for managed urban open space and analyses that indicate a relative lack of utility in existing urban open spaces can only create a sense of frustration and confusion in the minds of City Councillors. The resultant decisions, one suspects, are less than optimal.

Parks: The Child's View

The history of play and the evolution of parks indicate that the need for play and recreation is not a new urban phenomenon and that the solution to the problem of play spaces in the inner city is not always satisfied by the creation of a large community park.

A four-year study (Jacobs and Derevensky, 1977) was designed to explore the urban child's perception of his environment. Children between the ages of five and seventeen years were interviewed in order better to understand the manner in which children perceive and use the city. Of the children interviewed, 26 per cent said they played on the sidewalk, 20 per cent used the backyard, 14 per cent the park, 11 per cent the street, 9 per cent the alley. When the data were reorganized into age groupings, they showed that the preponderance of 5–9-year-olds used the backyards[1] whereas the 10–13-year-olds played on the sidewalks, in the streets and alleys, and the 14–17-year-olds used the parks. The children in the sample tended to move from the confines of the yard out to the sidewalks, into the streets, and away to the parks as they grew older.

The 5–13-year-olds, who opted to play everywhere but in the park where one would expect to find them, offered the interviewers a number of interesting reasons for their avoidance of the community park.

1. The lack of open spaces throughout the inner city and the spiralling cost of land within the commercial sector has necessitated the designation of a large single area as the sole park of each inner-city community. In many cases, this makes the park inaccessible to the population living at the periphery of the community which it is intended to serve.

   Therefore, if the park is too far to reach by foot or by bike, the children resort to the use of the streets and will not consider paying public transportation costs to travel to the park when they can use the street in front of their home.

   Frequently, if the park is not within the immediate home territory, children have to cross 'dangerous and/or hostile turf'[2] to reach the park and do not consider the park worth the risk they have to take.

   Parents of younger children would rather have these children closer to home so that they can keep a periodic check on the children's whereabouts.

2. The children find that the over-designed park environment does not offer sufficient adventure, challenge, or the opportunity to take risks. Vast open spaces are too large for the young child to adapt to

and feel comfortable with, whereas the street is more confined and smaller in scale.

3. There are not enough perceptually exciting things about the parks; they are frequently large, barren playing fields or iron jungle-gyms, and there are very few visual, auditory and/or kinesthetically stimulating things in pre-designed parks.

4. The parks' sports schedules are so rigidly organized that there is little opportunity for children to form 'pick-up' teams for a spontaneous game of hockey, football, baseball or soccer. Because of the monopoly of the parks by the junior sports leagues, the children resort to the use of the streets for pick-up games and practice.

5. In Montreal, autumn heralds the time when the parks department employees remove the playground equipment, leaving the playground as barren as the vast baseball diamonds for several months before the snow falls. The boards erected for the hockey and skating rinks are the only vertical structures on the horizon and there is literally nothing for the children to do in the parks between the time when the first leaves fall and the time when the temperature drops low enough for the skating rinks to become operative.

This age group's responses indicate that playgrounds need not be vast, green open spaces in order to attract them; easy accessibility and the freedom to explore, experiment, create and take risks are essential. All too often adults who design play areas for children are far too conservative, overly cautious and protective in their designs; as a result, they settle for specific rather than integrated recreational areas. One can certainly begin to understand the children's reluctance to use the parks under these circumstances.

On the other hand, there is an increase in the frequency of the use of parks with the rise in age level. This is due in part to the following:

1. Older children have usually been granted permission to wander farther from home.

2. The physical design of the parks — large open spaces — provides suitable meeting places for the older children as these spaces are more difficult to supervise.

3. The large open spaces are not too large a scale for the older adolescent to cope with.

4. The older children are more involved with league sports and the existence of a large number of league games at these parks draws

adolescent players and their peer supporters to the parks.

These observations, derived from several recent research studies (Jacobs and Derevensky, 1977; Gold, 1977), suggest that an exclusive focus on the park as the solution to urban recreation, particularly for younger children, is unresponsive to the total community's needs.

Towards a Community Recreation Network

If the older children are the only ones using the parks which are seen as a safe play area and the younger set are staying away, then changes must be proposed in the park system to make it more exciting and challenging than the street or alley, or conversely streets and alleys must be made into secure yet challenging play areas. The tendency has been to set parks aside for young children rather than integrating parks into the framework of the neighbourhood street. In so doing, the children are segregated from the rest of the community — the infants, adults and elderly are not thought of as having a place in the park systems. This creates an unnatural break in community life and, in fact, children react to this by staying close to home and making the street their park. Being close to home means that children can remain an integral part of the fabric of the community — they can chat with the elderly neighbours sitting on galleries, wheel an infant around, keep an eye on the toddlers and nip into their own house for refreshments.

It is becoming increasingly important that the community serve as the child's extended family in order that the child may learn more about the very young and the very old. Communities were not designed to be age-segregated. That play areas are an extension of the community should follow suit. The street and/or alley provides the natural link, a link that is neither socially nor spatially segregated. The street is and has been the prototypical 'unofficial public space' in nineteenth-century urban civilization, as opposed to the parks and park systems which were officially sanctioned for community recreation purposes. Yet the very obviousness of the street contrasts, curiously, with the benign neglect accorded it. Streets in Canadian settlements occupy the majority of all the public urban open space resources. They structure the form, and frequently the content, of cities and towns, and serve as the primary module of public community identification — 'our street' — beyond the immediate private domain — 'my house'.

The street is, by definition, a public resource. Important and highly visible sectors of the population are dependent upon the street: the young, the old and the poor depend singularly on the street for play, watching, meeting – in short, recreation. While the street functions to organize urban space, it also presents a high proportion of the available stock of public open space most accessible to the vast bulk of housing units in this country: the street is, in effect, a doorstep community open space.

The street not only offers children the proximity to home which they relish, but it also offers challenge and an element of risk which the pre-designed park does not. Children require an environment in which they can take risks, meet a challenge and control the amount of danger to which they expose themselves. When one climbs a tree to an exhilarating, heart-thumping height one is in control of the amount of danger to which one will expose oneself. When the environment does not provide this type of opportunity for controlled risk taking, the child often turns to social challenges and frequently finds him/herself in a situation in which it is not possible to control the amount of danger. Breaking windows and stealing cars set in motion societal retributions which cannot be controlled and which are far more traumatic than a bone fracture incurred by a fall from a tree which was climbed too high. Until the parks system can offer as much challenge and adventure as the street, children will continue to shun the parks.

Children possess a natural curiosity to explore and observe, and the elderly with their free time and years of experience possess a natural ability to discuss and explain. Streets facilitate the interaction of young and old, whereas parks tend to segregate them.

Immediately adjacent to urban streets are many small spaces created by the razing of abandoned buildings. These spaces may be integrated into the street's recreation network by creating vest-pocket 'turfs' on these sites. In discussions with the children, it was felt that they are more content in smaller, less heavily equipped play areas, and that adventure is a key factor in the attraction of a particular area. The hollowed-out piece of land which exists between two buildings can meet all of the prerequisites by which children rate a play area. These vest-pocket parks, which may be viewed by adults as a rubble site, offer children challenge and an opportunity for adventure and exploration. In many cases, these small pockets of land are scheduled for redevelopment at a future date and, rather than permitting parking lot franchises to occupy the land, socially conscious communities might advocate that the land be used for the children of the community. Whatever structures are placed in this play space should be portable, so that they can be dismantled easily and transported to the next site when construction on that lot begins. A vest-pocket turf might also provide the adults in the area with an outdoor ground-level seating area and the elderly would not have to travel far out of the neighbourhood to be in a park setting.

An 'undesigned' community recreational network which involves streets, alleys and vest-pocket parks can meet the needs of the adventure seekers and risk takers. A community worker would be needed for turf areas with support from parents in the area. Employment of stay-at-home parents as play supervisors would legitimize the adult desire to be outdoors in communication with peers and children. Under careful guidance, children would be able to create their own environments and to control their environments and their experiences. An area which could easily and naturally become part of the community recreational network is the schoolyard (Moore, 1974). Inner-city schools are typically old, decaying structures surrounded by the city in which an ever-increasing lust for land results in schoolyards being turned into parking lots and many frontyards being paved to provide room for teachers' cars. If the land attached to the school could be used in a more imaginative and creative manner, a strong, meaningful link might be created between the home and the school in the inner city. In offering the space to the community, the children would be assured of a permanent play area where experiments begun in the neighbourhood turf could be recreated and enhanced under the supervision and sympathetic guidance of the homeroom teacher. Perhaps with the promise of interesting outdoor experiments and activities the truancy rate might diminish. Parents tend to be more receptive and responsive to teacher suggestions when their children express enthusiasm and interest in school activities. Thus an adventure playground in the community schoolyard can serve only to enhance the parent—teacher relationship.

The winter in Montreal and most Canadian cities adds another dimension to the recreational network. Frequently, it is too cold for extended periods of outdoor play and it is during these long winter months that the need for exciting and innovative outdoor play areas becomes more pronounced. When asked about winter recreation, city administrators point to the outdoor skating rinks and mention the handful of community centres which provide indoor recreation. The problem with these centres lies in their inaccessibility for the majority of the population and the lack of a sufficient number of trained staff members to make the programmes so enticing that children will either walk, bike or travel by bus to reach the centre. The mention of public transit evokes tales of woe and howls of complaints from the children. A Metropolitan Toronto Report (Durlak, 1974) states that as far as public transportation is concerned, children (1) do not feel accepted; (2) are treated as 'second class citizens'; (3) believe that none of the transportation is designed for them — the seats and bellcord are too high, the windows are hard to open and the bars are too high to hold; (4) are afraid of accidents with buses and subways; and (5) feel that the distance which they wish to travel is just too far to walk, yet not far enough to warrant a 10-cent bus fare and a long wait in the cold weather.

As a strategy for the problem of inaccessibility, Gold (1977) has proposed that existing obsolete or abandoned buildings within the urban core be examined and that these buildings be converted for public or private recreational use. A project of this nature was carried out in one of Montreal's most disadvantaged areas where an abandoned funeral parlour was converted into a large recreational centre. Over the years 'Project 80' has become the mainstay of the children and youth in the area and has served significantly to reduce delinquent behaviour.

Conclusion

The majority of the inner-city population has never had the opportunity to control or to effect changes in its environment. With the advent of the 'undesigned' recreational network, a new vista will be opened which should provide the urban dweller with the opportunity to plan, create and control his environment. Both calculated risks and trial-and-error testing are essential to the play experience, and must be conceived of as integral parts of the spatial fabric of the community. What is suggested is a change of perception of the city on two levels. First, the totality of urban space should be reconsidered as an integral whole such that new activities might be assigned to previously segregated and frequently isolated uses. Second, the process of organizing and using urban space for play should be accorded at least as much energy as the products that are all too frequently designed simply to fill these spaces.

In so far as the physical model of a park meets the social demands for play and recreation, the planning, design and implementation of the physical place called a park, tot lot, playground, etc. could proceed with little discussion. These designated spaces for play, while consistent with the prevailing philosophy of segregated land use and the social polarity of work and play, are not consistent with the child's use of the city. The very identification of this gap provides opportunity to redefine and re-educate communities in the use of urban space by stressing their participation in the decision-making process through which such spaces as streets, vacant lots and alleys become used.

Initial community action in Montreal and other Canadian cities has begun to provide a more balanced public attitude to the question of the wise use of public space, for whom, and at what cost? The results of such a community- and process-oriented approach to the planning of public space are not yet clear. One suspects that they will not necessarily match existing perceptions of 'the garden city', but will develop their own physical models of play places for yesterday's, today's and tomorrow's children consistent with current social thought and action.

Notes

1. In the urban core of Montreal there is a preponderance of dwellings called flats, each with its own backyard. Although these yards are unlike those of single-family dwellings, they are none the less enclosed areas which offer a safe play space for the younger urban children, who graduate from there to the heavily trafficked streets.
2. In the colloquial sense, 'turf' refers to the child's sense of territoriality.

References

Allen of Hurtwood, Lady. 1968. *Planning for Play*. Norwich: Harrold and Sons.
Ariès, Phillipe. 1962. *Centuries of Childhood*. (Translated by Robert Baldick.) New York: Knopf.
Bengtsson, A. 1970. *Environmental Planning for Children's Play*. New York: Praeger.
Bruner, J. S., A. Jolly and K. Sylva (eds). 1976. *Play*. England: Penguin.
Butler, A., E. Gotts and N. Ouisenberry. 1978. *Play as Development*. Ohio: Merrill.
Caplan, F. and T. Caplan. 1974. *The Power of Play*. New York: Anchor.
Cass, Joan. 1972. *The Significance of Children's Play*. Wiltshire, California: Redwood.
Chase, John. 1971. 'Street games of New York City', in R. F. Herron and B. Sutton-Smith (eds), *Child's Play*. New York: Wiley.
Durlak, J. 1974. 'Suburban children and public transportation in Metropolitan Toronto.' Report to Canada Ministry of State for Urban Affairs.
Friedberg, P. and E. P. Berkley. 1970. *Play and Interplay*. New York: Macmillan.
Gold, Seymour M. 1977. 'Urban open space: 2000.' Paper presented at the Royal Australian Institute of Parks and Recreation 50th Annual Conference, Canberra, Australia.
Hartley, R., L. Frank and R. Goldenson. 1952. *Understanding Children's Play*. New York: Columbia University Press.
Herron, R. E. and B. Sutton-Smith (eds). 1971. *Child's Play*. New York: Wiley.
Jacobs, E. and J. Derevensky. 1977. 'Changing teacher perceptions: a look at the inner city child's environment', in R. Granger and J. Young (eds),

Demythologyzing the Inner City Child. Washington, DC: NAEYC.
Jacobs, Peter. 1973. *Urban Space.* Ottawa: Canada Ministry of State for Urban Affairs.
——1975. *Parc Habité.* Citizens Planning Committee of the Municipal Council, Stanstead, Quebec.
——and M. Charney. 1975. *Street Works: Generating Public Open Space.* Ottawa: Canada Ministry of State for Urban Affairs.
Moore, Robin. 1974. 'Anarchy zone: encounters in a school yard', *Landscape Architecture Quarterly*, October.
Piaget, Jean. 1962. *Play Dreams and Imitation in Childhood.* New York: Norton.
Stone, Gregory P. 1971. 'The play of little children', in R. E. Herron and B. Sutton-Smith (eds), *Child's Play.* New York: Wiley.
Sutton-Smith, Brian. 1971. 'Play preference and play behaviour: a validity study', in R. E. Herron and B. Sutton-Smith (eds), *Child's Play.* New York: Wiley.

17 BEYOND PLAYGROUNDS: PLANNING FOR CHILDREN'S ACCESS TO THE ENVIRONMENT

Cecilia Perez and Roger A. Hart[1]

Introduction

There is too much concern with playgrounds and not sufficient concern with the environments where children spend most of their time. Playgrounds are only one kind of recreational setting for children. They are relevant to the lives of children during only a small part of their development and for a small part of their time (Department of the Environment, 1973; Pollowy, 1973). It is time for the recreation, child-care and design professions to change their focus and to explore ways of maximizing the opportunity for children to find safe access to a diverse environment. Social science can aid these professions by helping to identify the forces which restrict access and by helping children and parents define those environmental qualities which they deem important. The authors' research and this paper are based on this premise.

Remarkably little is presently known about how children living in different physical and social contexts spend their days. From earlier investigations (op.cit.), it is clear, however, that there are extremes of children's access to the out-of-doors. Some children are trapped inside their own homes and their immediate environs due to serious physical, social and psychological forces, to the extent that their situation represents a serious social injustice. It is the purpose of the authors' current research to study in detail the complex interaction of these restrictive forces. It is hoped that from this improved understanding those professionals responsible for environmental planning and design, as well as those persons more directly responsible for the health and welfare of children, will be better able to improve the quality of their environments.

The research question arises out of a study on the relationship of children to the outdoor physical environment in a small Vermont town (Hart, 1978a). This investigation was designed to describe the development of the relationship of children to the landscape, focusing on their physical and experiential engagement with it from the door of their home to the fringes of their known world. This required the

252

simultaneous study of those aspects of child—environment relations commonly investigated separately: spatial activity, place use, spatial cognition and place values and feelings. This work revealed the importance of parents' and children's feelings about danger and other negative forces in the environment influencing children's spatial ranges out-of-doors. Subsequently, the United States Forest Service contracted the authors to investigate children's access to, and use of, vegetated spaces in New York City. These studies suggested how dramatically children's access to the environment varies not only in relation to children's ages and sex but also as a function of the degree of traffic, crime, type of housing, social fears and amount of time parent(s) are able to spend at home. These, and other forces not yet identified, must be clearly understood if ways of improving the quality of environments with children in mind are to be found.

The Rationale behind Playgrounds

Organized recreation programmes and facilities began as a response to a growing need in the late nineteenth century for a place for children to pursue leisure activities. This was at a time when the family was becoming less and less the institution which satisfied the recreational needs of children. The early founders of playgrounds had as their aim a place both safe and morally sound, which would counteract the vice which they felt children would encounter left on their own, in the streets (Grotberg, 1977). This aim, rather than the recognition of children's needs to explore the total environment, led to the construction of playgrounds which were devoid of elements interesting to children. As early as 1914, social welfare workers were citing incidents of playgrounds lying idle while children roamed the streets in search of danger and adventure (Russel-Sage Foundation, 1914).

Gold (1972, 1977), in highlighting the 'non-use' of neighbourhood parks, outlined the major categories of factors which influence the non-use phenomenon in order to move the recreation, planning and design professions towards policies which would increase the use of playgrounds by children. The authors consider this too narrow a conclusion from his observation of non-use; rather, it is believed that children − not playgrounds − should be the basis for planning. What can be said from present knowledge of the development of children and from the behaviour of their caretakers, about the environmental opportunities which need to be created for children?

The Development of Children's Exploration and Use of the Environment

Very little research has been undertaken of a truly ecological nature with children in their everyday environment. Recently Bronfenbrenner (1973a, 1973b, 1975) has encouraged research on ecological studies of children in the context of their families, but there have not to date been any studies of ecological forces influencing children's access to use of the out-of-doors.

The most relevant background material may be found only through a broad survey of anthropology, sociology, developmental psychology, geography and urban planning (Hart, 1978a, Appendix A). Some of the most relevant literature is summarized below.

The major forces influencing children's exploration of the physical world are represented in Figure 17.1 which draws considerably from the writings of Bowlby (1969) on the attachment behaviour of children and their caretakers. The diagram emphasizes that consideration of a child's environmental exploration also necessitates thinking of the child as part of an interactive system made up of child and 'caretaker(s)'. As women's roles and family structures change and more women find employment outside the home, child care is shared with other people. The term 'caretaker' represents all of these people and institutions.

Children want to learn how to engage competently with the environment. They want to know how to climb steps, cross streams and play in the street. At the same time, they have no desire to get hurt, and they grade the challenges in the environment which they set up for themselves, setting each challenge just a little beyond their existing experience with the phenomena. It is for this reason that a single tree can often satisfy the same child's climbing aspirations for many years.

Even though children have a desire to become competent, the extent to which they can experiment within realistically safe bounds varies according to the particular attachment/caring relationship they have developed with their caretaker(s). Important variables in this relationship are the child's age, the conflicting demands on the caretaker, and the particular environment which the child faces. It is necessary to look closely at the elements of this dynamic relationship.

Exploration is the outward vector in Figure 17.1. It expresses the urge found in all healthy children to move out from their home base to explore the environment in order to learn about it and about themselves

Figure 17.1: Schematic Representation of the Balance of Safety and Adventure in Child Development

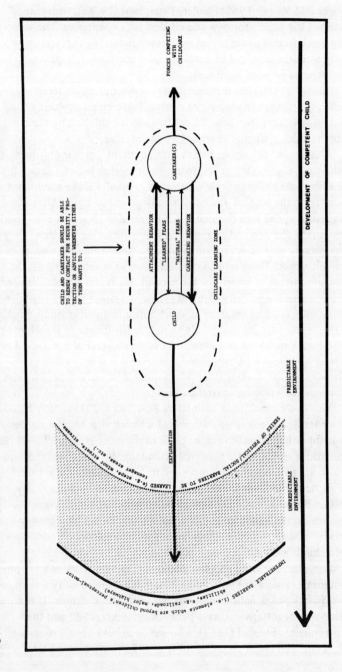

(Fiske and Maddi, 1961; Fowler, 1965; Hart, 1978a). 'Adventure' involves the search for new and challenging experiences. The value expressed in this paper is that serious restriction of exploration will deny a child the ability to develop into a competent, happy individual and is to be avoided at all costs.

Bowlby (1969) has distinguished two dynamically interacting forces which guarantee the renewal of contact between an exploring child and his/her caretaker: attachment behaviour exhibited by the child; and caretaking, usually practised by the mother.

Attachment behaviour begins with an infant's proximity-maintaining behaviour, e.g., crying or following when mother leaves a room (Bowlby). As children grow older, they gradually make excursions away from the mother and occasionally go out of sight. After three years of age, children become much better able to accept their mother's temporary absence and to engage in play with other children. They are increasingly able to accept surrogate attachment figures, such as a schoolteacher. There remain conditions on such substitutions, the most important of which for the present discussion is a child's need to know where the primary caretaker is; he/she needs to feel confident that contact can be resumed at short notice in an emergency. In this way, children are gradually able to reduce the degree of attachment with their caretakers, but even at six or seven years of age a child often attempts to hold a parent's hand and resents it if they refuse. Throughout the development of a normal child, attachment behaviour continues as a dominant strand of life.

Maternal caretaking is defined by Bowlby (p. 291) as 'any behavior of a parent, a predictable outcome of which is that the young are brought either into the nest, or close to the mother, or both'. Of the conditions that activate maternal caretaking, Bowlby mentions two which are environmental as opposed to organismic and are, therefore, of particular interest to this paper: (1) when an infant strays beyond a certain distance, and (2) when an infant cries for some external reasons. In both situations, a mother is likely to act by recovering the infant to her arms. This retrieving or protective function continues into childhood.

Together, the child and the maternal caretaker work as a learning system to experiment with and evaluate the child's ability to explore new places and situations without serious physical danger. It is a three-way negotiative process between caretaker, child and the environment. Froebel (1887), who seems to have been a particularly observant and sensitive philosopher of child—environment transactions

Figure 17.2: Fire Escapes are Used for a Variety of Activities both by Adults and Children

Secure access is an interactive process. Both parent and child seek the security of visual access to each other. Here, parents may watch over their children without directly interfering in the children's activities.

described the crucial balance between protective parents and an environment which must be explored and learned by the child. Sometimes during a child's development he/she will retreat more from exploring and engage in strong attachment behaviour; at other times, the caretaker finds it necessary to pull tightly on the reins of what he/she considers to be too adventuresome a child (Bowlby). The particula pattern of restrictedness which is adopted undoubtedly has an important socializing influence on children, having implications beyon the development of their environmental competence to their general sense of competence and an influence on their personalities, but it is n possible to consider these aspects in this paper. (See Bowlby, 1969; Hart, 1978a.)

Certain forces operating on the caretaker side of the model work negatively on the system. These forces act to deny those qualities of love, care and understanding which enable a person (or persons) to act sensitively in negotiating with a child over his/her exploration of, and learning to deal with, the environment. Such forces are seriously in need of study. Some of the negative forces of child caretaking have been identified by Bowlby and sub-categorized into 'withdrawing behaviours' and 'competing behaviours'. The reasons for the development of these behaviours may originate within the caretaker; dislike of contact with an infant is an extreme case of such withdrawir behaviour. More commonly they are due to competing behaviours suc as the demands of other household duties. Economic hardship and the work demands of poor families are surely another cause of these behaviours. Moreover, the current changes in Western societies of family structure and women's work roles are probably causing difficulties for many child caretakers and increasing the need for substitute caretakers. As children spend more and more time in institutional settings, their opportunities to face uncertainty in environments are reduced. This results in schools which dare not use the outdoor environment and larger community, and playgrounds which are static and boring. In all of these instances, the role of the caretaker as a sensitive person who understands the particular abilities and fears of the child, who is always available to the child and who dares to allow the child to experiment (often because of fears of legal liability by substitute caretakers) may be seriously threatened.

Research on Children's Accessibility to and Use of the Environment

There have been a number of studies which attempt to document children's use of the total urban environment (Morville, 1969; Hole,

1966; Department of the Environment, 1973; Coates and Sanoff, 1973; and Aiello and Gordon, 1974).[2] Probably the most useful findings of these studies is that even very well-equipped playgrounds attract children for only a small part of their time outdoors. Unfortunately, most of the research has been poorly designed and is piecemeal. It is extremely difficult to extract generalities with sufficient confidence to allow for any comparisons across different studies. The authors themselves seem to have made a concerted effort to avoid replicating any other investigators' methods or categories of observation and analysis. (For an exception, see Cooper (1974) who attempted to make comparisons with the British studies.)

Children's Accessibility to the Environment in a Small New England Town

In research conducted in a small New England town with the fictitious name of Inavale (Hart, 1978a), all 80 of the town's children, aged between four and twelve years, were involved in the research, but with a particular focus on a few families of children. A mixture of formal observational, interview and testing procedures were used, but the primary approach was ethnographic: a participatory pursuit of understanding through work with children 'in the field'.

Figure 17.1 summarized the major forces which, in combination, operate to different degrees upon children's exploration of the environment. It is difficult to express these forces diagrammatically because they are usually transactional rather than uni-directional. The primary force lies within each child in the form of his/her desire to explore and come to know the larger environment, but it would be simplistic not to recognize that there are many forces leading children to set limits for themselves. For this reason the diagram should be read with the text and the arrows should be read as expressions of the predominant direction of a force only.

Operating as something of a deterrent to children's explorations of their environment are their fears for certain kinds of places. A certain degree of fear of the unknown is perhaps a component of much of children's experience of new places; psychologists have observed how infants in strange (unfamiliar) environments will explore more when the secure face of their mother is present than when she is not. In the family's home environment, it may be reasonably assumed that the home (or at least the normal living space within the home[3]) is the secure base from which children explore. From this secure harbour, children gradually extend their range of familiarity with the environment. As they do so, children are repelled from some places more than others because of fears which children associate with them. Some of these fears are unique to a child, based on some personal experience, such as an inexplicable noise once heard coming from a certain building, while others are common to more than a single child. A most interesting feature of the relationship of children to these places is that, while they express fear of them, they also commonly express an attraction to them. The suggestion by Maslow (1968) that knowledge may have not only a growing-forward function but also an anxiety-reducing function, a protective, homeostatic function, is relevant here. This conforms with the more general notion that children have an urge to know the physical world in order to feel comfortable in it.

In addition to fears of the physical dangers of rivers, busy highways, wells, etc., parents have social fears for children, leading to restrictions which are less subject to gradual erosion through experience and learning. For Inavale mothers, these fears of bad influences on their children usually arise from their fear of drug abuse, petty crime, bad language and sexual permissiveness.

All of these forces operate in different degrees and combine to create a very different geographical range of experience in different children. Not only age, but also gender and differences in the physical environment, had a marked effect on children's abilities to extend their horizon. If there can be wide variation in children's ranges due to physical dangers in a small town, it is not difficult to imagine how dramatic the constraints on children's movements might be in the centre of some cities.

The 'suburban' area in Inavale is ideal for parents who wish to find their children quickly for meal-times or for preparation for a shopping expedition, etc. A few loud shouts are usually all that is required. The landscape qualities which make them convenient in this respect are common to new suburban housing tracts. First, there are the landscape qualities which combine to provide excellent visual access: mild topography, absence of vegetation other than lawns, and low density of buildings. Second, there is the relative quiet of the neighbourhood which, coupled with the presence of other parents, enables shouting to be an effective means of communication. Third, there is the relatively high proportion of children which means that any single child need not travel far afield to find playmates. A further advantage of the 'suburban' tract — and no doubt also true of other types of housing — is that, because of the high proportion of families with young children, parents can share the responsibility, implicitly and occasionally explicitly, of watching over children other than their own.

A large spatial range seems to be one common positive feature for young children living in such suburban landscapes. This feature of suburban parental caretaking, however, seems to become a somewhat negative force in later years. The continual process of negotiation by children with their parents on the extension of range, which had been observed in other parts of the town, whether it be to get candy and comics or to visit a friend, is reduced here. The mothers not only watch over but provide for their children by driving them to places and fetching things for them. This use of the car for children is another feature which it is believed resembles the pattern in the most middle-class suburban settings.

While children and parents in other parts of the town were respectively learning to negotiate and to accept traffic, physical dangers and the various social 'ills' of small-town main-street life, the 'suburban' children were still 'contained' in their own neighbourhood, punctuated with visits to specific locations (e.g., stores, friends' homes, school sports) chauffeured by their parents. They therefore miss opportunities to learn by dealing with uncertainty and by making decisions for themselves. The 'containment' quality of suburbs may be just one reason why they are not the ideal environment for children that they were once thought to be.

Children's Accessibility to the Environment in Manhattan, New York City

Inavale was chosen for the first in-depth study in order to simplify the complex problems of designing and executing such ecological research with untried methods. For environmental planners and designers, however, it is the urban and suburban landscapes which need to be evaluated and which require suggestions to be made for improving the quality of children's opportunities. One of the primary questions to be investigated is accessibility. This involves two factors: (1) how far can children go and what are the forces restricting them; and (2) what are the important environmental qualities that lie within this range of access and do they constitute a suitably rich environment for children's development?

A programme of research has been developed to begin to answer these questions for the children of Manhattan, New York.

Figure 17.3: Beyond Playgrounds: Diversity of Environmental Opportunity

Playgrounds are used for only a small amount of time by children because they can only satisfy a small range of activities. Accessibility to the larger environment is the key to whether or not children are able to find a diverse environment for their activities.

Exploring and Physical Activity

Quiet/Solitude

Constructive Play

Fine Manipulation

The Research Design

The primary purpose of the first phase of the research in the Inwood neighbourhood of Manhattan is to describe in depth the dynamics of city children's access to the out-of-doors. The reason for choosing this area was its physical and cultural diversity necessary for a rich exploratory study. A variety of interviews are being conducted to provide information on children's accessibility, where they go and do not go, what activities they engage in and with whom.

Interviews have been conducted with children to discover what they consider their range of movements in the city to be and, within that range, what places are inaccessible to them. Within these interviews are questions which seek to discover some of the primary forces which influence this spatial range and restricted place use, whether they be subjectively defined by the child, specific restrictions made by their parents, other persons and institutions, or physical barriers such as roads and railroad tracks, etc. In addition, interviews are being conducted with parents, local police officers, recreational personnel and former and current long-term residents of the area. The parental and professional interviewees give some added perspectives and insights into the use and non-use and the accessibility to elements these populations consider to be of value for children. The historical perspective of long-term residents, who either experienced the area as children themselves or raised children in this area, provides information about social and physical changes the neighbourhood has undergone and subsequently about changes in children's accessibility.

Through the interviews on range and place use with individual children, the extent to which children are able to travel away from their homes unaccompanied by adults has been examined. Some initial statements concerning the different types of environmental opportunities accessible to them within those ranges can now be made. The extent of free range (i.e., range alone without asking special permission each time) varies by age, sex, location of home and cultural background of the children, and in all cases is extremely limited. The current research has provided the following results.

First Grade children (6–7 years) of both sexes are the most restricted. Generally, First Grade children may not travel beyond the sidewalk immediately in front of their homes. Those children living near parks, may, however, play in the park area either next to or across the street from their homes, but only after being taken there by an adult.

Third Grade children (8–9 years) have slightly greater 'free' ranges. Both boys and girls may travel to the ends of their blocks and occasionally to a nearby store to run an errand. Some of these children may also make special trips to park areas unaccompanied by an adult, but only with parental permission and in the company of older or other children.

By Fifth Grade (10–11 years), boys' free ranges are considerably larger. They are commonly determined by specific places that they may go to rather than by boundaries. Girls of this age, however, are often as limited in the extent of their free range as are Third Grade girls.

These limitations on children freely to range away from their homes are affected by a multitude of forces which vary in both quality and degree in different social and physical environments. While traffic is sometimes recognized as important by urban planners, there are numerous other forces which limit children's spatial range. Some of these (e.g., social prejudices and crime) lead parents to restrict their children's movements. Other forces reside in: institutional restrictions on the use of territory; children's limited knowledge of available resources; their limited transportation access; and their social and environmental fears. All of these forces combine to create a limited range of free access.

The data from the historical interviews has so far revealed that, in the eyes of the residents, the physical neighbourhood of Inwood has remained much the same for the past 20–25 years. The type of physical changes described by long-term residents are the removal or deterioration of some recreational facilities that they or their children used. A much greater emphasis is placed by residents on the changing social and cultural character of the area. Without opportunity to contact incoming cultural groups, fears deriving from myths and stereotypes learned long ago take their toll on the children's lives in the form of restrictions placed on the current generation of children of all cultural backgrounds growing up in this area. While the Irish, Jewish and Italian children have some access to parks and playgrounds, their use of sidewalks and streets is very limited. Hispanic children, on the other hand, use the streets and sidewalks close to home somewhat more frequently. Black children for the most part are restricted to the confines of their housing project.

The research continues, providing more findings about the interplay of forces which comprise accessibility. The objective in trying to get a handle on the accessibility question is directly relevant to the work of those who participate in any capacity in the planning, building or programming of environments for children. It is the intention at the culmination of the research to make recommendations for urban planning policy and provide guidelines so that those professionals will know how to conduct briefer analyses of accessibility in their own unique, social, political and physical context. It is not desired to imply, by producing these guidelines, that there exists a universal solution for providing children with access to the environment. The research is, however, revealing a set of forces — physical barriers such as traffic or steep inclines, and social barriers such as parental fears of crime and fears associated with unfamiliar populations — which combines in a unique way in each unique context either to enhance or to restrict children's free movements and opportunities for transaction with the environment. It is for this reason that accessibility research needs to be carried out as a standard part of all cities' urban planning practice.

The Definition of Children's Landscapes

Connected to the important issue of maximizing children's free access to the environment is another major issue for children's environmental planning. What kinds of environments should children have access to? This is a difficult question. There is great danger in dogmatically specifying any universal truths. Parents should certainly have a great deal to say on this issue through their participation in the environmental planning process. The environment of cities, however, is currently being shaped by certain planning and political forces; therefore, professionals with a particular concern for children need to take a personal stand on this issue.

Although this question should not be limited to the qualities of the physical environment, the landscape is an extremely important factor in children's outdoor recreational opportunity. It is necessary for urban and recreational planners to discover what landscape qualities within cities (exemplified by New York) are discriminated by children and specifically what unique opportunities these different settings offer to children. There are a variety of environmental resource categories available to children which can be discerned by adult researchers. These categories include sidewalk pavement, street tarmac, vacant lots and associated dirt and rubble, abandoned vegetated spaces, backyards and courtyards, to name a few. The problem with this sort of environmental categorization is that the categories have been defined in adult terms rather than being grounded in the children's own discriminations and use of environmental qualities and resources.

In order to understand what qualities of the environment children discriminate and utilize in their recreation, attention must be turned to the experts — the children. Otherwise, planners are unlikely to meet the recreational needs of children, who are easily the greatest recreational users of the city environment. They will continue to limit their activities to the provision of under-utilized, behaviourally inadequate, and expensive traditional playgrounds and to the provision of expensive — and consequently highly restricted — out-of-city recreation programmes. With information provided by children, urban planners could work to produce better-balanced city environments offering children a choice from a suitable diversity. Once it has been discovered what diversity means to children by asking them to taxonomize the environment, adults can then use their own standards, as determined by existing developmental theories, and the (often implicit) developmental theories of parents, of what recreational opportunities (activities and experiences) all children should have available to them for their physical and mental health.

There have been some interview studies which explore children's city landscape perceptions and preferences, but the majority of these deal with institutional settings only (e.g., Peterson's (1974) playground equipment preference studies). In all of these studies, the land categories were defined by the investigators rather than by the children. What is needed at this point is a method by which children generate accounts of environmental qualities/resources.

One small piece of research — by the Detroit Geographical Expedition — came very close in basic approach to the kind of study proposed here, but is so loosely and briefly reported that one can have no confidence in the statements or learn anything about the methods (Colvard, 1971). This study involved interviewing children about their land categories and then mapping these data in two markedly different areas: around five houses in an inner-city, poor, black-populated ghetto of Detroit; and in a white-populated, relatively rich suburban area of Detroit. The land categories which were mapped for the two areas are suggestive of how different children's categories are likely to be from the existing adult-generated land-use categories currently used for mapping by all urban planners and recreational planners: dirt areas were distinguished from grass areas, green shrubs and trees from dead shrubs and trees; and dogs, cats, rubbish, trash, broken bottles, paper, litter and cans were mapped. In addition, columnar graphics express dramatic differences between the frequency of these elements in the two contrasting neighbourhoods, but again no figures are given to indicate even the sample sizes involved.

The closest suggestions of how most validly to proceed with children's classification of the landscape come from the sub-field of anthropology termed ethnoscience. In recent years, certain ethnoscientists have begun to use linguistic methods to discover how people from other cultures classify vegetation ('ethnobotany') and landforms and agricultural practices (sometimes called 'ethnogeography') (Berlin *et al.*, 1972; Conklin, 1967; Frake 1962; Johnson, 1978; Knight, 1971, 1974; Murton, 1973). While these methodological developments are still young and subject to considerable debate, they represent the beginning of an important attempt by social scientists to break away from the pretence that there are hard and fast objectively given categories which may be used for studying human behaviour. At the present time, no attempts have been made to utilize ethnoscientific methods for studying how urban environments are classified by their residents simply because the professions of anthropology and psychology have only recently shown any interest in investigating urban environmental problems. The problems of the classification and meaning of vegetation to urban populations, for example, is made particularly clear through the frequent, and often heated, debates on the definitions of what is 'natural' and what is 'man-made' in the environment, whenever environmental social scientists, urban planners or recreational planners come together (as for example in the United States Department of Agriculture (1977)). It is time to inform this debate with some careful empirical investigation of how urban populations classify the environment. Children, as the greatest users of the city outdoor environment for recreation, are the most natural special interest group to begin with. This will be Phase II of the Manhattan research. It is hoped that others will explore the problem. The authors are anxious to share the methodological problems and findings with other investigators.

The investigation by Hart (1978a) in the New England town went half-way towards developing a taxonomy of children's places. It was not an objective of the study to develop a systematic and comprehensive approach to children's place differentiation. The interview procedures did, however, reveal many place discriminations that were unique to children (see also Southworth, 1970, and Lynch, 1975). While these environmental categories were often very different from those of adults, they were not unique to each child. Many of the child-generated categories such as 'dirt-for-building', 'climbing-trees', and 'long grass for hiding and building' show a high degree of consensus.

Figure 17.4: Use of Commonland for Play

A new approach to planning and design is required. We need to incorporate an understanding of children's behaviour in the total environment. We know, for example, that one important aspect of children's environmental behaviour is the finding or making of places for themselves. This small commonland is in the middle of three British housing estates. The children ignore the playgrounds and 'play areas' (small triangles of mown grass) in favour of this extremely 'rich' setting which cost nothing to develop (from the BBC/Open University film 'Play and Place: Transforming Environments'; programme notes available from Roger Hart).

Figure 17.5: Breaking Down Barriers

In search of diversity and opportunity for play, without direct and constant supervision, children break down the barriers that restrict their activities. It is our responsibility as social scientists concerned with the welfare and healthy development of children to provide opportunity for their safe yet adventurous exploration of the environment.

The development of an ethnoscientific approach for the comparative study of children's place naming would be an extremely valuable step towards understanding what constitutes diversity of experience for children.

Going beyond playgrounds opens up new arenas for the child-recreation and planning professionals. It is necessary to carry out new kinds of research and to work in a participatory manner with communities in recreation and planning practice. In summary form, some of these new arenas are:

1. the need to understand how the major serious forces combine to restrict children's free movement in cities: how can traffic, crime and physical barriers be dealt with in planning policy?
2. the need to carry out good design of new residential areas which incorporate an understanding of children's environmental behaviour (see Hart, 1978b);
3. above all, the need to work with communities in a participatory manner; this includes the production of simple research guidelines which will enable people to identify their own problems of accessibility and to identify needed landscape qualities.

Notes

1. The research for this paper was funded in part by the Pinchot Institute for Environmental Forestry Studies, United States Department of Agriculture Forest Service.
2. This paper is limited in focus to pre-adolescent children. Excellent, ecological research has been carried out with adolescents by Southworth (1970) in Cambridgeport, Mass., and under the co-ordination of Kevin Lynch (1975) by UNESCO.
3. There are often frontiers of fear within the home, notably the cellars, but over all the home seems to represent a secure and safe base to children.

References

Aiello, J. and B. Gordon. 1974. 'Description of children's outdoor activities in a suburban residential area: preliminary findings.' *Proceedings of the Environmental Design Research Association, Conference 5.* Milwaukee.
Berlin, B., P. Raven and D. Breedlove. 1972. 'The origins of taxonomy', *Science,* 174, pp. 1210–13.
Bowlby, J. 1969. 'Attachment and loss. Experimental human ecology: a reorientation to theory and research on socialization.' Mimeographed paper. Ithaca: Cornell University.
Bronfenbrenner, U. 1973a. *An Emerging Theoretical Perspective for Research in Human Development.* Ithaca: Department of Human Development and Family Studies, College of Human Ecology, Cornell University.

—— 1973b. *Developmental Research, Public Policy and the Ecology of Childhood.* Draft copy. Paper presented at the President's Symposium, 'Interactions among theory, research and application in child development', Society for Research in Child Development, Philadelphia.

—— 1975. 'Experimental human ecology: a reorientation to theory and research on socialization.' Mimeographed paper. Ithaca: Cornell University.

Coates, G. and H. Sanoff. 1973. 'Behavioral mapping. The ecology of child behavior in a planned residential setting.' *Proceedings of the Third Annual Conference of the Environmental Design Research Association.* Los Angeles: University of California at Los Angeles.

Colvard, Y. (ed.). 1971. *Field Notes: The Geography of the Children of Detroit.* Detroit: Detroit Geographical Expedition, Discussion Paper No. 3.

Conklin, H. 1967. 'Ethnographic semantic analysis of Ifugao landform categories', *Transactions of the New York Academy of Sciences*, Series III, 30, 1, pp. 99–121.

Cooper, C. 1974. 'Children in residential areas: guidelines for designers', *Landscape Architecture*, 65(S), pp. 372–8 and 415–16.

Department of the Environment. 1973. *Children at Play.* London: Her Majesty's Stationery Office.

Fiske, D. W. and S. R. Maddi (eds). 1961. *Functions of Varied Experience.* Homewood, Ill.: Dorsey Press.

Fowler, H. 1965. *Curiosity and Exploratory Behavior.* New York: Macmillan.

Frake, C. 1962. 'Cultural ecology and ethnography', *American Anthropologist*, 64, 1, pp. 53–9.

Gold, S. 1972. 'Non-use of neighbourhood parks', *Transactions of the American Institute of Planners*, November, pp. 369–78.

—— 1977. 'Neighbourhood parks: the non-use phenomena', *Evaluation Quarterly*, 1, p. 2.

Grotberg, E. (ed.). 1977. *Two Hundred Years of Children.* Washington, DC: Department of Health, Education and Welfare.

Hart, R. A. 1978a. *Children's Experience of Place: A Developmental Study.* New York: Irvington Publishers.

—— 1978b. *Reading the Landscapes of Childhood.* New York: Center for Human Environments, City University of New York.

—— 1979. 'Children's exploration of tomorrow's environments: some changing forces influencing children's outdoor accessibility', in J. Tyrwhilt (ed.), *Children in the World of Tomorrow.* New York: Plenum.

Hole, V. 1966. 'Children's play on housing estates.' *Building Research Station: National Building Studies Research Paper 39.* London: Her Majesty's Stationery Office.

Johnson, K. 1978. 'Do as the land bids: a study of Otomi resource use on the eve of irrigation.' Unpublished Ph.D. dissertation, Clark University, Department of Geography.

Knight, C. G. 1971. 'Ethnography and change', *Journal of Geography*, 70, pp. 47–51.

—— 1974. *Ecology and Change: Rural modernization in an African community.* New York: Academic Press.

Lynch, K. (ed.). 1975. *Children in Cities: Young Adolescents and Their Environment in Cracow, Melbourne, Salta, and Warsaw.* Unpublished draft report for UNESCO.

Maslow, A. 1968. *Toward a Psychology of Being.* Princeton, New Jersey: Van Nostrand.

Morville, L. 1969. *Borns Borg of Friaracker (Children's Use of Recreational Areas)*, with English summary. Copenhagen: Statens Byggeronskingsitut, Teknisk Forlog.

Murton, B. J. 1973. 'Folk classification of cultivated land and ecology in Southern India', *Proceedings of the Association of American Geographers*, 5, pp. 199–202.

Peterson, G. 1974. 'Evaluating the quality of the wilderness environment', *Environment and Behavior*, 6, pp. 169–94.

Pollowy, A. 1973. *Children in the Residential Setting.* Montreal: Université de Montréal, Centre de Recherches et d'Innovation Urbaines.

Russel-Sage Foundation (1914). *West Side Studies.* Russel-Sage Foundation.

Southworth, M. 1970. 'An urban service for children, based on analysis of Cambridgeport boys' conception and use of the city.' Unpublished Ph.D. dissertation, Massachusetts Institute of Technology, Cambridge.

United States Department of Agriculture. 1977. *Children, Nature and the Urban Environment.* Proceedings of a USDA–Forest Service Conference. Washington, DC: United States Department of Agriculture.

CONTRIBUTORS

Edgar Boehm: Bund der Jugendfarmen und Aktivspielplätze Ev. (Association of Youth Farms and Adventure Playgrounds), Stuttgart, West Germany.

Elizabeth Chace, BA: Environmental Planner, Department of Environmental Protection, State of New Jersey, Trenton, New Jersey, USA.

Paul Davidoff, BA, MCP, LL.B.: Executive Director, Suburban Action Institute, New York, USA; Adjunct Professor, Columbia University; former Professor and Director, Graduate Program in Urban Planning, Hunter College, New York.

Brenda Fjeldsted, B.Occup.Ther., Dip.Occup.Ther.: Senior Occupational Therapist in Psychiatry, Occupational Therapy Program, Children's Centre, Health Sciences Centre, Winnipeg, Manitoba, Canada.

Louise Gaunt, B.Arch., M.Arch. and Urb.Design: Project Leader, Building Planning Division, The National Swedish Institute for Building Research, Gävle, Sweden; Architect SAR, Svenska Arkitekters Riksförbund.

Roger A. Hart, BA, MA, PhD: Assistant Professor, Environmental Psychology Program, City University of New York, USA; Co-editor, *Childhood City Newsletter.*

Polly Hill, BA: Adviser, Children's Environments Advisory Service, Central Mortgage and Housing Corporation, Head Office, Ottawa. President, International Playground Association; Commissioner, Canadian Commission for the International Year of the Child.

George Ishmael, BSc, Dip.L.Arch.: Landscape Architect, City of Norwich, England.

Ellen Jacobs, BA, M.Ed.: Assistant Professor, Department of Education, Concordia University, Montréal, Québec, Canada.

Peter Jacobs, BA, M.Arch., M.L.Arch.: Vice-Doyen et Professeur, Faculté de l'Aménagement, Université de Montréal, Montréal, Québec, Canada.

Robert S. Lockhart, BA, MES: Director, Rethink Ltd, Kitchener, Ontario, Canada; former Consultant, Balmer, Crapo and Associates, Waterloo, Ontario, Canada.

Ethel M. Luhtanen, BA, MES: Consultant, James F. Maclaren Ltd, Toronto, Ontario, Canada.

Robin C. Moore, Dip.Arch., MCP: Consultant, People—Environment Group, San Francisco and Inquiring Systems Inc., Berkeley, California, USA; Editor, *Newsletter*, International Playground Association.

Cecilia Perez, BA: Research Assistant, Environmental Psychology Program, City University of New York, USA; Co-editor, *Childhood City Newsletter*.

Anne-Marie Pollowy, B.Arch., M.Env. Plan., PhD: Associate, Social Systems Management Consultants, Yellow Springs, Ohio, USA.

Harvey A. Scott, BPE, MA, PhD: Professor, Faculty of Physical Education and Recreation, University of Alberta, Edmonton, Alberta, Canada.

Domien Verwer, BA, MA: Study Secretary, Stichting Ruimte, Rotterdam, The Netherlands; Consultant, Information and Consultation Group Woonerven, Ministry of Transport and Public Works, Den Haag, The Netherlands; Secretary, Consultation Group Recreation and Living, Foundation Recreation, Den Haag, The Netherlands; Councillor, International Playground Association.

William B. Watkins, BA Ed., MS, Ed.D.: Professor, Faculty of Health, Physical Education and Recreation, Pima Community College, Tucson, Arizona, USA.

Otto Weininger, BA, MA, PhD: Professor, Department of Applied Psychology, Ontario Institute for Studies in Education, Toronto, Ontario, Canada; Co-editor, *The Journal of the Canadian Association for Young Children*.

Galia Weiser, B.Arch., M.Arch.: Architect, Brixen and Christopher Architects, Salt Lake City, Utah, USA.

Paul F. Wilkinson, BA, MA, PhD: Assistant Dean (Academic) and Associate Professor, Faculty of Environmental Studies, York University, Toronto, Ontario, Canada.

INDEX